# ASAD'S LEGACY: SYRIA IN TRANSITION

EYAL ZISSER

# Asad's Legacy
## Syria in Transition

WITH A FOREWORD BY
ITAMAR RABINOVICH

NEW YORK UNIVERSITY PRESS
WASHINGTON SQUARE, NEW YORK

© Eyal Zisser, 2001
All rights reserved.
First published in the U.S.A. in 2001 by
NEW YORK UNIVERSITY PRESS
Washington Square, NY 10003


Cataloging-in-Publication Data available from
the Library of Congress

ISBN 0-8147- 9697-4


Printed in England

# CONTENTS

v

## Part III
## SYRIAN FOREIGN POLICY IN THE 1990s

# FOREWORD

## by Itamar Rabinovich

It is difficult to overstate the role played by Hafez al-Asad in the brief history of the Syrian state. That state is fifty-five years old, and in this period Asad was its dominant leader and ruler for the last thirty years. Together with the previous seven years during which he was a senior member of the Ba'th regime, his tenure at or near the helm added up to thirty-seven years.

During Asad's thirty years Syria was transformed from a weak state buffeted by domestic pressures and external currents into a powerful one, a major regional actor and a significant voice in the international politics of the Middle East. The ground for this transformation had been prepared during the Ba'th regime's first seven years, but it was Asad who was able to exploit this potential and convert it into the changes of the 1970s and 1980s.

Clearly there was also a darker side to these developments. Syria is governed by an authoritarian regime that has crushed opposition to it with terrible brutality. Influence or control over Syria's weaker Arab neighbors was acquired through violence and suppression. While Asad's regime was durable and stable, it remained highly personalized. The deficient institutionalization and the excessive role of primordial groups (family and community) in Asad's Syria were put into stark relief by the struggle over Asad's succession. The initial transfer of power to Asad's son unfolded smoothly, but beneath the placid surface the old demons of sectarian tensions and personal and factional conflicts threaten to return to the forefront of Syrian politics.

The sense of an ending also had an important impact on the efforts to settle Syria's conflict with Israel. I personally believe that Asad had made the decision to sign a peace agreement with Israel under very specific terms. He was able to make it after concluding that he could reconcile his peacemaking with Israel with more than forty years of fierce opposition to the idea and practice of the Jewish state, thus including a "dignified peace" with Israel in his legacy.

We do not know whether the present stalemate in the Israeli-Syrian negotiations will be resolved under his successor and, if so, within what time-frame. But in this matter, as in so many others, Asad left a complex legacy – the Arab leader who, in contradistinction to Anwar al-Sadat, symbolized the lingering oppositions of Arab nationalism to Israel, and who came to accept the notion of peace with Israel while continuing to display reluctance and ambivalence.

Eyal Zisser's choice of title is thus very apt. In the aftermath of Asad's death, Syria is clearly in transition. And whatever directions its domestic politics and foreign policies will take in the coming years, they are certain to unfold in the shadow of Asad's legacy.

*Tel-Aviv, June 2000*

# AUTHOR'S PREFACE AND
# ACKNOWLEDGEMENTS

During the first week of June 2000, Damascus was alive with activity preparatory to the investiture of Bashar, son of the Syrian President Hafiz al-Asad, as successor to his father. The Ba'th Party Congress was to convene on 17 June and elect him as a member of the Party's Regional Command, which would facilitate a quiet and orderly transition – at least in a formal sense. On 10 June 2000 Hafiz al-Asad died, and this rite of investiture was replaced by a funeral rite. The deterioration in Asad's state of health was an open secret and it was known that his days were numbered. Bashar's cultivation as successor had been accelerated in the previous few years, thus enabling him to prepare himself for the moment of his father's death. When the moment came, he took over in what seemed to be a smooth transition. Bashar became President, but many of the questions concerning the country's future raised during the last years of his father's rule in Syria remain unanswered. Indeed, Asad's legacy seems to be a country that is in a state of transition, like a train that has left a station but not yet arrived at its destination.

In 1965 Patrick Seale, the Damascus correspondent for the British *Observer*, published *The Struggle for Syria*.[1] To this day it is considered an important source for studying the history of Syria in the early years of its independence (1946-58). In his book Seale attempted to emphasize the key role that Syria has played in the Arab political arena since achieving independence. This was because in his interpretation whoever wished to lead the Arab world at the time had first to rule Syria.

Yet it becomes apparent that Syria's centrality in the Arab world was no guarantee of immunity and strength. Its image in those years, as Seale himself depicted it in his book, was that of a weak and unstable state. As the title suggests, Syria was given to endless power struggles – over orientation and identity and, in practice, even for its very existence. This image was that of a passive player who plays not a key role but, at most, a role that is the key to leadership and hegemony in the Arab world. Not by chance did Seale's book end in 1958, the year the Syrians decided to give up their national independence and merge with Egypt to form the United Arab Republic (UAR). This union led to a temporary loss of independence for the Syrian state, and its amalgamation with its Arab elder sister.

Two decades after publishing his first book on Syria, Seale published another about this state and, more precisely, its leader since November 1970: *Asad of Syria: The Struggle for the Middle East.*[2] Like its predecessor, this book is considered an important source for the study of modern Syrian history and, in particular, for understanding the personality of President Asad, his political path and his policy. Needless to say, it also bears evidence of Seale's efforts to emphasize the centrality of Syria under Asad in the regional and inter-Arab arena.

Nonetheless there is an essential difference between Seale's two books. This stems from the passage of time between their writing, and perhaps also from a change in perspective on Seale's part. His first book, *The Struggle for Syria*, depicts this state as a pawn in the hands of its Arab neighbors and the great powers, but in *Asad of Syria* he portrays Syria under Asad's leadership as a regional power that has maneuvered successfully to achieve a position of influence and seniority in the region. Seale's biography of President Asad was published in 1988, and is devoted mostly to the period between his coming to power (November 1970) and the mid-1980s. This period, particularly its end, is notable for the Syrian regime's success in consolidating and strengthening its position at home and abroad after successfully dealing with a series of challenges to its stability and to its very existence. Domestically, it managed to suppress the Islamic Revolt of 1976-82 which, at its peak in 1980, threatened the regime. Later Asad was able to settle peaceably a conflict between himself and his brother Rif'at, at that time second in the Syrian hierarchy, which broke out over Rif'at's attempt to advance his position as successor following the President's heart attack in November 1983.

In the regional arena Syria consolidated its position and prevented Israel, the United States and neighboring Arab states from marginalizing it. In the late 1970s it established a front against the Egyptian President Anwar al-Sadat's peace initiative, and by so doing kept other Arab states and the PLO from joining Egypt, Israel, and the United States in their efforts to advance the Arab–Israeli peace process at Damascus's expense. Syria also emerged with the upper hand from the confrontation with Israel in Lebanon which culminated in "Operation Peace for Galilee" ( June 1982), and thus assured itself full control over Lebanon. With Soviet assistance the Syrians began actively to pursue a policy of strategic parity with Israel. Syria's immediate goal was deterrence, but in the long term it hoped to defeat Israel on the battlefield. Finally, its backing of Iran in the latter's protracted war against Iraq from September 1980 was also perceived in the mid-'80s – i.e. from the time the tide turned in Tehran's favor – as a wise and fruitful step.

This state of affairs in the mid-1980s is what motivated Patrick Seale to give his book the portentous title, *Asad of Syria: The Struggle for the Middle East.* With this title he – and perhaps even Asad himself, who granted the author a long series of interviews for the the book – sought to express a feeling of relief and self-confidence, a sense that in the wake of difficult years full of challenges and perils – some of them threatening its very existence – the Syrian regime had safe-guarded its position domestically, regionally and in the wider world.

Seale's main argument, namely that Asad's leadership has so changed the Syrian state as to turn it into a regional power that takes action from a position of strength and influence, quickly found numerous adherents in the West and in Israel. Indeed, a long line of academics, journalists and, especially, government officials (Western and Israeli) were impressed by Asad's political successes in his various spheres of activity. They were enticed into seeing some kind of proof of great personal and political stature in the mystique that seems to surround Asad and his regime. This mystique was the product both of his own solitary nature and the deliberate inaccessibility of his regime and his country to the Western media. For some it provides evidence of the Syrian state's immunity and power.[3]

It thus comes as no surprise that President Clinton was quoted in June 1996 as saying that of all the Middle Eastern leaders he had met, none was smarter than President Asad "as far as IQ is concerned". Equally intriguing was Clinton's reference to the abortive peace negotiations between Israel and Syria mediated by the United States between 1992 and 1996. He said that Asad had wasted his brilliance on "small issues...missed critical opportunities", and perhaps "lost his chance to get back the Golan".[4]

This begs the question: to what extent did Asad's image as a talented, successful and, indeed, "omnipotent" leader correspond with reality? In other words, were his chosen path and policy truly responsible for the accomplishments attributed to him, or (asks the iconoclast), might a different path, or another leader, have brought better results?[5] Indeed, the Syria that Asad left behind when he died in June 2000 three decades after taking up the reins of government, remains in the throes of deep social and economic distress and finds itself utterly isolated, both internationally and regionally. Moreover, uncertainty for the future still hovers over the country and over Asad's handiwork, the Ba'th regime.

Hence, it seems that the sense of relief and self-confidence that Asad radiated in the pages of Patrick Seale's book was exaggerated and premature. Likewise, studies of Asad and his regime published in recent years aggrandized Asad's Syria when they painted it as an omnipotent regional power. Doubts over the invulnerability of the Syrian regime and state under Asad's leadership had multiplied since the late 1980s, when the decline of the Soviet Union hurled the regime into a protracted crisis that challenged Asad and eroded Syria's regional and international standing. At first, the Soviet decline led to the collapse of both components of Syria's national security doctrine: one was the effort to reach strategic parity with Israel, and the other was reliance on the "Soviet umbrella" in the event of an Israeli or even a US threat against Syria. The Syrians perceived the latter as real, at least in part due to accusations in the late 1980s that Damascus was involved in international terrorist actions. Although the American threat dissipated in the early 1990s, Damascus was not appeased. The Soviet collapse led to the emergence of a new world order – and, to some extent, a new regional one as well – in which the United States would set the tone. This new order, which included the emergence of a "new Middle East", naturally has implications for Syria's regional and international standing. It could also affect the status of the regime domestically, making it appear anachronistic and irrelevant – its chosen path and worldview no longer standing the test of reality.

The significance of the collapse of the Soviet Union and its East European allies was not lost on many in Syria. By the early 1990s many people in Syria, including individuals within the regime itself, even in the upper echelons, began to express their desire for social and economic reform. The globalization process began to make itself felt in Syria (as in most states) at the same time, threatening to demolish the walls with which the Syrian regime surrounded itself – as a kind of guarantee of its stability and very existence. Furthermore, globalization emboldened those voices in Syria that called for change.

Under these pressures the regime had to introduce a change in policy, and from the late 1980s Syria seemed to have indeed taken a new turn. It acted to improve relations with Western countries, chiefly the United States, in an effort to lift the possible threat posed by Washington, and hoped too that better relations would yield such political benefits as financial aid. As part of this effort Syria allied itself with the US-led anti-Iraq coalition during the Gulf crisis (August 1990-February 1991), and in October 1991 it joined the Middle East peace process, expressing for the very first time a readiness in principle to sign a peace treaty with Israel. Limited changes took place in areas of domestic, economic and social policy at home with the regime adopting in particular a policy of economic and, to a limited extent, political openness. Alongwith this policy came a readiness to modify the national order of priorities in an effort to raise the people's standard of living. The projected aim of this limited change was to assure "domestic harmony" or, in other words, to guarantee continued social and economic stability and thereby political stability as well.

The regime's domestic and foreign policy changes did not reflect a vision of reform; they ushered in no "new Syrian order". On the contrary, it seems that they were tactical moves engineered to preserve the existing situation. The then US Secretary of State, James Baker, said that the Middle East at the end of the 1980s stood before a "window of opportunity". If so, the regime did all it could to shut it or, at least, to keep out the "winds of change". The limited measures it has taken since the early 1990s have brought no real and encompassing answer to Syria's problems. Especially noticeable is the gap between what Syria has and what it hopes for in social and economic terms. Critical problems have hammered the regime relentlessly, the demographic question most of all. The population's rate of increase, one of the highest in the world, threatens to upset the state's existing socio-economic order. An ageing President Asad and his contemporaries in the elite needed to tackle the wider issue of succession and the next generation of leaders, and following his death that burden has fallen on Bashar, his son and successor. Mere engagement with these questions may be enough to shake Syria's political stability and influence the future of the regime.

These factors have led to debate in Syria since the mid-1990s (even if it does take place behind closed doors) over the state's future direction. The conflict is between those who call for change and reform and others for whom maintaining the *status quo* is the key to continuing political and economic stability. The latter maintain that any radical change – such as that introduced by Mikhail Gorbachev in the Soviet Union – would bring the country to a state of social, economic and hence political crisis which it would have difficulty withstanding. The very existence of this controversy, coupled with the reluctance to suppress it (or, in other words, its indecisiveness in the face of current challenges), suggests that the regime lost its way in the 1990s.

This is far from saying that the Ba'th regime in Damascus is about to meet its end. It still has at its disposal formidable sources of power and support. For instance, President Asad during his lifetime enjoyed significant support within Syria and beyond. This was not blind admiration, nor was it the passionate and messianic fervor that was felt for Jamal Abd al-Nasir. Asad was too closed and reticent a personality to inspire this sort of relationship between leader and subjects. On the other hand, Syrian citizens did not live in perpetual dread of the leader like their counterparts under such rulers as the Iraqi President Saddam Husayn. Asad may not have been loved, but he was respected; it was not so much fear as awe that his people felt for him. They esteemed his achievements. First, he preserved Syria's stability over the course of three decades. This unprecedented achievement was the result of political acumen combined with moderation, but also a willingness to resort to aggressive tactics and even use an iron hand when called for, as during the suppression of the Islamic Revolt in Syria in 1976-82. Another factor contributing to the public's admiration for Asad was his policy over the years on the conflict with Israel. His handling of this issue apparently reflected accurately the attitude toward Israel of the ordinary Arab citizen – not just in Syria. Finally, the Syrian regime, for all its weak points, has been run by a coalition of social and political forces which still represent the majority. This coalition binds together the once re-pressed and discriminated-against sectors of Syrian society – members of the minorities, the rural and peripheral populations and, finally, the lower classes of society. In three decades they have become the rulers of the state. The 'Alawi community dominates the coalition and holds it together.

In various ways the Syria of the late '80s and early '90s differed from what is described in most existing studies, chief among them Seale's biography of Asad already mentioned. It is now a weaker Syria, a state at a crossroads under the shadow of the "new world order". Perhaps it is this very order that has put Syria at the crossroads. Should the Syrian state accelerate down the road that began to open up in the early 1990s, or should it stick with the *status quo*? The regime seems either to hesitate before the question of its future path, or else to prefer that things remain as they are. In the short term it will presumably have its way, but of course the question is: what will happen in the long term, especially now that Asad has finally left the scene?

This study is an attempt to describe the crossroads at which Syria has found itself since the beginning of the 1990s and its related di-lemma. Moreover, it endeavors to sketch a portrait of President Asad, and his son Bashar, the Ba'th regime, and the Syrian state, and to examine and analyse their policy at home and abroad in face of the challenges and difficulties of the 1990s. The study consists of five sections that survey, chronologically and thematically, the main problems which together form a comprehensive picture of Syrian affairs in the 1990s.

The introduction, "From 'The Struggle for Syria' to 'The Struggle for the Middle East' ", reviews Syria's history from its establishment by the French in the 1920s until the mid-1980s. It concentrates on the period beginning with Asad's rise to power in November 1970 until 1985, when he reached a high point of his political career. Part I: "Syria under Asad – Regime and State" describes the state and the regime as shaped by Asad after he came into power. Part II: "A New Path" explores the crisis Syria has undergone since the mid-1980s following the collapse of the Soviet Union. This part also surveys the regime's early efforts to extricate itself from this crisis, efforts that include joining the anti-Iraq coalition led by the United States during the Gulf War. Part III: "Syrian Foreign Policy in the 1990s" covers the country's relations with its neighbors Iraq, Turkey and Jordan; its treaty with Iran; its status in the international arena; its relations with the great powers; the Israeli-Syrian peace process; and Syrian involvement in Lebanon. Domestic developments within Syria over the last decade are the subject of Part IV: "Inside Syria – A Country at a Crossroads". This part treats social and economic problems, the Islamic religious revival and the regime's relations with the Islamic movement in Syria, and of course the renewed power struggle in the Syrian elite around the key question of succession.

Visiting Syria is still not feasible for Israeli scholars, but fortunately the wealth of primary material available to the researcher compensates for this regrettable circumstance. This material includes speeches and interviews with President Hafiz al-Asad; Syrian, Arabic, and foreign newspapers and collections of radio and television broadcasts; and economic and political reviews and studies published in Syria and abroad. For the purposes of the study, ample use was also made of secondary sources treating Syria. Examination and analysis of this abundant material yields a reliable picture.

## Acknowledgements

It gives me great pleasure to thank all those who assisted in the preparation of this work. First, Professor Itamar Rabinovich, who introduced me to the study of Syria. I am indebted to my colleagues in Israel and abroad for their thoughtful advice and for generously sharing their information. Colleagues and friends in Syria and Lebanon gave me their personal impressions of events within Syria, but regretfully I cannot, for obvious reasons, divulge their names. Thanks are also due to Jacqueline Teitelbaum for her fine translation of this book. Personal thanks are due to the Colton family who generously granted me a scholarship that made it possible for me to devote my time to the study, and encouraged me while it was being written. Finally, I thank my friends at the Moshe Dayan Center and the Department of Modern Middle Eastern and African History at Tel Aviv University for their support and encouragement through the years. The publishers in London, C. Hurst and Co., have been helpful in a variety of ways; the cover photograph was taken by Christopher Hurst in 1999. Last but certainly not least, my affectionate gratitude to my wife Shirley and my children Liron, Lilakh and Toam, who have been with me every step of the way, and who give meaning to my work.

*Tel Aviv*                                                      EYAL ZISSER
*May 2000*

# NOTES

[1] Patrick Seale, *The Struggle for Syria* (Oxford University Press, 1965).

[2] Patrick Seale, *Asad of Syria: The Struggle for the Middle East* (London: I. B. Tauris, 1988).

[3] In their book *Syria and the Middle East Peace Process*, Raymond A. Hinnebusch and Alasdair Drysdale, two of the most prominent scholars of Syria in the West, describe Asad as "thoughtful, cautious, pragmatic, tough, determined, ruthless, energetic, patient, astute, calculating, remote, and intelligent", and as "tower[ing] over everyone else in the elite and ... widely respected for protecting Syria's interests". Even Syrians who detest the regime, it is said, "reluctantly acknowledge his Machiavellian brilliance". See Drysdale and Hinnebusch, *Syria and the Middle East Peace Process* (New York: Council on Foreign Relations Press, 1991), p. 24; see also Richard T. Antoun and Donald Quataert (eds), *Syria: Society, Culture, and Polity* (Albany, NY: State University of New York Press, 1991); Eberhard Kienle, *Contemporary Syria: Liberalization between Cold War and Cold Peace* (London: British Academic Press, 1994); Raymond A. Hinnebusch, *Authoritarian Power and State Formation in Baa'thist Syria: Army, Party, and Peasant* (Boulder, CO: Westview Press, 1990).

[4] *Jerusalem Post*, 12 June 1996.

[5] For more on the question of Asad's leadership, see Eyal Zisser, "Asad of Syria: The Leader and the Image", *Orient* 2, 1994, pp. 247-60.

# ABBREVIATIONS

| | |
|---|---|
| AFP | Agence France-Presse (Paris) |
| ASQ | *Arab Studies Quarterly* |
| CP | *Country Profile* (Economist Intelligence Unit) |
| CR | *Country Report* (Economist Intelligence Unit) |
| DR | Daily Report, Foreign Broadcast Information Service, Middle East and Africa. |
| FT | *Financial Times* |
| JP | *Jerusalem Post* |
| JIME Review | A review of Middle Eastern and energy affairs, the Japanese Institute of Middle Eastern Economies. |
| IHT | *International Herald Tribune* |
| INA | Iraqi News Agency (Baghdad) |
| IRNA | Islamic Revolution News Agency (Tehran) |
| IJMES | *International Journal of Middle Eastern Studies* |
| MBC | Middle East Broadcasting Center ( London ) |
| MECS | *Middle East Contemporary Survey* (Moshe Dayan Center, Tel Aviv) |
| MEED | *Middle East Economist Digest* |
| MEJ | *Middle East Journal* |
| MENA | Middle East News Agency (Cairo) |
| MEQ | *Middle East Quarterly* |
| MERIP | *Middle East Research and Information Project Report* |
| MES | *Middle Eastern Studies* |
| MM | *Middle East Mirror* |
| NYT | *New York Times* |
| PKK | Parti Kerkeren Kurdistan (Kurdistan Workers' Party) |
| PLO | Palestine Liberation Organisation |
| PPS | Parti Populaire Syrien (Syrian National Socialist Party) |
| SANA | Syrian Arab News Agency |
| WP | *Washington Post* |
| WT | *Washington Times* |

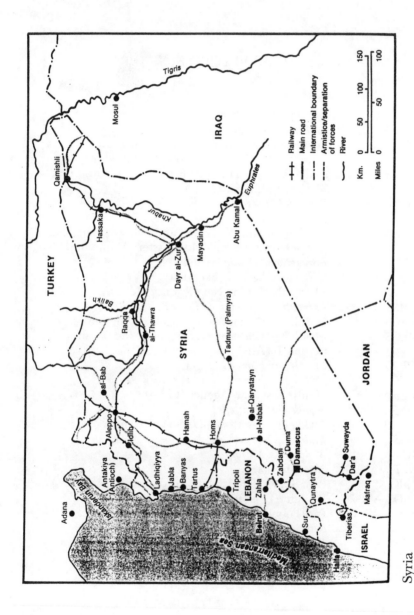

Syria

Reproduced courtesy of *Middle East Contemporary Survey*,
Moshe Dayan Center, Tel Aviv, Israel.

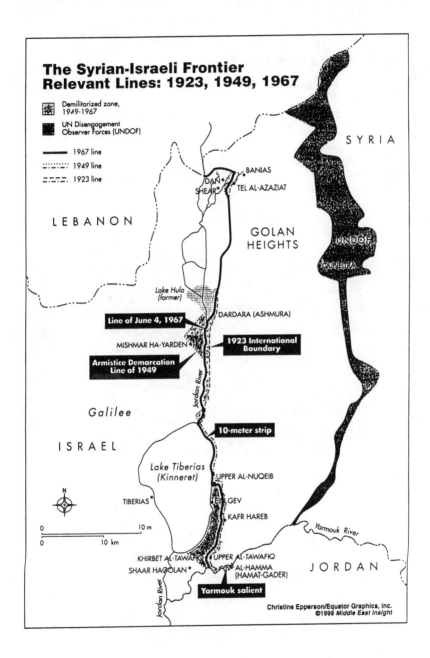

# The Syrian-Israeli Frontier
## Relevant Lines: 1923, 1949, 1967

Demilitarized zone,
1949-1967

UN Disengagement
Observer Forces (UNDOF)

——— 1967 line
········· 1949 line
-·-·-·- 1923 line

SYRIA

BANIAS

DAN
SHEAR•  • TEL AL-AZAZIAT

LEBANON

GOLAN
HEIGHTS

UNDOF

QUNEITRA

Lake Hula
(former)

DARDARA (ASHMURA)

Line of June 4, 1967

1923 International
Boundary

MISHMAR HA-YARDEN

Armistice Demarcation
Line of 1949

Jordan River

Galilee

10-meter strip

ISRAEL

Lake Tiberias
(Kinneret)

UPPER AL-NUQEIB

N

TIBERIAS•

EIN GEV

KAFR HAREB

0        10 m

Yarmouk River

0        10 km

KHIRBET AL-TAWAFIQ•  • UPPER AL-TAWAFIQ

SHAAR HAGOLAN•

AL-HAMMA
(HAMAT-GADER)

JORDAN

Jordan River

Yarmouk salient

Christine Epperson/Equator Graphics, Inc.
©1999 Middle East Insight

xxi

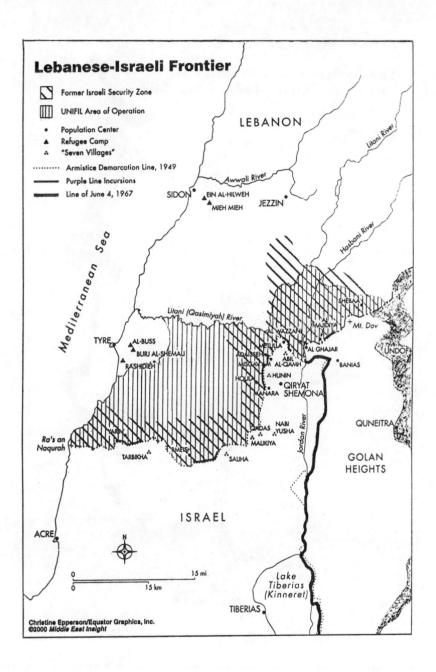

**Lebanese-Israeli Frontier**

- Former Israeli Security Zone
- UNIFIL Area of Operation
- • Population Center
- ▲ Refugee Camp
- ⚬ "Seven Villages"
- ·········· Armistice Demarcation Line, 1949
- ——— Purple Line Incursions
- ▬▬▬ Line of June 4, 1967

LEBANON

Litani River

Awwali River

Hasbani River

SIDON
EIN AL-HILWEH
MIEH MIEH
JEZZIN

*Mediterranean Sea*

Litani (Qasimiyah) River

SHEBAA
MAJIDIYA
+ Mt. Dov

TYRE
AL-BUSS
BURJ AL-SHEMALI
RASHIDIEH

AL WAZZANI
METULLA
AL GHAJAR
ADAISSEH
ABIL
MISGAV AM  AL-QAMH
⚬ HUNIN
HOULA
MANARA
QIRYAT SHEMONA

UNDOF

BANIAS

QUNEITRA

*Ra's an Naqurah*

ZARIT
RMEISH
TARBIKHA
SAUHA
QADAS
MALIKIYA
NABI YUSHA

Jordan River

GOLAN HEIGHTS

ISRAEL

ACRE

N

0 ——— 15 mi
0 ——— 15 km

Lake Tiberias (Kinneret)

TIBERIAS

Christine Epperson/Equator Graphics, Inc.
©2000 *Middle East Insight*

INTRODUCTION

# FROM "THE STRUGGLE FOR SYRIA" TO "THE STRUGGLE FOR THE MIDDLE EAST"

## The roots of the Syrian state

The Corrective Revolution ( *al-Thawra al-Tashihiyya*) brought Hafiz al-Asad to power in Syria on 16 November 1970. For many the Revolution marks a turning-point in this state's history, for it seemed to conclude the "Struggle for Syria", to use Patrick Seale's term. The struggle over Syria's future course, policy, identity and indeed its very existence had been waged and won. Asad's political acumen and talents, combined with favorable circumstances within Syria's borders and beyond, facilitated his founding of a centralized and powerful regime. The ensuing political stability and economic prosperity, unknown in the past, made Syria a regional power.

Asad's achievement brought with it the eradication, at least temporarily, of the uncertainty over Syria's future that had prevailed since its establishment by the French in the 1920s. This uncertainty was, in part, an outgrowth of the Syrian state's lack of roots and historical legitimacy, in that it was established to serve French interests and not in response to its inhabitants' wishes. The uncertainty that hovered over Syria's future loomed still larger after the last French soldier left Syrian soil on 17 April 1946 (a date celebrated ever since as Syrian Independence Day). This was due mainly to the internal political fragility that characterised Syria in its first years of independence.

The Syrian state with its current borders and demographic composition is thus the distinct product of Anglo-French understandings and arrangements reached at the end of the First World War. Until its establishment by the French, a Syrian political entity had never existed in any of the territory then known as *bilad al-Sha'm* or, since the nineteenth century (clearly under Western influence), by the

1

name "Syria" (i.e. geographical Syria). Moreover, throughout Arab and Muslim history and for the duration of the Ottoman rule that began in 1516, the term lacked any political significance. It was primarily a geographical designation for the territory that includes, in addition to contemporary Syria, Transjordan, Palestine and Lebanon. For a short time in the 1860s the term had administrative significance as well, because in 1864 the Ottoman authorities established the *vilayet* (district) of Syria, based on the district of Damascus to which they attached adjacent districts.[1]

Nonetheless, in the course of over 1,300 years of Arab and Muslim history, a series of events marked this expanse as distinct in its own right, at least in the collective memory and consciousness of its inhabitants. First, roughly between 650 and 750 the Umayyad dynasty which ruled the Muslim empire made Damascus its capital. It was only later that the heirs to the Umayyads, the Abbasids, moved the seat of the caliphate to Iraq and, later still, made Baghdad their capital.[2] Second, Syria (*Bilad al-Sha'm*) was the site of two momentous battles in Arab and Islamic history. One was Salah al-Din al-Ayyubi's rout of the Crusaders in 1187 at the Horns of Hittin, which brought about the end of the Crusader presence in the region. Salah al-Din himself hailed from Tikrit, in Iraq, but spent most of his adult life in Syria as the founder of the Ayyubid dynasty which ruled Syria and Egypt.[3] The second battle was that of 'Ayn Jalud in 1260 in which Baybars, the Mamluk sultan, defeated the Mongolian army and thus halted its invasion of the heart of the Arab and Islamic world. Lastly, at the close of the nineteenth and start of the twentieth centuries, the Arab national movement sprang up from Syrian soil, with Damascus as its center. For a time this gave Syria special status, at least in its own eyes, as the bellwether of the Arab world. In the words of the Syrians themselves, it served to turn Syria into the "beating heart" of that world and to keep it so up to the present.[4]

The notion of Syria as an entity geographically and sometimes in other ways as well was fertile soil for the appearance of thinkers and writers from the mid-nineteenth century onwards who sought to emphasize the distinction and unity of *Bilad al-Sha'm*. Some viewed inhabitants of the region as a distinct nation, and the territory in which they lived as a discrete political unit which should serve as a national home for its inhabitants. The first of these was Butrus al-Bustani, a mid-nineteenth-century Christian intellectual of Maronite origin. In his writings he stressed the distinctness of Syria territorially but stopped short of affirming the existence of a Syrian people. His writing is therefore an expression of local patriotism rather than of nationalist sentiment. Indeed Syrian identity, limited as it may have been, enveloped Bustani in the more encompassing mantle of Arab and Ottoman identities. He was, incidentally, editor of the newspaper *Nafir Suriya*, the organ of the district of Syria which the Ottomans had established in the 1860s (see above).[5]

Another writer of the period was Henri Lammens, whose book *La Syrie* was published in 1920. This Belgian Jesuit priest living in Beirut posited the existence of a Syrian nation which was neither Arab nor Muslim but had roots older still, some of them Christian, and had been vanquished and subjugated by Arab and Muslim conquerors. Encouraged by the French, Lammens aimed to lay the ideological foundations for the French presence in the Levant; under the French aegis, the Syrian state and nation would be restored to their former glory.[6] Similar notions had in fact been current as early as the close of the nineteenth century among some Christians in the Levant. For example, at the end of the First World War Shukri Ghanim, a Maronite from Mount Lebanon living in Paris, demanded that the Levant be placed in French hands in order to *re-establish* the Syrian state.[7]

Antun Sa'ada, a Greek Orthodox intellectual from Mount Lebanon who in 1932 founded the Syrian National Socialist Party (the PPS), espoused a similar view, though with a different background and objective. Influenced by the success of Fascism in Europe, he proclaimed the existence of a Syrian people who were neither Arab nor Muslim, and advocated the establishment of a greater Syrian state that would serve as a home for this nation. Sa'ada himself was executed by the Lebanese authorities in July 1949, but even after his death his movement continued to enjoy a certain influence in Lebanon and in Syria.[8]

Lastly, King Abdallah I should be mentioned in this context. He founded the Emirate of Transjordan, which later became the Kingdom of Jordan, and from the 1920s until his assassination in July 1951 pressed for the establishment of a Greater Syria (*Suriya al-Kubra*) under his leadership. Abdallah's vision was anchored in the previously mentioned Arab-Islamic worldview that regarded Syria (*Bilad al-Sha'm*) as a homogeneous area – not merely in geographical terms – that constituted a part of the Arab and Islamic world. In this spirit and in keeping with his Hashemite lineage, Abdallah advocated the establishment of a Syrian state under his leadership as a way-station *en route* to comprehensive Arab unity.[9]

These notions of Sa'ada, Abdallah and of course Lammens never aroused the enthusiasm of the majority in geographical Syria or even in the Syrian state after its establishment by the French. Theirs were fringe ideas, pushed aside altogether in favor of the reigning nationalist and Arab perception that pursued the establishment of a large and unified Arab state.

Indeed, even before the demise of the Ottoman empire secret societies began to organize with the goal of achieving independence, or at least autonomy, for the Arab parts of the empire. The appearance of these societies rejected a shift in orientation among the population away from Ottomanism toward Arabism. The extent of support for Arabism and opposition to the Ottoman empire is not clear, but during the course of the war, Jamal Pasha, the Ottoman governor of Syria, executed dozens of Arab nationalist activists on the charge of acting against the empire.

After conquering Syria, the British transferred control of most of its territory to their allies, the Arab nationalists under the leadership of the Hashemite family. Between 1918 and 1920 an Arab kingdom took shape in Syria under King Faysal, with Damascus as its capital, and its establishment was perceived as the first step on the way to attaining Arab sovereignty and independence in these territories. The kingdom was not, however, seen as a territorial state limited to the area circumscribed by its borders, congruent to the territory of the contemporary Syrian state.[10]

Given this background, it is clear why the Syrian state established by the French at the end of the 1920s was perceived as an artificial entity which disturbed the inherited natural harmony of *Bilad al-Sha'm:* the Syrian state was not founded in response to a demand by its inhabitants, but in utter opposition to most of them who demanded the establishment of an Arab state that would stretch across all the lands of geographical Syria at the very least, and if possible embrace Iraq and the Arabian Peninsula as well. Also the French did not regard the establishment of the Syrian state, except for Lebanon, as a fundamental objective of their colonial presence in the region. If they espoused such a goal at the start of their involvement in the Levant, they very soon abandoned it in the face of the prevailing reality in Syria. Indeed, immediately after taking control of the entire Levant in 1920, the French acted to fragment the area. The internal region of Syria was divided into two states; Aleppo and Damascus (based on the Ottoman *vilayets*), which were only united in 1924. In addition, the French established states for the ethnic and religious minorities in the Syrian territory: a Druze state in the area of Jabal Druze, with its capital Suwayda, and an 'Alawi state along the 'Alawi coast, with its capital Ladhiqiyya. Autonomous districts were also established in the Jazira (then populated mostly by Kurds and Turkmen) and in Alexandretta, which also had a large Turkish population. The establishment of the state of Lebanon should also be seen as, *inter alia*, part of the effort to fragment Syria. The French intention was to assure their future control over this territory, once it had fallen into their hands. Even when they set up the Syrian state at the end of the 1920s, they hampered the establishment and operation of its governmental institutions. Rather, they continued to strengthen and entrench the forces of disunity and divisiveness in Syrian society, including sectarian and regional rivalries and the gulf between the urban and rural populations.[11] The legacy of French Mandatory rule would later prove a handicap for the post-independence Syrian regime.

Aside from this, the independent Syrian state (as from 17 April 1946) had to deal with other complex challenges, which stemmed from its demographic composition and other social and political characteristics. Gideon Gera (Avi-Dan), in his article "Elites and Center in Syrian Society", published in 1968, lists seven causes of Syria's lack of stability in those years:

(1) Its geographical location made it a crossroads in the Middle East and hence the battleground for clashes in inter-Arab and international conflicts.

(2) Its ethnic and sectarian divisions included particularly the existence of compact minority communities that constitute the local majority; some 60% of the population of Syria is Sunni Arab, half living in the cities and the other half in the rural areas and the periphery. Christians accounted for some 13% of the population; 'Alawis some 12%, mostly in the 'Alawi region; Druze, approximately 5%, mostly in Jabal Druze; Kurds and Turkmen, some 10%, mostly in the Jazira area; and finally the Ismaili population, accounting for less than 1%.

(3) There was a deep and ancient gulf between urban and rural peoples.

(4) Rivalry existed between the urban centers of Damascus in the south and Aleppo in the north.

(5) The West presented an acute challenge, continuing cultural and political influence and legacy;

(6) A tradition of sovereign independence was lacking, and local communities had no faith in Syria's ability to exist as an independent political unit.

(7) There was no single recognized and accepted governmental center.[12]

The country's political instability hindered the efforts of most of the regimes that governed from Damascus to institute systematic and effective policy. It pushed them into radical, ill-conceived policies and obliged them to give priority to overall Arab interests over purely Syrian ones. Syria's policy on the Palestine question from 1948 onwards[13] and the neo-Ba'th regime's foreign policy in 1966-70, are examples of this.[14] Public opinion therefore found coming to terms with the state's very existence difficult in the first decades of independence, and tended to question its future. Many Syrians instead leaned toward a more sweeping type of identity, not circumscribed by the state's territorial borders; such would be "pan-Arabism" or, among more closely defined circles, "pan-Syrianism" and the notion of a "Greater Syria". At the same time, the individual's primary loyalty focused on the regional, the sectarian, the tribal and sometimes the familial. Lack of stability made Syria prey to an increasing involvement of inter-Arab and Western forces in its affairs. These forces aimed to exploit its fragility to achieve influence, and in so doing exacerbated an already shaky situation, sometimes undermining its very existence as an independent state. Notable examples were Abdallah's "Greater Syria" program, Nuri al-Sa'id's "Fertile Crescent", and the formation of the United Arab Republic (UAR) under Jamal Abd al-Nasir.

Syria's history from independence until Asad's rise to power in November 1970 can be divided into two main periods:

(1) *From independence in April 1946 to the Ba'th Revolution in March 1963.* During this time the Sunni urban elite, which had played a leading role in the social and economic life of geographical Syria for centuries, ruled the country. However, this elite had become weak and was incapable of coping with the challenge of independence – managing an independent Syrian state with acute problems and an uncertain future; and various forces in the social and political system sought to take its place and in so doing the elite fought among themselves. Their internecine struggle was waged partly on ideological grounds (between communists, Ba'thists, and members of the PPS) and partly on socio-economic ones (urbanites versus those from the periphery) with regional, sectarian and personal rivalries also adding to the bitterness.[15]

Foreign powers did not remain impartial observers of the struggle for Syria. Her Arab neighbors, Israel and the superpowers all sought to assure themselves a hold on the Syrian state, which was seen as a key to attaining influence and indeed hegemony in the region. This struggle contributed more than anything else to Syria's image as a weak, unstable state fraught with protracted crises and chronic military coups.[16] In 1958 the crisis that had begun with independence reached a peak when the Syrians decided to merge with Egypt in forming the UAR. Yet what at first seemed like national suicide ultimately turned out for the best. The Syrians were disillusioned with the consequences of the merger, and in September 1961 decided to dismantle the UAR. From that point on they were resolved, whatever happened, to adhere to the political framework of an independent Syria.[17]

(2) *From the Ba'th Revolution of March 1963 to Asad's rise to power in November 1970.* The Ba'th Revolution overturned Syria's traditional pyramid of authority, and the previously dominant Sunni urban elite gave way to a broad coalition of new political and social forces. These forces represented sectors of Syrian society that had previously been denied access to political or economic power, or even to political and socio-economic mobility. Although the Ba'th Party's founders, Michel Aflaq (Greek Orthodox) and Salah al-Din al-Bitar (Sunni), were from the urban middle class, the party drew its strength from society's lower classes – the minority communities and rural and peripheral regions. [18] Consequently the Ba'th regime's rise to power encountered fierce opposition from various sectors in Syrian society that had lost ground with the changes in government. Spearheading this opposition were the Islamic circles whose mainstay consisted of the middle classes of the Sunni urban sector. [19]

The Syrian Ba'th regime also experienced a bitter internal feud during these years. On one side was a group of young military officers, mostly from minority communities, called "the Military Committee" (*al-Lajna al-'Askariyya*), who had been behind the Ba'th Revolution in March 1963. They were at odds with Michel Aflaq and Salah al-Din al-Bitar and their supporters – the founders and veteran leaders of the party. Feuds in Syria were always multi-faceted and this was no exception. The two sides differed in age, ideology and socio-economic orientation. Military officers, mostly from rural and peripheral areas and minority communities, made up the Military Committee under the leadership of Salah Jadid. Beside him stood the 'Alawis, Hafiz al-Asad and Muhammad 'Umran; the Druze and Ismailis; and a group of party colleagues from the Sunni community of the periphery, including Nur al-Din al-Atasi and Yusuf Zu'ayyin, respectively President and Prime Minister of Syria from 1966 to 1970. This group, known as the "neo-Ba'th", adopted radical political views, especially on society and the economy (their socialism followed the East European model). The group quickly began to demand an immediate and drastic social and economic revolution in the spirit of its views, with the aim of improving the lot of the social sectors it represented. At odds with them were Aflaq, Bitar and their supporters. Joining them were other Ba'th Party members from the army and the party hierarchy who mostly belonged to the Sunni urban middle class. On personal, sectarian, political and ideological grounds the Aflaq-Bitar group opposed the radical demands presented by the Military Committee and its supporters, and advocated restraint in implementing social and economic reforms. [20]

In February 1966 the struggle was decided with the triumph of the neo-Ba'th faction under the leadership of Salah Jadid. However, the radical social, economic and foreign policy of Syria's new and inexperienced rulers quickly came to be regarded as divorced from reality and the road to ruin. This policy widened the political divide in Syrian society and reawakened, with increased vigor, opposition to the regime from broad sectors of the population led by the Islamic circles. The foreign policy of Jadid and his colleagues pushed Syria into isolation in the Arab world and ultimately propelled the entire region into the Six-Day War of June 1967. [21]

Syria's defeat in the war spelt an end to the neo-Ba'th regime in Syria. Its top echelon quickly fell to wrangling: the acting Defense Minister, Hafiz al-Asad, led the military faction which advocated restraint and discretion in the face of the harsh realities at home and abroad, while at odds with them were representatives of the civilian faction-party members and representatives and government bureaucrats led by Salah Jadid – an 'Alawi like Asad, though from another tribe. The latter held to their extreme and impassioned stance. In 1969-70 the quarrel reached its climax when Asad, with the backing of the army and security forces, overcame his rivals and seized control of the state. For the first time in its history, a single authority governed Syria, sharing rule with no one else and in effect free of contenders or rivals for power. [22]

## Syria under Asad (1970-85)

Asad's rise to power with the Corrective Revolution of 16 November 1970 was a watershed in the history of the state. Although it has enjoyed continuity, this period, like its precursors, can be subdivided.

*The first six years, 1970-76.* These are most commonly described as "the good years", [23] characterized by relative political stability and economic growth. Thanks to a pragmatic policy and the exploitation of convenient regional and international circumstances, Asad successfully strengthened Syria's regional and inter-Arab position. Domestically he acted to mollify and attract the various sectors in Syrian society which in the past had displayed reservations, if not outright hostility, toward the Ba'th regime. To this end he was prepared to backtrack from the ideological articles of faith that the regime had upheld in the past. He directed these efforts mainly to the Sunni urban sector, hoping to win it over with a policy of economic openness designed to restore the sector's former status in economic life. [24]

Asad also sought a way into the hearts of the Islamic circles in

Syria, by softening his regime's secular image. He began attending prayers in Damascus's Sunni mosques, made a pilgrimage to Mecca, and even tried to win religious legitimacy for his fellow 'Alawis. Indeed, in 1972 Imam Musa Sadr, leader of Lebanon's Shi'ite community, issued a religious edict recognizing 'Alawis as Shi'is, and hence as Muslims.[25] Asad invested particular effort into forging a system of governmental institutions consisting of the People's Assembly, the government, the institution of the presidency, and the National Progressive Front – an umbrella organization covering all the political parties permitted in Syria. This system was meant to confer legitimacy on Asad and his regime, and to guarantee for the regime the support of various sectors of the population who for the first time were represented in these institutions. Finally, it was designed to afford a sense of stability to a state whose lot had for many years been instability and a lack of governmental and legislative institutions.[26]

In the regional and inter-Arab arena Asad acted to defuse the tension, the ideological polarization, and the rivalry and political acrimony which had characterised the Syrian regime's relations with neighboring Arab regimes throughout the 1960s. Syria, of course, bore a considerable share of the responsibility for this hostility, and Asad improved beyond recognition its ties with Jordan, rehabilitated relations with Iraq, and began to acquire for the country a position of influence in Lebanon. A crucial motivation behind these efforts was his ambition to establish an Arab front *vis-à-vis* Israel. The Six-Day War put the conflict with Israel squarely at the top of the Syrian agenda. At issue were the future of the Golan Heights, which Israel captured in June 1967, but also, where Asad was concerned, the future of Syria itself and indeed of the entire Arab nation. He believed Israel to be an enduring threat not only to his country but to all Arabs. He responded to the Israeli challenge by building up a domestic front and, as already mentioned, an inter-Arab front designed to facilitate the achievement of strategic parity between Israel and the Arabs.[27] In this light the significance of the October War becomes clear. The Syrians call it "the October War of Liberation" (*Harb Tishrin al-Tahririyya*), seeing it as the crowning achievement of Asad's regime in those years. This war reflected a new phase in the process of maturation of the Syrian regime and of President Asad himself. For the first time Arabs had taken the initiative, and in the early stages of the war they made impressive gains. The October War did not end in victory, but the Syrian public saw it as an achievement. It was a stark contrast to the Six-Day War, a baptism of fire that had seared failure on to Asad's developing worldview (he was, at that time, a youthful Minister of Defense).[28]

*The struggle for survival, 1976-83*. In 1976, six years after they had come to power, the halcyon days of Asad and his regime ended. The President was soon facing a series of grave crises that threatened his regime. Domestically, Syria was pitched headlong into an economic slump generated by fluctuations in world oil prices. These fluctuations led to a reduction of Gulf aid to Syria and in the numbers of Syrian workers in the Gulf countries. Fewer expatriate workers meant fewer currency-transfers, which had constituted a significant portion of the national balance sheet in the early 1970s.[29] The economic crisis formed a fitting backdrop to the outbreak of the Muslim Brotherhood's Revolt in February 1976. The revolt at first gathered momentum and broad public support, as it seemed at the time, mostly among the urban population in the northern cities of Aleppo, Homs and Hama. It sought to protest against the regime's socio-economic policy, its sectarian character (predominantly 'Alawi), and its secularist worldview. Early in 1980, at the height of the Revolt, the feeling swept Syria and beyond that "the days of the Ba'th regime are numbered".[30]

In June 1976, shortly after the Islamic Revolt broke out, Syrian military forces entered Lebanon at the invitation of the Maronite Christian leadership then in control of the political institutions. Syria's overt involvement in Lebanon's internal affairs was a direct continuation of its active participation in this arena, which had begun in the early 1970s and intensified after the outbreak of civil war in Lebanon in 1975. Syria's intervention manifested its determination to play an active, if not pivotal role in the regional and inter-Arab arena, and its desire to reap the benefits of its relatively stable internal politics.[31]

However, Syria soon began to feel Lebanon as a heavy burden. Its own domestic problems, combined with a lack of readiness among Lebanon's powerful factions to resolve their conflict under its aegis, kept Syria from bringing the civil war in Lebanon to an end. Instead of acquiring the patronage it sought and dictating a new Lebanese order to suit itself, Syria thus found itself struggling through the quagmire of its involvement in Lebanon with no clear means of extricating itself. Most of the forces in Lebanon, among them some of Syria's natural allies in that state (i.e. the PLO and the Muslim leftist camp), took a stand against Syrian involvement. In addition, the heavy economic, military and political burden of that involvement damaged the Syrian army's ability to stand up to the Israelis in the Golan Heights. Furthermore, it stirred sharp domestic criticism, diminished Syria's stature in the Arab world, and harmed its relations with the Soviet Union.[32]

On 19 November 1977 the Egyptian President Anwar Sadat

arrived in Israel. His visit led to the signing of the Camp David Accords in September 1978 and the March 1979 peace treaty between Israel and Egypt. These accords left Syria alone at the forefront of the military and political struggle with Israel, and damaged its chances of regaining the Golan Heights. In 1978 it did succeed in founding, with Iraq, an Arab rejectionist front as a counterweight to Sadat's peace initiative, and thwarted US efforts to widen this initiative to include Jordan and the Palestinians. However, relations between Syria and Iraq soon showed the strains of the longstanding Ba'th Party schism, one faction of which ruled in Iraq, the other in Syria. Personal rivalry and mutual distrust between Saddam Husayn, President of Iraq since July 1979, and President Asad contributed still further to the looming rift.[33]

Ties between Iraq and Syria were ruptured beyond repair with the outbreak of war between Iran and Iraq in September 1980 and Syria's decision to back Iran. Before this – Syria had cut itself off from Egypt over the Israeli-Egyptian peace agreement, but it now severed its connections with the Gulf states and with Iraq and Jordan. Syria's relationship with the last two had been continuously at a low ebb since the late 1970s. The clearest manifestation of Syrian isolation was the refusal by the Gulf states to continue the generous financial aid they had provided to Damascus throughout the 1970s (Iran's financial aid and supply of oil compensation did not cover this loss). Finally, Iraq, Jordan and Saudi Arabia mobilized to help the Islamic movement in its struggle against the Syrian regime until 1982.[34]

Syria's domestic and foreign woes did not escape the notice of Israel, which in 1981-2 exploited them to further its political and security interests at Syrian expense. On 14 December 1981 it applied Israeli law to the Golan and on 6 June 1982 went to war in Lebanon ("Operation Peace for Galilee"). With this war Israel aimed, at least in part, to drive Syria out of Lebanon and establish there a new order of its own.[35] The Israeli move came at the end of Leonid Brezhnev's reign, as the Soviet leader lay ill and his condition denied Syria effective Soviet support and left it alone in the military and political conflict with Israel. In the battles waged in Lebanon, Syria suffered a humiliating military defeat that led to a temporary loss of its grip on that state and checked its aspirations to play a leading role in the region.

Israel's descent into the morass of Lebanon from late 1982 onward did not restore to Syria its lost status there. First, Israel successfully forced the Lebanese regime under Amin al-Jumayyil to sign the Israel-Lebanon agreement of 17 May 1983 (although the agreement ultimately proved meaningless). Second, the United

States sought to take Israel's place in Lebanon: it srengthened its
ties with Amin al-Jumayyil's government and sent marines to Beirut,
and late in 1983 reached the brink of armed conflict with the Syrians in the course of the military and political struggle for control in
Lebanon.[36]

Finally, on 13 November 1983, strained to breaking-point by
mounting tensions and fatigue, President Asad suffered a near-fatal
heart attack. In the ensuing power struggle in the Syrian elite, Rif'at,
the President's brother, till then viewed as the number-two man in
the hierarchy, tried to exploit his brother's illness to advance his
standing as successor. Other forces in the Syrian elite opposed Rif'at,
and later, after he had recuperated, President Asad joined their
efforts to block Rif'at and settle accounts with him for his behavior
while he had lain ill.[37]

*Recovery, 1983-85.* The regime in Damascus had taken a pounding
from 1976 on, but it coped with the successive crises. In the mid-
1980s it emerged with the upper hand from its long struggle for
survival on the home and foreign fronts. Domestically, the violent
suppression of the Revolt which climaxed with the events in Hama
in February 1982, meant the liquidation of the Islamic movement
as an organized and active movement in the country, and assured
the regime many years of calm. It seems also that, despite the widespread sense (at home and abroad) during the period of the Revolt
that the regime was about the collapse, Asad and his regime continued to enjoy the support of broad sectors of Syrian society, including
many in the Sunni community. Furthermore, the regime succeeded
in unifying the ranks and consolidating the power bases that had
made its rise to power possible in the first place. Among these were
the army and security forces, the members of the 'Alawi community
and other minorities, the governmental and party bureaucracy, and
the rural Sunni sector.

Later, at the beginning of 1984, Asad recovered from his illness
and managed to bring the succession struggle to at least a temporary close. In this instance too the Syrian elite demonstrated a large
measure of internal cohesion, in particular an awareness of the need
to prevent a break in its ranks at all costs. Attesting to this is the fact
that Rif'at al-Asad and his associates were prepared to give up their
positions for the good of the regime.[38]

In Lebanon, Syria managed to regain the upper hand. Terrorist
actions carried out by Lebanese and Palestinian organizations with
overt Syrian encouragement succeeded in convincing Israel and the
United States that they were unlikely to achieve anything in Lebanon, and would be wise to leave Syria as the only power in the state.

Taken together, these events turned Syria's military downfall on the battlefield into an important political victory. The Lebanon war made tangible to the Syrians not only Israel's military superiority but also its weaknesses and vulnerabiliy. Indeed, in the war's aftermath and as a lesson drawn directly from it, the Syrians adopted the concept of strategic parity with Israel. At its foundation lay Syrian determination to achieve a balance of power that would give it the capability to face Israel alone on the battlefield. In the short term this meant defense against a possible Israeli threat along the lines of the Lebanon war; in the long term it translated into the ability to launch a successful assault against Israel.

The strengthening of ties with the Soviet Union after Brezhnev's death and Yuri Andropov's rise to power facilitated Syria's achievement of the goal it had set for itself. The Soviet Union bent itself to the task of aiding Syria in its efforts to achieve strategic parity with Israel and supplied it with advanced weaponry. The Syrian national security doctrine, as formulated at that time, had two interlocking elements: gaining independent fighting capability against Israel and reliance on the Soviet Union for political, economic and military support, and especially strategic backing in the event of a possible threat from Israel or the United States. In the mid-1980s both objectives seemed within Damascus's reach.[39]

At that point the Syrian regime could therefore look back with satisfaction on its life-and-death struggle with rivals at home and abroad. From the vantage point of the mid-1980s it seemed to have emerged as the absolute victor: the regime enjoyed apparent immunity, internal cohesion, and support from broad sectors of the Syrian population. Asad regarded this not only as a victory for his policy and proof of his stature as a man and as a leader but also, as is recorded by his biographer Patrick Seale, as a victory for his convictions and his chosen course: it was Syria's unwavering adherence to its positions and views – domestically, in Lebanon and in the regional arena – that had ultimately led to victory.[40] Finally, the regime's achievements enabled it to raise its sights for the first time to targets not mentioned in the past. The struggle for Syria thus ended, and with its close began – with a clear Syrian advantage, as it seemed to Damascus at the time – the struggle for the Middle East.

## NOTES

[1] On the origins of the terms "Syria" and "*Bilad al-Sha'm*" and their evolution through the years see Daniel Pipes, *Greater Syria: The History of an Ambition* (New York:

14 *Introduction*

Oxford University Press, 1990), pp. 13-51, and Kamal Salibi, *A House of Many Mansions: The History of Lebanon Reconsidered* (London: I. B. Tauris, 1988), pp. 57-71.

[2] On the modern Syrian view of the Umayyad period see the interview with the Syrian Foreign Minister, Faruq al-Shar', Syrian Television, 20 August 1998 (DR).

[3] On the Syrian approach to Salah al-Din, see Moshe Maoz, *Asad: The Sphinx of Damascus* (London: Weidenfeld and Nicolson, 1988), pp. 103-5; Henry Kissinger, *Years of Upheaval* (Boston: Little, Brown, 1982), p. 779.

[4] The quote is taken from a newspaper interview with the Syrian Vice-President 'Abd al-Halim Khaddam, *Al-Quds al-'Arabi*, 14 June 1997; see also the remarks of the Syrian Foreign Minister Faruq al-Shar' in the same vein – Syrian Television, 20 August 1998 (DR). For more on the growth of Arabism in Syrian lands see Eliezer Tauber, *The Arab Movements in World War I* (London: Frank Cass, 1993); *idem, The Emergence of the Arab Movements* (London: Frank Cass, 1993); and *idem, The Formation of Modern Syria and Iraq* (London: Frank Cass, 1995); see also Rashid Khalidi, Lisa Anderson, Muhammad Muslih, Reeva S. Simon (eds), *The Origins of Arab Nationalism* (New York: Columbia University Press, 1991); Malik Mufti, *Sovereign States, Pan Arabism and Political Order in Syria and Iraq* (Ithaca, NY: Cornell University Press, 1996).

[5] Albert Hourani, *Arabic Thought in the Liberal Age, 1798-1939* (Cambridge University Press, 1983), pp. 99-102.

[6] For more on this see Kamal Salibi, "Islam and Syria in the Writing of Henri Lammens" in B. Lewis and P. M. Holt (eds), *Historians of the Middle East* (London: Weidenfeld and Nicolson, 1962), pp. 331-42.

[7] See Meir Zamir, *The Formation of Modern Lebanon* (Ithaca, NY: Cornell University Press, 1988), pp. 38-96.

[8] For more on Anton Sa'ada's movement see Labib Zuwiyya Yamak, *The Syrian Social Nationalist Party: An Ideological Analysis* (Cambridge, MA: Harvard University Press, 1966).

[9] See Yehoshua Porath, *In Search of Arab unity, 1930-1945* (London: Frank Cass, 1986), pp. 39-57.

[10] *Ibid.* See also Yusuf al-Hakim, *Suriya wal-'Ahd al-Faysali* (Syria under Faysal) (Beirut: Dar al-Nahar lil-Nashr, 1966); Khayriyya Qasimiyya, *Al-Hukuma al-'Arabiyya fi Dimashq 1918-1920* (The Arab government in Damascus, 1918-1920) (Beirut: al-Mu'assasa al-'Arabiyya lil-Dirasat wal-Nashr, 1982); Malcolm B. Russell, *The First Modern Arab State: Syria Under Faysal, 1918-1920* (Minneapolis: Bibliotheca Islamica, 1975).

[11] For more on the French Mandate period see Philip S. Khoury, *Syria and the French Mandate: The Politics of Arab Nationalism, 1920-1945* (Princeton University Press, 1987); Itamar Rabinovich, "The Compact Minorities and the Syrian State", *Journal of Contemporary History*, 14(4) 1979, pp. 683-712.

[12] Gideon Gera (Avi-Dan), "Elitot ve-Merkaz ha-Hevra ha-Surit" (Elites and the Center in Syrian Society), *Ha-Mizrah ha-Hadash*, 18(3-4) 1968, pp. 205-22.

[13] For more on the Syrian stand on the Palestine question see Philip S. Khouri, "Divided Loyalties? Syria and the Question of Palestine, 1919-1939", *MES*, 21, 1985, pp. 324-48; Itamar Rabinovich, "Syria and the Palestine Question", *Wiener Bulletin*, XXXI (47-8) 1978, pp. 135-41.

[14] See Nikolaos Van Dam, *The Struggle for Power in Syria* (London: I. B. Tauris, 1996), pp. 15-88; Yaacov Bar-Siman-Tov, *Linkage Politics in the Middle East: Syria Between Domestic and External Conflict, 1961-1970* (Boulder, CO: Westview Press, 1983). See also the lecture by Itamar Rabinovich, "Politica Pnimit ve-Mediniyot Huts be-Surya" (Domestic politics and foreign policy in Syria), 9 October 1996) text of the lecture available in the Moshe Dayan Center Library).

[15] For more on power struggles in Syria during the period 1946-63, see Patrick Seale, *The Struggle for Syria*; Nikolaos van Dam, *The Struggle for Power in Syria*; Michael H. Dusen, "Intra- and Inter-generational Conflict in the Syrian Army" (unpubl. Ph.D

thesis, Johns Hopkins University, 1971).

[16] Seale, *The Struggle for Syria*; see also Andrew Rathmall, *Secret War in the Middle East: The Covert Struggle for Syria, 1949-1961* (London: I.B. Tauris, 1994).

[17] On the UAR, see Monte Palmer, "The United Arab Republic: Assessment of its Failure", *MEJ*, 20, 1966, pp. 50-67. See also Itamar Rabinovich, *Syria under the Ba'th 1963-66: The Army-Party Symbiosis* (Jerusalem: Israel Universities Press, 1972), pp. 11-25.

[18] For more on the Ba'th Party, see Kamel Abu Jaber, *The Arab Ba'th Socialist Party: History, Ideology and Organization* (Syracuse University Press, 1966); David Roberts, *The Ba'th and the Creation of Modern Syria* (New York: St Martin's Press, 1987).

[19] On the Islamic movement and its struggle against the Ba'th regime in those years see Umar F. Abd-Allah, *The Islamic Struggle in Syria* (Berkeley, CA: Mizan Press, 1983), pp. 88-103; Itamar Rabinovich, *Syria under the Ba'th*, pp. 109-26. See also Eyal Zisser, "Tenu'at ha-Ahim ha-Muslemim be-Surya: bein Hashlama leMa'avaq" (The Muslim Brotherhood in Syria: between coexistence and struggle), in Meir Litvak (ed.), *Islam ve-Democratia ba'Olam ha'Aravi* (Islam and democracy in the Arab World) (Tel Aviv: Kav Adom, HaKibbutz haMeuhad, 1997), pp. 96-122.

[20] On Syria under the Ba'th regime during the years 1963-6, see Itamar Rabinovich, *Syria under the Ba'th*.

[21] See Nikolaos Van Dam, *The Struggle for Power in Syria*, pp. 34-89; see also Eyal Zisser, "Surya ve-Yisrael: Milhemet Sheshet ha-Yamim ule'ahareha" (Syria and Israel: the Six-Day War and its aftermath), *Iyyunim bi-Tekumat Yisrael*, 8, 1998, pp. 205-52.

[22] See Nikolaos Van Dam, *The Struggle for Power in Syria*, pp. 62-74.

[23] Moshe Maoz, *Asad*, p. 84.

[24] *Ibid.*, pp. 84-9; see also Volker Perthes, *The Political Economy of Syria under Asad* (London: I. B. Tauris, 1995), pp. 23-180.

[25] Moshe Maoz, *Asad*, p. 62.

[26] See *ibid.*, pp. 58-62; Seale, *Asad of Syria*, pp. 169-84; Eyal Zisser, *Decision Making in Asad's Syria* (Washington Institute for Near East Policy, February 1998 – Policy Focus no. 35), pp. 12-16.

[27] See Eyal Zisser, "Israel and Syria – The Six-Day War and Its Aftermath"; see also Moshe Maoz, *Yirael-Surya, Sof haSikhsukh* (Syria and Israel: From War to Peace-Making) (Or Yehuda: Sifriyat Ma'ariv, 1996), pp. 74-124 (for the English edition see Moshe Maoz, *Syria and Israel: From War to Peace-Making*, Oxford: Clarendon Press, 1996).

[28] See Moshe Maoz, *Syria and Israel: From War to Peace-Making*, pp. 96-101, 112-24; Seale, *Asad of Syria*, pp. 125-47.

[29] See Eliyahu Kanovsky, *What's Behind Syria's Current Economic Problems* (Moshe Dayan Center for Middle Eastern and North African Studies, Tel Aviv University, occasional papers, 1985).

[30] Umar F. Abd-Allah, *The Islamic Struggle in Syria*; Eyal Zisser, "The Muslim Brotherhood in Syria"; Hana Batatu, "Syrian Muslim Brethren", *Merip Report*, 12(110) (November-December 1982), pp. 12-20; Thomas Mayer, "The Islamic Opposition in Syria, 1961-1982", *Orient*, 24, 1983, pp. 589-609.

[31] See Reuven Avi-Ran, *Ha-Me'oravut ha-Surit biLvanon 1975-1985* (The Syrian involvement in Lebanon, 1975-1985) (Tel Aviv: Ma'arachot, 1986), pp. 9-76.

[32] *Ibid.*, pp. 77-124; see also Itamar Rabinovich, *The War for Lebanon, 1970-1985* (Ithaca, NY: Cornell University Press, 1986), pp. 89-120.

[33] See Eberhard Kienle, *Ba'th v Bat'th: The Conflict Between Syria and Iraq: 1968-1989* (London: I. B. Tauris, 1990); see also Amatzia Baram, "Ideology and Power Politics in Syrian-Iraqi Relations (1968-84)", in Moshe Maoz and Avner Yaniv (eds), *Syria under Assad* (London: Croom Helm, 1986), pp. 125-39.

[34] Seale, *Asad of Syria*, pp. 355-8.

[35] Ze'ev Schiff and Ehud Ya'ari, *Milhemet Sholal* (Israel's Lebanon War) (Hebrew)

( Jerusalem: Schocken Books, 1984), pp. 40-142 (for the English edition see Ze'ev Schiff and Ehud Ya'ari, *Israel's Lebanon War,* New York: Simon and Schuster, 1984).

[35] Seale, *Asad of Syria,* pp. 391-420.

[37] Eyal Zisser, "*Syria – The Struggle for Power*" in Moshe Maoz, Joseph Ginat and Dan Winckler (eds), *Modern Syria: From Ottoman Rule to Pivotal Role in the Middle East* (Brighton: Sussex Academic Press, 1999), pp. 33-54.

[38] Seale, *Asad of Syria,* pp. 411-28; Itamar Rabinovich, "Syria" in Itamar Rabinovich and Haim Shaked (eds), MECS, vol. IX (1984-5), pp. 643-9.

[39] See Amos Gilboa, "Tfisat haBitahon haLleumi" (The national security doctrine) in Avner Yaniv, Moshe Maoz, and Avi Kover (eds), *Surya veBitahon Yisrael* (Syria and Israel's security) (Tel Aviv: Ma'arachot, 1990), pp. 143-54.

[40] Seale, *Asad of Syria,* pp. 492-5.

# Part I

# SYRIA UNDER ASAD – REGIME AND STATE

## 1

## ASAD'S REGIME – THE THREE ORBITS: 'ALAWI, SYRIAN AND ARAB

The mid-1980s was a peak period in Asad's political career, when he enjoyed regional and international recognition as a prominent leader of the Middle East. He seemed to have succeeded where his predecessors had failed: unlike them, he had held firmly to the reins of power over an extended period, in which he advanced Syria's position to that of a regional power. Many analysts attributed this success to two principal causes. One was the clear sectarian nature of the Syrian regime – it depended on the support of President Asad's own 'Alawi community, whose members controlled the military and security forces. The second was its dictatorial and violent nature. In the course of suppressing the1976-82 Islamic Revolt, it proved its readiness to take drastic steps to maintain control. But in the opinion of these observers, the source of the regime's strength was also, ironically, its Achilles heel. Should future developments undermine the sectarian-security bonds that guarantee the state's stability, the regime and possibly the state itself could collapse – a fate which nearly overtook Saddam Husayn's regime in Iraq in early 1991 after the end of the Gulf War.[1]

Others have argued that neither the regime's sectarian aspect nor its aggressive and violent nature provides an adequate explanation of the state's long run of political stability. What is more, overemphasis on these aspects obscures the political, economic and social processes that took place in Syria under Asad's rule. Raymond Hinnebusch, in his *Authoritarian Power and State Formation in Ba'thist Syria*, offered the counter-argument that the Ba'th regime has successfully entrenched itself in Syria. Its traditional power bases within the 'Alawi community, the army and the security forces, he maintained, have broadened to include more of the Syrian public. Hinnebusch attributed this success to the moderate and pragmatic policy of the regime and its leader, which in turn generated the stability that Syria has enjoyed since Asad seized power.[2]

In this context some qualification of the praises that have been

17

heaped upon Asad and his regime is in order. There is nothing in the following reservations to detract from Asad's achievements; they merely serve to cast in a more realistic light the overall backdrop to his actions between coming to power and his death. First, despite Syria's relative stability under him, and the regime's strong image, his period of rule was marked by a protracted struggle for survival in the face of domestic and foreign challenges. These threatened repeatedly to undermine, if not topple, his regime. The two salient challenges were the 1976-82 Islamic Revolt against the Ba'th regime, and Asad's power struggle with his brother Rif'at in 1983-4. Asad did indeed emerge from this long battle for survival with the upper hand, but it seems that he could not altogether dispel the uncertainty that always hung over his regime, particularly when the time of his own inevitable exit from the political stage arrives. Second, Asad could not claim sole credit for the relative stability that marked his rule. Rather, it was largely a ready-made reality. Years of ruthless struggles for control of the state preceded his rise to power. The feuds, which had to do with ideological, political, socio-economic, sectarian and personal issues, generated the instability that gripped Syria and characterized the state for so long. Asad came to power after these struggles had mostly ended, and after most of the parties involved had exhausted, neutralized or liquidated each other. The stage was nearly empty save for Asad himself. In the 1940s and '50s, the veteran Sunni urban elite which had ruled Syria for hundreds of years lost all its power and influence. Moreover, political opponents had eradicated such powerful political forces as the Syrian National Party (the PPS) and the Communist Party. In the 1960s the Ba'th Party's radical leftist faction ousted the veteran leaders of the Party, Michel Aflaq and Salah al-Din al-Bitar. The senior Sunni military officers – who also played an important role at that time – exhausted themselves in incessant struggles for control over the military and the state. Between 1966 and 1970, members of the Druze and Ismaili communities, who had participated in the neo-Ba'th revolution of February 1966, were expelled from the top echelon. Finally, Salah Jadid and his supporters, Asad's last remaining adversaries, pulled the rug from under their own feet with their radical, not to say adventurist, policy. All that remained for Asad – himself once a member of Jadid's group – was to give the final shove to topple the regime of Jadid and his associates. This was the last obstacle between Asad and the founding of his regime.[3]

Yet Asad's record speaks for itself. Over the years, he proved himself a skillful and sophisticated politician, able to exploit conditions fully to serve his interests. Furthermore, his regime was, relatively at least, a sturdy and stable structure; it was a true representation and reflection of Syrian society, more so than is conventionally assumed outside Syria, and certainly more so than any previous Syrian regime.

Abd al-Nasir once claimed that Egypt exists and acts in a system of three interlocking orbits – Arab, Islamic and African.[4] By the same token it can be said that Asad's regime (and likewise Asad himself) acted in three orbits: 'Alawi, Syrian and Arab. 'Alawi by background and origin, Asad was 'Alawi within, Syrian without, and Arab in his soul. These also shaped the character of the regime: the 'Alawi orbit gave it its internal core; the Syrian orbit its outer shell or body; and the Arab orbit (or the Arab roots from which the regime drew sustenance), its soul, its *raison d'être*, and the legitimacy for its authority.

## The 'Alawi orbit

The Syrian regime was a personal one that surrounded President Asad, and to a significant extent was the work of his own hands. At the same time, it was also a family and even a tribal regime, owing to the central role played by members of Asad's family, chiefly his son Bashar who succeeded him as President and likewise members of his tribe, the Kalbiya. Notwithstanding Syria's close-knit relations with the communist regime of the Soviet Union, it was the personal, family-dominated regimes of Nicolae Ceauşescu in Romania and Kim Il Sung in North Korea that influenced and inspired the Syrian regime. Thus it was no surprise that Ceauşescu's fall in December 1989 was a difficult experience for Asad and an encouragement to his opponents.[5] Kim Il Sung's death in 1993 also shook Asad, and in an unusual step he paid a visit to the North Korean embassy in Damascus to express his condolences, declared a national day of mourning, and sent a personal letter to North Korean leaders stressing the close ties between the two states. In it he described North Korea as a source of inspiration for him and his regime.[6] Yet Asad's regime was also a sectarian one: it depended on the support of the 'Alawi community, which was an important binding agent for the rest of its components. In this perspective the regime was clearly the product of the Syrian 'Alawi community's rise from the humble status of a minority community to pre-eminence. Until the early 1960s, as will be recalled, this community was at the bottom of the social ladder and in the margins of Syria's political and economic system. But in the wake of the February 1966 neo-Ba'th revolution, the 'Alawi officer corps became a power to be reckoned with in Syria, although it continued to act behind the scenes. The 'Alawi takeover of Syria came out into the open after the Corrective Revolution of November 1970, when Asad took on the role of President himself and appointed fellow-'Alawis to key leadership positions.[7]

## The Syrian orbit

The roots of the Syrian regime under Asad spread beyond the 'Alawi community. This regime was the result of the social and political revolution that took place in Syria after the Ba'th Party seized power in 1963, and as such it clearly reflected the ensuing socio-economic and political order in the state. Central to that order was the coalition of forces that brought down the one that preceded it, which had rested on the hegemony of the Sunni urban elite. At its core were the members of the 'Alawi community – a dominant factor which, by virtue of its strength and relative advantage over its partners, guaranteed the coalition's unity and durability. Members of the Sunni community from the rural areas and the periphery constituted a senior partner in this coalition, but under the rule of the Sunni urban elite this sector was denied all social and political mobility, and remained at the bottom of the social ladder, along with members of the minority communities. Its rise up the ladder became feasible only after the 1963 Ba'th revolution and the 1966 neo-Ba'th revolution, i.e. after it joined forces with members of the 'Alawi community – in the army and in the party – while accepting its predominance.

Most of the (visible) Syrian elite since the beginning of the 1970s came from this sector, attesting to its power and importance in the regime. This group included the Vice-President for Foreign Affairs 'Abd al-Halim Khaddam, the Prime Minister Mustafa Miru, the Foreign Minister Faruq al-Shar' and the Defense Minister Mustafa Talas. Other Sunnis, representing the urban class of Syria's Sunni majority, also served in government, including Vice-President Zuhayr Mashariqa and Hikmat Shihabi, who served as Chief of Staff for nearly a quarter of a century (1974-98).[8]

The coalition also included members of the other minority communities in Syria – Christians, Druze and Ismaili – who regarded 'Alawi dominance as a guarantee of their own status and security. They undoubtedly preferred the existing situation to renewed Sunni hegemony in the state. Since Asad rose to power, a fourth group had been making headway slowly and steadily in his coalition, though as a junior and marginal partner. This was the Sunni economic elite, especially in Damascus, which managed over the years to reap the fruits of the policy of economic and political openness that Asad's regime adopted after November 1970 (a trend which gathered momentum in the 1990s – see below), but its influence and access to power-brokers and decision-makers are minimal. It seems, even today, that it will be a long time, if ever, before it becomes an integral part of the ruling apparatus.[9]

Representatives of this coalition of forces, which gave the Ba'th regime its leg-up, held the key positions in Syria's political, social and economic systems during Asad's time. There were only two ways for these individuals to make their way up the social and political ladder before the 1963 Ba'th Revolution. One was the army, which since its inception had drawn to it the minorities and the socially underprivileged. Many who joined were 'Alawis and Sunnis from rural areas and the periphery. For various reasons the 'Alawis acquired a position of dominance in the army, and made it the springboard for their leap to the top echelon of government in the state.[10] The second means of advancement was the Ba'th Party. Like the army, it attracted members of social circles and sectors on the margins of Syrian society. Founded on 7 April 1947 by two high-school teachers from Damascus, Michel Aflaq and Salah al-Din al-Bitar, it was initially a radical party located on Syria's political fringe. Its socio-economic platform, like its secular character, encouraged and assisted 'Alawis and members of other minority communities, as well as rural Sunnis, to join its ranks. Once the Ba'th Party had seized power, members of these social sectors made their way into the rest of the state's institutions, especially the apparatus of civilian government. In the wake of the broad process of nationalization of the Syrian economy in the 1960s they also entered the economic institutions.[11]

Asad's regime was thus anchored more deeply than its predecessors in reality, namely in the political and socio-economic order instituted in Syria following the March 1963 Ba'th revolution, which remained almost unchanged till Asad's death. This argument bears on the current discussion, since it leads to the conclusion that Asad's regime genuinely represented the constituent parts of Syrian society. The regime also reflected quite accurately the balance of power between these components, and enjoyed their support, which helped him in difficult times, such as during the 1976-82 Islamic Revolt. That revolt obviously placed the Syrian regime in jeopardy, and the regime in turn suppressed it with force. However, support for the rebels throughout the various stages of the rebellion was limited to urban concentrations of Sunnis in the north. By contrast, the rural Sunni sector, the members of the minority communities and even the urban Sunni sector in Damascus either supported the regime or at least refrained from backing the Revolt. In so doing, they contributed decisively to its defeat.[12]

It is important to note that the cohesion of the ruling coalition in Syria depended for years on two conditions. The first one was the

ability to satisfy, if only in part, the various elements of this coalition, and it was met on the whole by affording them a sense of belonging
and of participation in the management of state affairs, and by providing an answer – even if incomplete – to their social and economic
needs. In these areas the Syrian regime made significant strides, at
least according to the official statistics. These show an improvement
in both the political representation of these sectors and in their
economic situation. State-funded social and economic services expanded in scope.[13] The second condition for keeping the coalition
together was sustaining 'Alawi predominance in the army and security forces.

Incidentally, Asad's policy (foreign policy in particular) since his rise
to power in 1970 was remarkable for being concerned solely with Syrian
interests and has consistently endeavored to promote them. This
represents a departure from the pursuit of all-Arab interests that came
before. Nevertheless, his regime held back from fostering a sense of
Syrian nationalism or even Syrian uniqueness, in sharp contrast to
neighboring Arab states in which (most prominently Iraq) local
regimes actively encouraged a sense of particularism and historical
uniqueness which, they hoped, would imbue their states and regimes
with legitimacy and historical roots. Thus, neither Syria's long history
nor the abundant archaeological finds made there were used to im-
part legitimacy and uniqueness to the Syrian entity established by
the French in the 1920s and independent since 1946. Although pan-
Arabism as a dominant worldview faded, the regime's reluctance to
cultivate a sense of nationalism or Syrian uniqueness did not change,
even after the Damascus regime's socio-economic concepts and policy
crumbled at the start of the 1990s.[14]

## The Arab orbit

While the 'Alawi and Syrian dimensions gave the regime its outer
shell or body, the Arab roots from which it drew sustenance gave it
its soul. Indeed, the Syrian regime presented itself as an ideological
one, genuinely committed to its worldview and vision for the future.
This commitment was a source of inspiration as well as legitimacy at
home and abroad. It is true that the response of more than a few
analysts was to see Asad as a cynical, unprincipled leader, totally bent
on ensuring his authority within Syria, and if possible also in the territorial area surrounding it ("Greater Syria").[15] However, Syria's more
recent history, Asad's personal background and, especially, his regime's
political record showed that pan-Arabism, not pan-Syrianism, was the
worldview to which he gave allegiance. This does not gainsay what,
in his opinion, was a necessary interim stage for the realization of this

vision, namely the establishment of Syrian hegemony in the area surrounding it – in Lebanon and Jordan, and over the Palestinians.

For years the regime and especially the man at its helm needed this ideological dimension to ensure allegiance to its worldview and vision. The various components of the ruling coalition in Syria, led by the 'Alawi element, had only recently arrived in the corridors of power, and were inexperienced, unprepared and lacking in confidence. The ideological allegiance that the regime had shown over the years provided the legitimacy for its authority, and was also essential to a sense of belonging and full acceptance in Syrian society for the other groups that made up the Syrian mosaic, and of course the Sunni urban element. Furthermore, this ideological commitment consolidated ranks within Asad's coalition by providing them with a platform or common basis for action around which a broad consensus could crystallize.

## NOTES

[1] See, for example, Daniel Pipes, *Syria Beyond the Peace Process* (Washington Institute for Near East Policy, 1996 – Policy Papers, no. 40); Middle East Watch, *Syria Unmasked: The Suppression of Human Rights by the Asad Regime* (New Haven, CT: Yale University Press, 1991).

[2] Raymond A. Hinnebusch, *Authoritarian Power and State Formation in Ba'thist Syria: Army, Party and Peasant*; see also Richard T. Antoun and Donald Quataert (eds), *Syria: Society, Culture, and Polity*.

[3] See Eyal Zisser, "Asad of Syria: The Leader and the Image"; and Nikolaos Van Dam, *The Struggle for Power in Syria*, pp. 48-79.

[4] See Jamal Abd al-Nasir, *Falsafat al-Thawra* (The philosophy of the Revolution) (Cairo, Al-Matba'a al-'Alamiyya, no date).

[5] See *Davar*, 8 March 1990; and also Eyal Zisser, "Syria" in Ami Ayalon (ed.), MECS, vol. XIV (1990), p. 653.

[6] *Al-Ba'th*, 14 July 1994.

[7] Daniel Pipes, "The Alawi Capture of Power", *MES*, 25 (4), 1989, pp. 429-50; Martin Kramer, "Syria's Alawis and Shi'is" in Kramer (ed.) *Shi'ism, Resistance, and Revolution* (Boulder, CO: Westview Press, 1987), pp. 237-54; see also Alain Chouet, "Alawi Tribal Space Tested by Power: Disintegration by Politics", *Maghreb-Machrek*, January-March 1995.

[8] Eyal Zisser, *Decision Making in Asad's Syria*, pp. 17-27; Alain Chouet, "Alawi Tribal Space Tested by Power".

[9] Moshe Maoz, *Asad*, pp. 84-7; see also Hans Hopfinger and Marc Boeckler, "Step by Step to an Open Economic System: Syria Sets Course for Liberalization", *British Journal of Middle Eastern Studies* 23(2), 1966, pp. 183-202; Matthew Gray, "The Political Economy of Tourism in Syria: State, Society, and Economic Liberalization", *ASQ*, 19(2) 1997, pp. 57-73.

[10] Petre Gubser, "Minorities in Power: the Alawites of Syria" in R. D. Mclaurin (ed.), *Political Role of Minority Groups in the Middle East* (New York: Praeger, 1979), pp. 17-48; Amos Perlmutter, "From Obscurity to Role: The Syrian Army and the Ba'th Party",

*Western Political Quarterly*, 22, 1969, pp. 827-45.

[11] For more on the Ba'th Party, see Kamel Abu Jaber, *The Arab Ba'th Socialist Party: History, Ideology and Organization*; David Roberts, *The Ba'th and the Creation of Modern Syria*.

[12] See Umar F. Abd-Allah, *The Islamic Struggle in Syria*, pp. 102-32; see also Eyal Zisser, "The Muslim Brotherhood in Syria", pp. 96-122.

[13] See Raymond A. Hinnebusch, "Local Politics in Syria: Organization and Modernization in Four Village Cases", *MEJ*, 30, 1976, pp. 1-24; "Political Recruitment and Socialization in Syria: The Case of the Revolutionary Youth Federation", *IJMES*, 11, 1982, pp. 143-74; and "Rural Politics in Ba'thist Syria: A Case Study in the Role of the Countryside in the Political Development of Arab Societies", *Review of Politics*, 44, 1982, pp. 110-30.

[14] See, for example, Moshe Maoz, *Asad*, pp. 203-8; see also Youssef M. Choueiri (ed.), *State and Society in Syria and Lebanon* (University of Exeter Press, 1993).

[15] See Daniel Pipes, *Greater Syria*, pp. 115-88.

# 2

## THE SYSTEM OF GOVERNMENT
## IN ASAD'S SYRIA

The Syrian regime that Asad established after coming to power in November 1970 and bequeathed to his son Bashar in June 2000 has two aspects. On the surface there is a formal governmental system – a system of legislative and executive institutions. Organized and hierarchical, it is anchored in the Syrian constitution and that of the Ba'th Party. It comprises the People's Assembly, the government and the presidency of the Republic, alongside the Ba'th Party institutions. Other political bodies, such as popular organisations, professional associations and trade unions, are claimed to represent additional sectors of Syrian society. This formal system reflects the numerical strength of the elements of the coalition on which the regime rests. The regime uses the formal system to create a sense of legitimacy and an air of legality for its actions, and to reward its supporters. By integrating them into the system, it is able to satisfy their expectations of proximity to political power and of economic and social mobility.

No less important is the hidden face of the Damascus regime. This is the informal ruling apparatus that consists mainly of the heads of the security services and senior military commanders. The regime depends on them to ensure stability in the state and to protect it. These officers are participants, some overt but most covert, in the apparatus of government. Their status and strength is a reflection not so much of the letter or spirit of the Syrian constitution as of the intrinsic balance of power among the coalition of forces which are the foundation of the regime.

The difference between the formal and informal systems is thus one of quantity *versus* quality. The formal governmental system is more representative and reflects the relative weight of the coalition's elements among the public at large. Thus, for example, Sunnis constitute some 60% of government ministers and delegates to the People's Assembly or the Party Congress. This figure corresponds to their percentage of the population. By contrast, the informal system reflects the qualitative relationship – the true balance of power among the forces in Hafiz and Bashar al-Asad's coalition. Because 'Alawis are the dominant element in this coalition, even though they form a minority of 12% of the population, almost 90% of the military commanders and heads of security services are 'Alawis.[1]

## The formal apparatus of government

In practice this system consists of two parallel, integrated subsystems: that of the party and that of the civilian government. The former has priority by virtue of the Syrian constitution, of which Clause VIII states: "The Ba'th Party leads society and the state and stands at the head of the National Progressive Front, which acts to unite the forces of the masses and to mobilize them in the service of the goals of the Arab nation."[2]

Through the branches, departments and cells of the Ba'th Party organization the word of the party reaches throughout the state. Every four years, party branches elect their representatives to the Party Congress and this in turn elects the party institutions: the 90-member Central Committee (*al-Lajna al-Markaziyya*) and the 21-member Regional Command (*al-Qiyada al-Qutriyya*). The latter is the highest body of both party and state, and this status is emphasised in the manner of electing Syria's President: first the Regional Command of the Party approves the candidate and then the People's Assembly may endorse him. Lastly the candidacy is submitted to a public referendum.[3] At the head of the party stands the Party's Secretary-General, a position held today by Hafiz al-Asad.

In theory the Ba'th Party in Syria, with all its national institutions, constitutes part of an overall network of Ba'th parties active throughout the Arab world. These pan-Arab institutions correspond to the national ones, but enjoy legislative superiority over them. At the apex stands the supreme leadership, called the National Command (*al-Qiyada al-Qawmiyya*), which in theory has supreme authority over Ba'th Party Regional Commands throughout the Arab world. In at least one instance the Ba'th Party National Command implemented its formal supremacy. In 1963, under the guidance of its leaders and founders Michel Aflaq and Salah al-Din al-Bitar, the National Command intervened in Iraqi affairs, dictating to the party leadership and its members their political moves in the midst of a domestic crisis. This step was seen in hindsight as disastrous, since it led to the loss of Ba'th Party rule in Iraq for a number of years.[4]

Today the distinction between the regional (i.e. countrywide) and national (pan-Arab) institutions has no practical significance. The two important centers of activity of the Ba'th Party remain, as before, in Damascus and Baghdad. However, neither of these centers recognizes the other as legitimate, nor do they maintain communications. This schism between Damascus and Baghdad has led to the division of many Ba'th Party branches in the Arab world. Thus, until Syria's full takeover of Lebanon, two factions of the party were active there: one pro-Syrian and the other pro-Iraqi. The latter was liquidated when Lebanon became a Syrian protectorate. Today the Syrian faction of the Ba'th Party exercises full control over most of the Ba'th parties in the Arab world, for example in Jordan and Lebanon and among the Palestinians. It also presides over the all-Arab institutions of these parties. Further more, owing to past experience as well as to a vision of the future, Asad has not only ensured his election as Secretary-General of the Syrian Ba'th Party but he also heads the National Command of all Ba'th parties throughout the Arab world, or at least those parts controlled by Syria.

As mentioned above, an executive system and legislative institutions function alongside the party system. These are controlled almost entirely by Ba'th Party members in key positions. The system of legislative bodies in Syria includes the People's Assembly (*Majlis al-Sha'b*), composed of 250 members elected in regional elections every four years, of whom some 60% are members of the National Progressive Front, which comprises all the political parties permitted in Syria, chief of them the Ba'th Party. More than 40% are independent candidates.[5] According to the Syrian constitution, the Assembly's authority includes, *inter alia*, endorsement of the candidate for the Presidency of the Republic following approval by the Ba'th Party Regional Command; ratification of laws; and approval of the budget, development programs, international treaties and contracts. The Assembly also has the authority to review and criticize government policy as necessary. The executive authority includes the President of the Republic and the government, defined as "the highest executive and administrative body in the state".[6] The prime minister and other ministers answer to the President who appoints them, but the government is required to report to the People's Assembly. Most of the communities of Syria are represented in the government according to their relative weight in the population. In the 1960s 'Alawis and members of other minorities – in other words, members of the peripheral regions – were represented in government institutions such as the party leadership or the Revolutionary Council disproportionately to their numbers in the population but this imbalance has been corrected, in part at least, under Asad's rule.[7]

Political parties other than the Ba'th are permitted in Syria. These are chiefly, leftist parties, such as both factions of the Syrian Communist Party and those parties with Nasserist roots, mostly a remnant of Syrian politics of the 1950s and '60s. These parties are united in the National Progressive Front, a body established in 1972 and headed by President Asad.

*The informal ruling apparatus*

There is more to the Syrian regime than its formal system: an informal one coexists with it. This informal apparatus reflects the qualitative balance of forces in Hafiz and Bashar al-Asad's coalition, a balance dominated by members of the 'Alawi community. It centers mainly on the chiefs of the security services and the senior army officers (see Ch. 2), whose contribution is critical to ensuring stability in the state. They also, in large measure, hold the key to its future, yet in daily life, and certainly in the social and economic spheres, their weight and influence are much less than is commonly supposed. This is because their orientation and consequently their interests lie firmly in military and security matters as opposed to social and economic issues.

Via the Ba'th Party institutions efforts are made to bridge the gap between the formal and informal systems. The party is in many respects where the two systems converge. It provides an ideological cloak which both can share, woven from the political and socio-economic worldview common to all the forces active in Syria – bureaucrats in the party and the administrative apparatuses, and senior military officers. Furthermore, the party institutions provide a meeting place for political leaders and army officers, since the party has branches in the military and security forces and these elect their own representatives to its top institutions. In these institutions, as in the Central Committee or the Regional Command, the party bureaucrats and government functionaries sit side by side with senior commanders of the army and the security forces.[8]

The integration of military and security chiefs into party institutions is meant to express the party's supremacy over other systems and institutions in Syria. Certainly this is the case where the army is concerned; the regime took care to present it as an ideological army, i.e. the emissary and executant of the Ba'th Party's directives. In a practical perspective, this integration is part of an effort to establish and maintain a bridge between the formal and informal wielders of power; to create a common language or perhaps a joint basis for action; and to facilitate a dialogue that could mitigate or resolve conflicts. In the past, efforts to ensure the supremacy of party institutions over the military have failed. Moreover, at the decisive moment the party institutions proved unequal to the task of restraining rival camps and imposing a compromise to facilitate dialogue between them. Thus in 1969-70 the overwhelming majority of the party and government institutions lined up behind Salah Jadid in his clash with Hafiz al-Asad, but Asad had won the support of the military-security system and with its help took over Syria in November 1970.

After Asad's coup the government and party institutions were purged of Jadid's supporters and replaced by those of Asad.[9] The conflict which erupted in 1983-4 between Asad and his brother Rif'at was played out primarily within the military system, in absolute disregard of the party and governmental apparatus. Asad had tried to work via the party establishment (the formal system), but the appointment of a six-man committee of senior government and party representatives to run Syria during his illness ran foul of an insurgency organized by senior 'Alawi officers. The latter had united around Rif'at to oppose the committee, which they saw as a possible threat to their status and to the ascendancy of the 'Alawi community in Syria. Later, when Asad had recovered and taken a stand against his brother, most of the officers abandoned Rif'at and flocked back to Asad's side. The fraternal conflict was thus played out exclusively within the military-security system. Only after Hafiz al-Asad defeated his brother within that system did he convene the January 1985 Ba'th Party Congress. New party institutions were elected and Rif'at's supporters were weeded out[10] (see Ch. 8: "The Struggle for Succession").

The distinction between these parallel systems in Syria sets in bold relief the centrality of the President – Hafiz and, today, Bashar al-Asad: he directs them both, presiding over the totality of party and legislative institutions in Syria with a firm hand. He is the Secretary-General of the Ba'th Party in Syria and head of its pan-Arab hierarchy. As President of the Republic, he steers the formal government system, by virtue of which role he is also Commander in Chief of Syria's armed forces. However, it should be remembered that President Asad's standing did not derive solely from the spirit and letter of the Syrian constitution. It stemmed from his absolute mastery over the informal system, i.e. over the commands of the military and security forces.

## The Syrian elite

President Asad was the central pillar of the Syrian regime. His personality and political status bound together its disparate, sometimes competing elements. His character and particularly his image both within and outside Syria constituted beyond doubt a powerful source of strength for the Syrian regime. Despite the regime's personal and sectarian nature and all the hatred and antagonism Asad inspired across broad swathes of the Syrian public, he inspired tremendous respect – or, more precisely, awe. The high regard for him in Syria and, to a great extent, in the Arab world beyond it was due to his political record: he succeeded in maintaining stability in his state for more than a quarter of a century and won admiration for his stand in everything connected with the Arab-Israeli conflict and other all-Arab issues. The steps he took were not necessarily characterized by great courage or a readiness to take risks, but insofar as they reflected the consensus view in Syria and the Arab world, they generally attracted the support and esteem of the man in the street. Asad's record, the respect or awe he inspired and his political power within the Syrian government system combined to make him an indispensable leader. However, although his status in Syria was clearly an advantage to the regime, it was also a potential drawback: reliance, if not outright dependence, on Asad the individual had clear implications for Syria's domestic stability when he quit the political arena in June 2000.

The ruling elite that functioned at Asad's side, helping him to maintain his regime and govern the state, reflected accurately the coalition of forces, if not the political and socio-economic order, on which the Ba'th regime was founded. At least some heads of the formal system were members of this elite – as, of course, are the principals of the informal apparatus. An individual's membership of the elite or of Asad's inner circle and status there did not necessarily derive from his official position: the determining factors are personal status or the standing of the body one controls in the overall range of forces in Syria. Thus, commanders of army divisions or heads of security services enjoyed and still enjoy immense respect and influence and form an integral part of the Syrian ruling elite. By contrast, most of the senior ministers in the government enjoy no such standing and are denied access to Asad's inner circle.

Acceptance into the Syrian elite came via ties to President Asad. By the same token, the key to the status of members of the top echelon is the degree of proximity to the President which they enjoy. Members of this elite reached the top thanks to one of the following four types of links to Asad: (1) family connections: e.g. his brothers or sons; (2) tribal or communal ties – belonging to Asad's tribe, the Kalbiya, or his community, the 'Alawis; (3) ties of personal friendship to Asad's circle of friends who shared his thinking and approach, some of whom had been his companions since the 1950s and '60s – the formative years of his journey to the top: and (4) occupational ties, being one of Asad's assistants and advisers, people who had long worked closely with him.

These were the basic groups that together formed the Syrian elite under President Asad. Although the nature of the connection to President Asad differs from group to group, all four share certain general characteristics: first and foremost, a common socio-economic background. As already mentioned, members of this elite reflected and represented the ruling coalition, namely the same social forces or socio-economic and political order that underpinned the Ba'th regime from the time it seized control in Syria to the present. The second characteristic was age and seniority in the job: most of those close to Asad were his contemporaries, and had performed the same functions for many years, in some cases for more than two decades. It was, in a sense, a sign of stability. It also made clear Asad's predilection for preserving the *status quo*, limiting change as much as possible, and avoiding the upheaval of replacing people to whom he had become accustomed and whom he trusted. Defense Minister Mustafa Talas had held his position since 1972, and Hikmat Shihabi served as Commander in Chief for nearly a quarter of a century, from 1974 to 1998. The situation was similar in the civilian sector. The Foreign Minister, Faruq al-Shar', had served in this post since 1985 and the Prime Minister, Mahmud al-Zu'bi, had served in his position from 1987 to 2000, to name but two.

A third characteristic prevalent among those in the Syrian elite is their political background: most of those surrounding President Asad grew from the same military or party roots. Furthermore, most studied in military or academic institutions in Eastern Europe and, as a result, developed a clear East European orientation in their approach to military, political and socio-economic issues.

*Members of Asad's family.* The inner core of the elite consisted of Asad's relations. Owing to the Syrian regime's personal and familial character, this group had particular importance. Three layers, or ranks, were discernible within this group. Specifically, these corresponded to three generations reflecting three stages in the expansion of the Asad family's grip on Syria's ruling institutions. The first layer was the brothers' generation, namely Rif'at and Jamil, who until 1985 played a leading role in the regime's top echelon. Then there were the second-ranking relations such as 'Adnan Makhluf, a nephew of Asad's wife Anisa, or 'Adnan al-Asad who played a prominent role in the regime's elite until the beginning of the 1990s. The third layer is the generation of the sons: Basil and, after his death in a car accident in January 1994, Bashar, and to a lesser extent Asad's third son, Mahir. This generation began making its way to the top with their father's encouragement and involvement early in the 1990s, and seized power following his death in June 2000 (see Ch. 8: "The Struggle over Succession").[11]

*The 'Alawi barons.* Commanders of the military and security forces, who were members of Asad's tribe and community, constitute another powerful group in the Syrian elite, and under Bashar al-Asad they still play an important role. Their control over those forces is the source of their strength because they maintain Syria's political stability and have been the bulwark of Asad's regime since the 1970s. Their power is indispensable to the regime, and they bind its constituent forces into a coalition. Moreover, they are a deterrent factor at home and abroad against any attempt to harm or overturn the Ba'th regime.

A significant number of analysts have referred to the Syrian regime, particularly its topmost echelon, in terms commonly used to describe the Mafia. President Asad and the surrounding elite were compared to a "godfather" and his associates.[12] Without being drawn into a debate over the appropriateness of this comparison one can say that it does have something to contribute to an understanding of the issue. To extend the metaphor, the 'Alawi officer' corps can be compared to strong-arm men in the service of the "godfather", the family patriarch, who defend his position and carry out his directives. Their importance comes to the fore when the patriarch dies and a struggle ensues over succession. Such strong-arm men were a recognized phenomenon in Middle Eastern societies of the past, e.g. the *Qabadiyat*, the fighting men of the Sunni urban notable families in the Levant, who played a key role in preserving and boosting their power.[13]

Under the protection and with the encouragement of the regime, these officers turned the military units and security agencies under their command into political and economic fiefdoms – a focus of power and support, not to mention sizeable sources of revenue. For example, a main source of income for these officers is commissions and brokerage fees from merchants and businessmen who seek to exploit the officers' ties and influence in the corridors of power to advance their interests. There have even been cases of 'Alawi officers serving as hidden partners in financial deals and partnerships. According to Western sources, highly-placed people in the army and security forces had a hand in drug cultivation and trade in the Biqa' Valley in Lebanon, and even in smuggling from Lebanon into Syria. During Rif'at al-Asad's tenure as commander of the "Defense Companies", his officers and troops would host a weekly market day in Damascus of goods smuggled in from Lebanon, most of which could not otherwise be had in Syria. Rif'at and his officers collected tidy commissions.[14]

This group of 'Alawi officers is loosely affiliated, and its members differ in age and in family and tribal origin. Tensions and power struggles intermittently break through the surface. Ranks have closed only in the face of external threats to this group or, of course, to the existence of the Ba'th regime. In practice it should be seen as a coalition of forces within the 'Alawi community which Asad forged from the time of his rise to power. Indeed, as the coalition of communities and minorities – Asad's largest coalition – assured his rule in Syria, so the coalition of 'Alawi forces safeguarded his rule within the 'Alawi community, and ensured the transition power into the hands of his son Bashar. This 'Alawi coalition is based primarily on ties of blood and marriage, and in addition, on political alliances and client–patron relationships. Together these brought Asad the support of other families in the community who were integrated into his family or joined it politically in exchange for political, economic or other favors from him. Incidentally, Asad's first step in politics was to wed Anisa: marriage into the Makhluf clan, an important one in Asad's village of Qurdaha and in his tribe, the Kalbiya, boosted his status there. It also extended his range of contacts, enabling him to establish firm ties with other 'Alawi elements such as members of the Haddadin tribe, with whom the Makhluf clan had connections.[15]

*The third group* of influential figures who supported Asad was made up of members of the Sunni community who shared his views regarding the future of the state. This group played a number of pivotal roles in the Syrian elite, i.e. the formal political system, but its strength was grounded in its strong ties with President Asad, deriving from long-term personal friendships and common ideas and purposes. The members were close and formed, together with Asad, something of a club. Within this "kitchen cabinet" important decisions were taken on the running of the Syrian state and in areas of foreign policy and security.

This group had several prominent characteristics. First, most of its members were rural Sunnis who reflected or, more precisely, represented this central component in the socio-political coalition of forces upon which the Ba'th regime was founded. Second, they were Asad's close friends, most of them his contemporaries, who had stood beside or behind him for decades, since his first days in Syrian politics. Third, they all filled senior roles in the top ranks of the formal government or party system and were in charge not only of defining policy but of executing it. Fourth, most of this elite grew out of the party system; only a minority reached their position via the military route.

Among the members of this group was 'Abd al-Halim Khaddam, who had served as Vice-President for Foreign Affairs since March 1984. Born in the coastal town of Banyas in the 'Alawi region, Khaddam's acquaintance with Asad began in the late 1940s, when they belonged to the Ba'th Party's students' association led at the time by Asad. While Asad climbed up the military ladder, Khaddam rose in the party system. He served as governor of Hama in 1964, of Qunaytra in 1967, and later of the Damascus district. Even before Asad's rise to power, he was appointed Minister of Finance and Foreign Trade, and in 1971 he became Foreign Minister.[16]

Hikmat Shihabi was born in Aleppo and from 1974 to 1998 served as Chief of Staff. Before that, in 1971-4, he served as chief of military intelligence, and from 1968 to 1971 was assistant to the head of the military security department, a position from which he aided Asad's ascent to the presidency. As the years passed, Shihabi carried out a series of sensitive secret missions for Asad that were a complete departure from his formal duties as Chief of Staff. At the end of 1973 he was sent to Washington for the opening of the US-mediated Israeli-Syrian negotiations over the signing of a disengagement agreement for the Golan Heights. Shihabi's counterpart in these discussions was the Israeli Defense Minister Moshe Dayan. In 1976 he prepared the ground for Syrian involvement in Lebanon, and late in 1978 went to Iraq as Asad's messenger in an effort to establish an Arab rejectionist front against the then Egyptian President Anwar al-Sadat's peace initiative. Shihabi was Asad's messenger again in talks with the Israeli Chiefs of Staff, Ehud Barak and Amnon Shahak, at the end of 1994 and in mid-1995, another clear sign of Asad's trust in him.[17] And yet when the time came, in July 1998 – owing to his health problems, and perhaps also out of a desire to ease his son Bashar's ascent to the top – Asad unflinchingly signed Hikmat Shihabi's retirement orders.[18]

Mustafa Talas, who served as Defense Minister from 1972, became acquainted with Asad in an officers' training course at the Hums Military Academy in 1950. In 1968-72 he served as Chief of Staff and Assistant Defense Minister and in this capacity helped Asad to seize power. In return he was awarded the defense ministry.[19] Others in this category included Abdallah al-'Ahmar, assistant secretary-general of the Ba'th Party's National Command, born in the village of al-Tall, north of Damascus; Ra'uf al-Kasm, a native of Aleppo, director of the Office of National Security; and Mahmud al-Zu'bi, born in Hauwran, who served as Prime Minister from 1987 till 2000 and in the past was Speaker of the People's Assembly.

As already mentioned, these men, individually and as a group, draw their power from their proximity to President Asad. There is no doubt, however, that Asad needed this political and personal association. Neverthless, he was occasionally capable, usually under duress, of dispensing with the services of one of its members, who mostly had no standing or power-base of their own. One noteworthy case is that of Naji Jamil, a member of the Syrian elite until 1979. A Sunni from Dayr al-Zur, Jamil went to flying school with Asad and has stuck by him ever since, climbing with him to the top. He was for many years commander of the air force although, unlike Asad himself, he never completed his flight training or served as a pilot. Jamil was also a member of Asad's inner circle, but his defiance of the President at the end of the 1970s shortened his career; he was relieved of his position and for a time placed under house arrest.[20] The case of Hikmat Shihabi, a devoted friend of Asad who one day suddenly found himself pensioned off, offers similar testimony.

These were the faces of the Syrian elite and, in a more general way, the image of Asad's regime – an image fashioned during the 1970s and which never lost its features thereafter. In the early 1980s it seemed that the character and composition of the regime and of the Syrian elite were Asad's trump card, the source of his own power and that of his regime. However, since the late 1980s this assumption has seemed uncertain as events have turned this source of strength into a handicap and even a weakness. Thus there was no surprise when President Asad had to remove many members of the elite from their positions in order to ensure his son Bashar's candidacy as his successor. It also seems likely that consolidating a loyal and committed elite will be a priority for Bashar as President.

## NOTES

[1] See Dar al-I'tisam, *Ma'sat al-'Asr alati Faqat majazir Sabra wa-Shatila* (The massacre that was greater than Sabra and Shatila) (Cairo: Dar al- I'tisam, no date), p. 150.

[2] For the full text of the Syrian constitution see *al-Thawra*, 1 February 1973; see also Syrian Arab Republic, "The Constitution of 1973", *MEJ*, 28(1), 1973, pp. 53-6.

[3] See Radio Damascus, 1 August 1984 – DR, 2 August 1984.

[4] See Itamar Rabinovich, *Syria Under the Ba'th*, pp. 80-4.

[5] See Eyal Zisser, "Syria – The Elections to the People's Assembly (August 1994): Exercising Democracy?", paper presented at the MESA (Middle East Studies Association of North America) Conference, San Francisco, 21–24 November 1997.

[6] See *Al-Thawra*, 1 February 1973.

[7] Michael van Dusen, "Political Integration and Regionalism in Syria", *MEJ*, 26, 1972, pp. 123-36.

[8] For the composition of government institutions in Syria, see Itamar Rabinovich, "Syria", in Itamar Rabinovich and Haim Shaked (eds), MECS, vol. IX (1984-5), pp. 645-7; Eyal Zisser, *Decision Making in Asad's Syria*, pp. 5-17.

[9] Nikolaos van Dam, *The Struggle for Power in Syria*, pp. 48-79; see also Mahmud A. Fakhsh, "The Alawi Community of Syria: A New Dominant Political Force", *MES*, 20, 1984, pp. 133-53.

[10] Patrick Seale, *Asad of Syria*, pp. 437-40.

[11] Eyal Zisser, *Decision Making in Asad's Syria*, pp. 5-28; Alain Chouet, "Alawi Tribal Space Tested by Power: Disintegration by Politics".

[12] See Daniel Pipes, *Syria beyond the Peace Process*, pp. 9-31; Eyal Zisser, *Decision Making in Asad's Syria*, pp. 3-12; Itamar Rabinovich, "The Godfather", *New Republic*, 3 July 1989, pp. 35-8.

[13] For more on this see Michael Johnson, *Class and Client in Beirut* (London: Ithaca Press, 1986), pp. 45-81.

[14] See, for example, Moshe Maoz, *Asad*, pp. 167-8; Zisser, *Decision Making in Asad's Syria*, pp. 21-5.

[15] Seale, *Asad of Syria*, pp. 55-7.

[16] See *al-Watan al-'Arabi*, 26 August 1988; Seale, *Asad of Syria*, pp. 35-9.

[17] *Yidi'ot Aharonot*, 30 June 1995; Seale, *Asad of Syria*, pp. 226-49, 311, 355; see also Uri Sagie, *Orot baArafel* (Lights within the fog) (Tel Aviv: Yidi'ot Aharonot, 1998), pp. 246-52.

[18] *Al-Hayat*, 3 July 1998; *Ha'aretz*, 3, 5 July 1998.

[19] See Talas's autobiography, *Mira't Hayati* (The story of my life) (Damascus: Dar Talas lil-Nashr, 1992, 1994), 2 vols.

[20] Seale, *Asad of Syria*, pp. 173-7.

# Part II

# A NEW PATH

# 3

## THE FRIENDSHIP THAT FAILED – SYRIA IN THE SHADOW OF THE SOVIET COLLAPSE

### *The rise and fall of Mikhail Gorbachev*

On 11 March 1985 Moscow released the news of Mikhail Gorbachev's appointment as General Secretary of the Soviet Union's Communist Party, replacing Konstantin Chernenko who had died after one year in office. The choice of Gorbachev, a young and energetic party functionary, was designed to give the Soviet Union stable and effective leadership after nearly a decade of ageing and frail Kremlin premiers.

The Syrian reaction to the news from Moscow was positive. Damascus hoped that Gorbachev's appointment would end the confusion and instability in the top Soviet echelon, and that Syria would again obtain a sympathetic hearing and helping hand from its long-standing and, in fact, only remaining ally. In his congratulatory remarks to the new Soviet leader, Asad spoke of the firm bonds of friendship and cooperation between the two states and expressed the hope that they would continue and deepen in the Gorbachev era. "Comrade Chernenko", wrote Asad, "was a partner who was devoted to the Soviet Union and to peace, socialism and the friendship between the Soviet Union and the other nations that fight imperialism and Zionism. It is my hope that Syrian-Soviet friendship will continue to grow stronger. We in Syria will work toward this end and I am convinced that the Soviet leadership will do so as well."[1] However, Asad, was soon to discover that the glory days of Syrian-Soviet relations were past. Later, when the extent of the calamity Gorbachev had brought upon the Soviet Union became clear, a senior Syrian official was quoted as saying, "We regret the Soviet collapse more than the Russians do."[2]

Gorbachev's rise to power in Moscow found the Syrian regime more dependent than ever on its ties with the Soviet Union, as the extensive arms deals in 1983-4 made clear. These had enabled Syria to

37

develop – as a lesson from the 1982 Lebanon war – its new concept of national security: strategic parity with Israel.[3] Syria even signed a treaty of friendship and co-operation with the Soviet Union on 8 October 1984, a step which it had never taken in the past.[4] This was something of a departure from Asad's traditional policy whereby Syria held back from becoming a client beholden to Moscow's favours and rubber-stamping its dictates. Until the early 1980s Asad also tried to maintain a high degree of maneuverability in the international arena and took care not to shut the door to dialogue and improved relations with the United States. Thus, after the October 1973 war he considered putting in motion an effort to step up contacts with Washington. One goal of such an effort would have been to improve the chances of Syria regaining the Golan Heights.[5]

Stronger ties and dependence on the Soviet Union were a blessing for Syria, at least in the short term. They facilitated its military rehabilitation and set it on a new course leading, or as the Syrians hoped, to a balance of power with Israel. The alliance with the Soviet Union boosted Syrian self-confidence, and on the eve of Gorbachev's emergence Damascus felt a sense of strength and satisfaction at having survived a long drawn-out struggle for survival. The overall feeling was that Asad's regime had reached a plateau of calm and security. The Islamic Revolt had been put down, an Arab rejectionist front against the Israeli-Egyptian-American axis was now established, and Syria had re-asserted its position in Lebanon and begun to drive Israel out of that country.

It must be emphasised that since mid-1967 the issue of the conflict with Israel had remained a top priority for Syria. Its importance redoubled after 1979, following the signing of the Israeli-Egyptian peace treaty which removed Egypt – the largest and strongest Arab state – from the front line of the Arab conflict with Israel. The latter did not wait long before moving to take advantage of the new regional circumstances created in the wake of the peace treaty; it soon began efforts to drive Syria out of Lebanon and, perhaps, also to advance much longer-term strategic goals by exploiting the Syrian regime's recent difficulties. Even after Syria had emerged from its troubles and regained its former status in Lebanon, the question of Israel continued to preoccupy the Syrian leaders, although other issues occasionally diverted their attention. These included the Islamic Revolt, which reached a peak and ended in 1982; the power struggle within the Syrian elite during 1983-4; and regional and inter-Arab issues such as the war between Iran and Iraq. However, once these problems were resolved, Damascus's focus reverted to the struggle with Israel and its practical manifestation at the time – the struggle for hegemony in the Lebanese arena.

The Syrian regime chose to deal with what it perceived as a real and enduring threat to Syria's national security and that of the entire Arab world by adopting, developing and perfecting the concept of strategic parity with Israel. The original goal had been to bring about an overall balance between the Arab world and Israel, i.e. to establish an all-Arab coalition of forces, but now that this had failed, the concept changed. Achieving strategic parity with Israel would make Syria independently capable of blocking Israel's future "attempts at aggression", and of defeating Israel and dictating to it terms for the establishment of an "Arab order" in the region to Damascus's liking.

In the years following Israel's Operation Peace for the Galilee (the Lebanon war of June 1982), the strength of the Syrian army increased significantly. Its military capacity mushroomed from 300,000 soldiers in 1983 to 500,000 in 1985, and new divisions and units were established. It acquired advanced Soviet weaponry, including fighter planes, surface-to-air and surface-to-surface missiles with much greater ranges, and electronic and air-control battle systems. Damascus hoped that these armaments would close, or at least narrow, the qualitative gap between Israel and Syria, to which the Syrians attributed their defeat in the 1982 Lebanon war.[6]

Syria's effort to expand and upgrade its fighting forces had exacted a price. It naturally involved a significant increase in military expenditure, with which the country had difficulty coping. Even in normal times real spending on the military accounted for nearly half the gross national product – although a far different picture emerged from the official national budget as published by the Damascus regime. The military expansion and upgrading since 1982 boosted expenditure even beyond this threshold.[7]

The growing security burden exacerbated the dismal circumstances of a failing economy run by a government and party bureaucracy following rigid socialist principles. Also, of course the practical implication of putting security requirements at the top of the national agenda was the neglect of other spheres of life in the state. Education, health and social services languished, as did the economic infrastructure – communications, transport, electricity and water supply, and so on. Unfavorable domestic, regional and international circumstances made the economic picture worse still. Syria's continuing isolation in the Arab world, its strained relations with most of the Gulf countries, and its latest clash with the West served to handicap the economy further during those years.

The upshot was a severe economic crisis that peaked late in 1985. Its effects included a dramatic drop in foreign currency reserves, down to a mere US$50 million, a drastic increase in the trade defi-

cit, and rampant inflation. To prevent total economic collapse,
severe restrictions were slapped on imports, which led to shortages
of basic goods and a sharp decline in living standards.[8] The inevitable result was anti-regime sentiment and criticism, and a resumption
of anti-government terrorism. In February 1986, for example, an
explosion was reported on a bus in the 'Alawi region, killing dozens
of passengers.[9] These terrorist acts were evidence that pockets of
opposition to the regime still existed, remnants perhaps of the Islamic movement, which might exploit the economic turmoil to
undermine the state's hard-won stability.

Mounting domestic tensions did not escape the watchful eyes of
the regime. It well knew that economic stability was the best guarantee of political stability – far better than either military strength or
efficient security services. Indeed, at the beginning of 1986 President Asad issued instructions to slow down, though not halt, military
expansion and upgrading, and to direct much more resources than
previously to social and economic needs.[10] Trimming security ex-
penses made possible at least a temporary check in the economic
downslide. After the discovery of oil fields in the eastern region in
the mid-1980s and the beginning of oil production in commercial
quantities toward the end of the decade, Syria's economic situation
showed some improvement. Thus the regime successfully arrested
the economic decline, even if the effort to achieve strategic parity
with Israel had to be abandoned. In his address to mark Ba'th Revolution Day on 8 March 1986, Asad explained his decision to stop
the military expansion drive: "When we took up the slogan of strategic parity several years ago, we were aware of the fact that this parity
meant not [pitting] tank against tank or cannon against cannon,
but parity in all walks of life – economic, social, political, cultural
and military." Later in the speech he admitted that such parity was
then beyond Syria's reach, not only in armaments but also in education and science.[11] Thus Asad's lesson from the mid-1980s economic
crisis was clear: Syria's resources were inadequate for building up
the military to the extent necessary for it to adhere to the path of
armed struggle with Israel. Moreover, economic and social problems that had been neglected in favor of promoting the struggle
called for renewed attention to prevent them developing into a renewed threat to domestic stability.

The impasse in how the struggle with Israel should be handled
had ramifications in the regime's other spheres of activity. The sense
of relief that spread through Syria with the regime's achievements
in Lebanon where  Israel (and incidentally, the United States as
well) were concerned was soon found to be premature. Between
1985 and 1989 Damascus failed to enforce a new "Syrian order" on

Another dangerous development, in the Syrian view, took place
November 1989. The Soviet ambassador in Damascus, Alexander
tov, in an interview with a Western newspaper, announced that
e supply of Soviet arms to Syria would henceforth be conditional
the recipient's ability to pay for it. Syria would have to be content
h acquiring weapons for the purpose of self-defense – in other
ds, it would have to abandon its aspiration to overpower Israel.[24]
m 1985 the Soviets rejected most of Syria's requests for advanced
ipment.

he death knell of the Soviet Union did not sound till early 1991,
by the late 1980s it was plainly imminent. The effectiveness of the
ral apparatus of Soviet government deteriorated, as did the
ts' regional and international standing. Significant in this con-
was the influence this process had on the communist regimes of
rn Europe, which began to fall like nine-pins. In December 1989
ae Ceauşescu's regime in Romania, and Ceauşescu himself, who
ng been an ally of the Syrian regime, were brought down. The
unist regimes of Poland, Czechoslovakia and East Germany
llapsed in 1989.

newest crisis to confront the Syrian regime, like the thorny
al and international circumstances in which it found itself,
d from previous crises in power and scope. President Asad
hide his fears for the future, and in his annual Revolution
dress on 8 March 1990 he painted a grim picture of the days
. He warned against the return of Western imperialism, i.e.
mpt to violate Syria's territorial integrity or threaten its in-
nce. Such a scenario would set the clock back for Syria and
e Arab world to the conditions of the first half of the twen-
tury. Asad explained: "The broad changes taking place today
rld, like the new constellation of forces created in their
re expressed not only in the economic domain but also in
cal domain. We must not, especially in the face of the les-
tory, discount the possibility of imperialism's return, or of
t to generate geographical changes, that is, changes in
aphical division of the world." Asad added: "History
that there have been nations that burgeoned and flour-
ng them were ones that established for themselves huge
nd empires, but later they vanished into the mists of
day not so much as a remnant or a memory remains of
refore,] we should learn from the past. It seems fitting
eats, which led to the loss of lands we held for genera-
d cause us to pause and take stock of what the future
e for us."[25]

later, on 12 March 1992, Asad addressed the Syrian

the powers in Lebanon. This order had been designed to end
Lebanon's civil war, rehabilitate its governmental institutions, and
compel the country to follow Damascus's dictates. Though victorious in the struggle for control in Lebanon which it had fought with
Israel and the United States in 1982-5, Syria failed to turn its victory
to advantage. Instead, it seems to have returned to square one –
that is, to where it had been on the eve of "Operation Peace for the
Galilee" (June 1982). Again Syria found itself completely enmeshed
in Lebanon, both militarily and politically, with no way of realizing
its long-term goals there.[12] Syria's relations with most of the Arab
world remained cool, if not hostile. The absolute break with Egypt
that it initiated after the signing of the Israeli-Egyptian peace agreement had not been mended, and President Asad's announcement
that he would never set foot in Cairo as long as Egypt upheld the
agreement made a renewal of these relations the near future unlikely. Relations also remained chilly, if not antagonistic, with the
Gulf states, which continued to withhold their formerly generous
financial aid for Syria in protest at its support of Iran in the Iran-
Iraq war.

Nor did the end of that war in August 1988 prove favorable for
Syria. Iraq's apparent return to the inter-Arab arena as victor in its
war with Iran pushed Syria into a corner and aroused grave concerns
in Damascus. These fears seemed well-founded because in the
aftermath of the war Iraq turned west, declaring its intention to settle accounts with both Israel and Syria for their anti-Iraq stance during the war (see Ch. 4). Lastly, United States efforts in 1987 and in
1989-90 to advance a political process in the region with the participation of Israel, Jordan and the Palestinians also made Syria anxious.
Such a process threatened to increase its isolation in the Arab world,
weaken its regional position, and lessen its chances of regaining the
Golan Heights as part of a future arrangement with Israel.[13]

In the international arena, Syria's relations with most Western
countries, especially the United States, were fraught with tension and
hostility. Damascus-US relations reached an unprecedentedly low
point in 1983-84 over American involvement in Lebanon. This involvement brought the Americans into direct confrontation with the
Syrians there (American warships and planes bombed Syrian positions on Mount Lebanon in the summer of 1983). Later, after Hizballah
attacked the American embassy and Marine headquarters in Beirut
in April and October 1983, killing some 300 servicemen and civilians,
the United States pulled out of Lebanon. Claims made by US sources
that Syria had had a hand in these attacks left deep rifts in relations
between the two countries. The break widened further when allegations were made that senior Syrian officials were involved in the drug

trade in the Biqa' Valley, were guilty of violations of human rights in Syria; and, especially, were connected with acts of terrorism against Israeli and Western targets.[14]

In April 1986 the British arrested the Syrian intelligence agent Nizar al-Hindawi after he attempted to smuggle a bomb on aboard an El Al flight awaiting take-off from London's Heathrow airport. The act was apparently in retribution for Israel's interception of a Libyan executive jet bringing back from Libya a delegation of senior Syrian officials, among whom was Abdallah al-Ahmar, Assistant General Secretary of the Ba'th Regional Command. Israel forced the plane down because it mistakenly thought that it was carrying the Fatah leader Abu-Jihad (Khalil al-Wazir). Once the error was discovered, the Israeli authorities quickly allowed the plane to continue on its way.[15]

It seems that the Syrian reaction to this was to try to blow up an Israeli passenger plane. In his biography of Asad, Patrick Seale claims that Muhammad al-Khuly, then head of air force security, took the decision without the knowledge or consent of President Asad.[16] It may be hard to believe that Khuly would have taken such a decision without informing Asad and obtaining his approval, but it is in keeping with Asad's character to make general decisions and issue broad and sometimes – as perhaps in this case – ambiguous guidelines, leaving his people free to decide the practical details of their execution themselves.[17] Either way, after the affair came to light, and after the British had tried and convicted Hindawi, Britain severed diplomatic relations with Syria, and Washington swiftly recalled its ambassador from Damascus. Most West European countries were obliged to follow Britain's lead and freeze political and economic ties with Syria.[18]

In December 1988 a Pan American airliner exploded over Lockerbie, Scotland, killing all 288 passengers. Syria was again accused of indirect responsibility for the explosion, because Ahmad Jibril – whose followers, so it was then believed, were involved in the attack – maintained his headquarters in Damascus.[19] Only in the early 1990s was Damascus exonerated, and the finger of blame pointed exclusively at the Libyan leader, Mu'ammar al-Qaddafi.[20]

From the mid-1980s, the United States took a stronger stand against all those whom it suspected of involvement in terrorist acts against American targets. This policy came to a climax with its aerial bombing of military targets in Libya on 15 April 1986 following the revelation that Libyan agents had been involved in terrorist acts against American targets in Europe. Asad had no reason to suppose that the US attitude toward Syria would be any different should the finger of blame point in its direction for such acts in which, at least accord-

ing to the Americans, Syria was involved. Indeed, As
Syrian involvement in international terrorism – at
ried out on West European soil against Western tar
is doubtful if that was enough to assuage his fear
can measures against him.

This state of affairs pushed Syria ever deeper i
brace, and it was ironic that just when it neede
than ever before, the winds of change began t
Soviet Union and across the entire Eastern Bl
long familiar with the leaders in Moscow and
Soviet ruling apparatus, was one of the first lead
perhaps in all the world, to read the politica'
correctly. He understood that the process of r
initiated was likely to lead to the Soviet regi
what happened in the country, and to the w
collapse of the Soviet Union. This understa
assessment that Soviet ability to help Syria w

Delivering an address in March 1992, As
Soviet leaders were losing touch with reali
ations he had had with Soviet leaders in 1
immigration from the Soviet Union to Isr

"The talks I had [in the USSR] were among
the leaders of that state. I am certain that
meant what he said to me during these talk
that the matter no longer depended, as i
intentions of the leaders of the USSR, an
liable to bring about a result far different
and they – had hoped for. That is indeed

During Asad's visits to Moscow in Ju
1990, Soviet leaders took the trouble
cance of recent and coming change
of welcoming remarks at a dinner
Gorbachev stated, in reference to
tegic parity with Israel, that this cc
military solution to the Arab-Isra
able. Gorbachev went on to say tha
between the Soviet Union and Is
that the Syrians could not prevent i
the change was already under w
to normalize relations with Isr
and Israeli diplomats met in H
lished their consulate in Tel Av
opened in Moscow. In 1989 th
Jews emigrate to Israel."

People's Assembly to mark the start of his fourth term in office. He defined the collapse of the Soviet Union as the most significant event for Syria since the end of the Second World War and, by extension, since Syrian independence. He elaborated on this:

"In the second half of the 1980s, unique and significant changes began appearing on the horizon. When we examine their influence on the Arab homeland, the conclusion is that by comparison with these changes, all earlier changes in the international arena – since the Second World War – seem lacking in importance or depth. Therefore we must make very clear to ourselves our point of view, and tighten the bonds between ourselves, the Arabs, to remain alert, and to foresee the future as soon as possible: to predict and to understand the advantages and disadvantages it holds, and its influence – for better or worse – on us and on our enemies....and especially the peril [that the future holds] for weak peoples and nations."[26]

The apocalyptic tenor of Asad's remarks may have been exaggerated, but he had good reason to fear the ramifications of the Soviet collapse for the future of his regime and for Syria. This became clear as events unfolded.

## The disappearance of the Soviet bulwark

The Soviet Union had been a prime source of political, military and economic aid and support for the Syrians, and moreover had provided strategic backing in the face of a possible Israeli or US attack on Syria. Damascus considered this a real possibility, given the prevailing regional and international circumstances in the late 1980s. The collapse of the Soviet Union thus left Syria vulnerable to the threat of such an attack at the very moment when it loomed larger than ever before. It is noteworthy that earlier clashes with Israel – e.g. over the application of Israeli law to the Golan Heights in December 1981 and, of course, the Lebanon war in June 1982 – had led Asad to conclude that Israel was again likely to exploit Syria's strategic problems. In particular, he was concerned that Israel would take advantage of the international imbalance resulting from the Soviet collapse to attack Syria, drive it into a corner it and try to advance Israeli and Western interests in Lebanon and other arenas at its expense. It will be recalled that Israel had made the most of international crisis situations earlier. In December 1981, when the Polish President, General Jaruzelski, declared a state of emergency in Poland, Israel promptly declared the application of Israeli law over the Golan Heights. Israel went to war in Lebanon, taking maximum advantage of the Syrian regime's domestic troubles and the leadership crisis then in progress in the Soviet Union with the protracted illness and subsequent death of the then General Secretary of the Communist Party and Soviet President, Leonid Brezhnev. The crisis in the Kremlin's upper echelons kept the Soviet Union from playing an effective role in the course of the Syrian-Israeli confrontation in Lebanon in June 1982. The same was true later, when Syria found itself engaged in a conflict with the United States in Lebanon in 1983.[27]

*Fears about the United States.* Asad also did not discount the possibility of a direct American assault. This concern arose from serious accusations directed at Syria, namely that Damascus was involved in the bombing of the Pan Am jet over Lockerbie; that Syria sponsored terrorist organizations; and even that highly-placed Syrian officials had a hand in the cultivation of and trade in illicit drugs. Such an attack became, in Asad's mind at least, a distinct scenario since his view of the United States at that time was not much better than his view of Israel. US policy in the region had contributed to this poor image during the Republican administrations of Reagan and Bush in the 1980s. Specifically, this policy had included US involvement in Lebanon, leading to a direct US Syrian confrontation in the summer of 1983, the air assault on Libya in April 1986 and the American effort since the mid-1980s to advance the Israeli-Palestinian-Jordanian peace process without Syria's participation. Nor did American military involvement in Grenada and Panama escape Asad's attention. He viewed it as a dangerous precedent with ominous implications for Syria.

## Soviet Jewish immigration to Israel

One consequence of the demise of the Soviet Union, as noted above, was the wave of Jewish immigration from Russia to Israel. More than half a million Russian Jews entered Israel within less than two years (1989-91). Asad perceived this as a factor likely to strengthen Israel even further and encourage it to proceed with new acts of aggression against the Arabs. In his 8 March 1990 address to commemorate Ba'th Revolution Day, he commented on this issue:

"Let us look at the intensive Jewish immigration to the land of Palestine. Did we ever anticipate that such a thing would take place? For the moment, it is not relevant that it is based on a lie and a fraud and that, in fact, Israel forced it upon the world, as no one argues with Israel. All support it and praise it under the slogan of man's freedom to migrate, and in the name of the right of the Jew to return to his homeland – the promised land, the land of Israel that God promised them according to their holy books. However, let us ask ourselves: in the name of what freedom of immigration are they speaking? Does no one see that the word freedom in practice means aggression? For the freedom to immigrate is in practice (in the case before us) the freedom to conquer another's land and evict him from his home. The Jewish immigrant does not come in search of work or a place to live, he believes he is returning to the land of his forefathers given to him by God. He also believes that this homeland is his property and that of his descendants, thus he believes in his right to return to it in order to rule it and evict its local inhabitants. He returns to it in order to fight the Arabs, since Palestine is part of the Arab homeland. Thus the freedom of man to migrate from place to place becomes a false slogan, for its meaning is in fact the right to conquer another's land and evict the other from his home and from his land."[28]

The collapse of the Soviet Union thus generated both an internal crisis and an ideological split within Syrian society and among the ruling regime as well. The USSR and the socialist states of Eastern Europe had been for the Syrian regime a source of inspiration and a role model, and their collapse was emblematic of the disintegration of the Damascus regime's professed outlook. Indeed, from many points of view the collapse of the socialist regimes in Eastern Europe made the Syrian regime irrelevant and anachronistic. This came nearly twenty years after a similar process had taken place in Egypt, though against a different background, and led to the end of the Nasser era.

Naturally, the Syrian regime rushed to launch a propaganda campaign designed to emphasize its own pluralistic nature and the dramatic difference between it and the Soviet and East European regimes. "The collapse of the East European regimes that called themselves socialist", said an editorial in *Tishrin* dated 2 October 1991, "does not mean the end of socialism or the collapse of the socialist method. This development expresses the collapse of one socialist method, and only history will decide. Against this background the importance of the Corrective Movement [of 16 November 1970] under the leadership of the warrior Hafiz al-Asad is clear. This revolution predated the principle of economic and political pluralism by some two decades, and took the steps necessary to reach the goal of bringing about the development of a political and social system that can withstand the most difficult external pressures."[29]

Nonetheless, the circumstances that gripped Syria from the late 1980s, in the shadow of the Soviet collapse, would one day force the regime effectively to abandon its ideological commitment to its fundamental concepts of socialism, Arab unity and the struggle against imperialism and Zionism. In the past, this commitment had been its life-blood and source of legitimacy. The end of Ba'thist ideology was of course liable to rouse from hibernation some of the regime's traditional enemies at home, chief among them being the Islamic circles, but also including the Sunni urban middle class. Indeed, after the fall of Ceauşescu's regime in Romania in December 1989, printed circulars and graffiti appeared in Damascus which indicated that at least some Syrian citizens made a connection between events in Eastern Europe and current events in Syria. Their content ("Every Ceauşescu has his day" [*kull ceauescu biyaji yumh*] or "Asadcescu"[30]) was, in this perspective, a warning sign to the rulers of Syria. The end of Ba'thist ideology was also liable to undermine several sources of power and strength on which the regime relied. Most important of these were the weak strata of society and citizens from rural areas, and the support of the party and government bureaucracy that had managed the Syrian economy hitherto.

The regime's characteristic passivity and propensity for defensive tactics since Asad's rise to power had virtually frozen all foreign, social and economic policy, as well as the roster of personnel in the upper echelons of politics, security and finance in Syria. Mounting difficulties now exacerbated the cumulative effect of this long freeze. Inertia made it all the more difficult for the regime to demonstrate the initiative, openness and creativity necessary to deal with the problem. One could, of course, argue that the crisis was one of perception, stemming from the way the regime had concepualized the circumstances that had prevailed since the late 1980s. But in that case, Damascus could only see itself as even more under threat.

Seen from the standpoint of the 1990s, the Syrian regime's achievements over the first half of the 1980s thus appear minimal. The regime had indeed proved remarkably adept at the art of survival over the years, but its policy of a determinedly defensive posture – successful as it may have been – did not look likely to help it achieve a breakthrough either at home or abroad. In any case it became clear that such a breakthrough was not anywhere on the regime's agenda. All its thoughts centered, as has been said, on holding firm to preserve the *status quo* – especially where Israel and the West were concerned. It slowly became clear, however, that standing on the spot in a changing world was tantamount to moving backwards.

This sense of real danger spurred the Syrian regime to acknowledge the need to adopt a new path and institute real changes in its policy. The regime could not, however, ignore the possibility that such changes might exacerbate rather than resolve the crisis, for a number of reasons. First, it feared a loss of control over these processes of change; once they were set in motion, halting them would be impossible, as the fate of the Soviet communist regime under Gorbachev made clear. Second, at least some of these changes involved abandoning the worldview to which the regime had clung and for which no suitable substitute had yet appeared. They were the powers in Lebanon. This order had been designed to end Lebanon's civil war, rehabilitate its governmental institutions, and compel the country to follow Damascus's dictates. Though victorious in the struggle for control in Lebanon which it had fought with Israel and the United States in 1982-5, Syria failed to turn its victory to advantage. Instead, it seems to have returned to square one – that is, to where it had been on the eve of "Operation Peace for the Galilee" ( June 1982). Again Syria found itself completely enmeshed in Lebanon, both militarily and politically, with no way of realizing its long-term goals there.[12] Syria's relations with most of the Arab world remained cool, if not hostile. The absolute break with Egypt that it initiated after the signing of the Israeli-Egyptian peace agreement had not been mended, and President Asad's announcement that he would never set foot in Cairo as long as Egypt upheld the agreement made a renewal of these relations the near future unlikely. Relations also remained chilly, if not antagonistic, with the Gulf states, which continued to withhold their formerly generous financial aid for Syria in protest at its support of Iran in the Iran-Iraq war.

Nor did the end of that war in August 1988 prove favorable for Syria. Iraq's apparent return to the inter-Arab arena as victor in its war with Iran pushed Syria into a corner and aroused grave concerns in Damascus. These fears seemed well-founded because in the aftermath of the war Iraq turned west, declaring its intention to settle accounts with both Israel and Syria for their anti-Iraq stance during the war (see Ch. 4). Lastly, United States efforts in 1987 and in 1989-90 to advance a political process in the region with the participation of Israel, Jordan and the Palestinians also made Syria anxious. Such a process threatened to increase its isolation in the Arab world, weaken its regional position, and lessen its chances of regaining the Golan Heights as part of a future arrangement with Israel.[13]

In the international arena, Syria's relations with most Western countries, especially the United States, were fraught with tension and hostility. Damascus-US relations reached an unprecedentedly low point in 1983-84 over American involvement in Lebanon. This involvement brought the Americans into direct confrontation with the Syrians there (American warships and planes bombed Syrian positions on Mount Lebanon in the summer of 1983). Later, after Hizballah attacked the American embassy and Marine headquarters in Beirut in April and October 1983, killing some 300 servicemen and civilians, the United States pulled out of Lebanon. Claims made by US sources that Syria had had a hand in these attacks left deep rifts in relations between the two countries. The break widened further when allegations were made that senior Syrian officials were involved in the drug trade in the Biqa' Valley, were guilty of violations of human rights in Syria; and, especially, were connected with acts of terrorism against Israeli and Western targets.[14]

In April 1986 the British arrested the Syrian intelligence agent Nizar al-Hindawi after he attempted to smuggle a bomb on aboard an El Al flight awaiting take-off from London's Heathrow airport. The act was apparently in retribution for Israel's interception of a Libyan executive jet bringing back from Libya a delegation of senior Syrian officials, among whom was Abdallah al-Ahmar, Assistant General Secretary of the Ba'th Regional Command. Israel forced the plane down because it mistakenly thought that it was carrying the Fatah leader Abu-Jihad (Khalil al-Wazir). Once the error was discovered, the Israeli authorities quickly allowed the plane to continue on its way.[15]

It seems that the Syrian reaction to this was to try to blow up an Israeli passenger plane. In his biography of Asad, Patrick Seale claims that Muhammad al-Khuly, then head of air force security, took the decision without the knowledge or consent of President Asad.[16] It may be hard to believe that Khuly would have taken such a decision without informing Asad and obtaining his approval, but it is in keeping with Asad's character to make general decisions and issue broad and sometimes – as perhaps in this case – ambiguous guidelines, leaving his people free to decide the practical details of their execution themselves.[17] Either way, after the affair came to light, and after the British had tried and convicted Hindawi, Britain severed diplomatic relations with Syria, and Washington swiftly recalled its ambassador from Damascus. Most West European countries were obliged to follow Britain's lead and freeze political and economic ties with Syria.[18]

In December 1988 a Pan American airliner exploded over Lockerbie, Scotland, killing all 288 passengers. Syria was again accused of indirect responsibility for the explosion, because Ahmad Jibril – whose followers, so it was then believed, were involved in the attack – maintained his headquarters in Damascus.[19] Only in the early 1990s was Damascus exonerated, and the finger of blame pointed exclusively at the Libyan leader, Mu'ammar al-Qaddafi.[20]

From the mid-1980s, the United States took a stronger stand against all those whom it suspected of involvement in terrorist acts against American targets. This policy came to a climax with its aerial bombing of military targets in Libya on 15 April 1986 following the revelation that Libyan agents had been involved in terrorist acts against American targets in Europe. Asad had no reason to suppose that the US attitude toward Syria would be any different should the finger of blame point in its direction for such acts in which, at least according to the Americans, Syria was involved. Indeed, Asad acted to halt Syrian involvement in international terrorism – at least those carried out on West European soil against Western targets. However, it is doubtful if that was enough to assuage his fear of future American measures against him.

This state of affairs pushed Syria ever deeper into the Soviet embrace, and it was ironic that just when it needed Soviet aid more than ever before, the winds of change began to blow through the Soviet Union and across the entire Eastern Bloc. President Asad, long familiar with the leaders in Moscow and the structure of the Soviet ruling apparatus, was one of the first leaders in the Arab world, perhaps in all the world, to read the political situation in Moscow correctly. He understood that the process of reform that Gorbachev initiated was likely to lead to the Soviet regime losing control over what happened in the country, and to the weakening and possible collapse of the Soviet Union. This understanding led to the Syrian assessment that Soviet ability to help Syria would only decrease.

Delivering an address in March 1992, Asad remarked that he felt Soviet leaders were losing touch with reality. He recounted conversations he had had with Soviet leaders in 1990 on the issue of Jewish immigration from the Soviet Union to Israel. In his words,

"The talks I had [in the USSR] were among the best we had ever had with the leaders of that state. I am certain that President Gorbachev sincerely meant what he said to me during these talks. Still, I understood even then that the matter no longer depended, as it had in the past, on the good intentions of the leaders of the USSR, and that the course of events was liable to bring about a result far different from the desired result that we – and they – had hoped for. That is indeed what took place."[21]

During Asad's visits to Moscow in June 1985, April 1987 and April 1990, Soviet leaders took the trouble to explain in detail the significance of recent and coming changes in their policy. In the context of welcoming remarks at a dinner honoring Asad in April 1987, Gorbachev stated, in reference to Syria's aspiration to achieve strategic parity with Israel, that this concept was out of date, and that a military solution to the Arab-Israeli conflict was no longer reasonable. Gorbachev went on to say that the absence of diplomatic relations between the Soviet Union and Israel was not a normal situation and that the Syrians could not prevent it from changing in the future.[22] Indeed, the change was already under way. In 1986 the Soviet Union began to normalize relations with Israel, and in August of that year Soviet and Israeli diplomats met in Helsinki; in July 1987 the Soviets established their consulate in Tel Aviv and in July 1988 the Israeli consulate opened in Moscow. In 1989 the Soviet Union opened its doors to let Jews emigrate to Israel.[23]

Another dangerous development, in the Syrian view, took place in November 1989. The Soviet ambassador in Damascus, Alexander Zotov, in an interview with a Western newspaper, announced that the supply of Soviet arms to Syria would henceforth be conditional on the recipient's ability to pay for it. Syria would have to be content with acquiring weapons for the purpose of self-defense – in other words, it would have to abandon its aspiration to overpower Israel.[24] From 1985 the Soviets rejected most of Syria's requests for advanced equipment.

The death knell of the Soviet Union did not sound till early 1991, but by the late 1980s it was plainly imminent. The effectiveness of the central apparatus of Soviet government deteriorated, as did the Soviets' regional and international standing. Significant in this context was the influence this process had on the communist regimes of Eastern Europe, which began to fall like nine-pins. In December 1989 Nicolae Ceauşescu's regime in Romania, and Ceauşescu himself, who had long been an ally of the Syrian regime, were brought down. The communist regimes of Poland, Czechoslovakia and East Germany also collapsed in 1989.

This newest crisis to confront the Syrian regime, like the thorny regional and international circumstances in which it found itself, differed from previous crises in power and scope. President Asad did not hide his fears for the future, and in his annual Revolution Day address on 8 March 1990 he painted a grim picture of the days to come. He warned against the return of Western imperialism, i.e. any attempt to violate Syria's territorial integrity or threaten its independence. Such a scenario would set the clock back for Syria and the entire Arab world to the conditions of the first half of the twentieth century. Asad explained: "The broad changes taking place today in our world, like the new constellation of forces created in their shadow, are expressed not only in the economic domain but also in the political domain. We must not, especially in the face of the lessons of history, discount the possibility of imperialism's return, or of an attempt to generate geographical changes, that is, changes in the geographical division of the world." Asad added: "History teaches us that there have been nations that burgeoned and flourished. Among them were ones that established for themselves huge kingdoms and empires, but later they vanished into the mists of time and today not so much as a remnant or a memory remains of them. [Therefore,] we should learn from the past. It seems fitting that our defeats, which led to the loss of lands we held for generations, should cause us to pause and take stock of what the future holds in store for us."[25]

Two years later, on 12 March 1992, Asad addressed the Syrian

People's Assembly to mark the start of his fourth term in office. He defined the collapse of the Soviet Union as the most significant event for Syria since the end of the Second World War and, by extension, since Syrian independence. He elaborated on this:

"In the second half of the 1980s, unique and significant changes began appearing on the horizon. When we examine their influence on the Arab homeland, the conclusion is that by comparison with these changes, all earlier changes in the international arena – since the Second World War – seem lacking in importance or depth. Therefore we must make very clear to ourselves our point of view, and tighten the bonds between ourselves, the Arabs, to remain alert, and to foresee the future as soon as possible: to predict and to understand the advantages and disadvantages it holds, and its influence – for better or worse – on us and on our enemies....and especially the peril [that the future holds] for weak peoples and nations."[26]

The apocalyptic tenor of Asad's remarks may have been exaggerated, but he had good reason to fear the ramifications of the Soviet collapse for the future of his regime and for Syria. This became clear as events unfolded.

## The disappearance of the Soviet bulwark

The Soviet Union had been a prime source of political, military and economic aid and support for the Syrians, and moreover had provided strategic backing in the face of a possible Israeli or US attack on Syria. Damascus considered this a real possibility, given the prevailing regional and international circumstances in the late 1980s. The collapse of the Soviet Union thus left Syria vulnerable to the threat of such an attack at the very moment when it loomed larger than ever before. It is noteworthy that earlier clashes with Israel – e.g. over the application of Israeli law to the Golan Heights in December 1981 and, of course, the Lebanon war in June 1982 – had led Asad to conclude that Israel was again likely to exploit Syria's strategic problems. In particular, he was concerned that Israel would take advantage of the international imbalance resulting from the Soviet collapse to attack Syria, drive it into a corner it and try to advance Israeli and Western interests in Lebanon and other arenas at its expense. It will be recalled that Israel had made the most of international crisis situations earlier. In December 1981, when the Polish President, General Jaruzelski, declared a state of emergency in Poland, Israel promptly declared the application of Israeli law over the Golan Heights. Israel went to war in Lebanon, taking maximum advantage of the Syrian regime's domestic troubles and the leadership crisis then in progress in the Soviet Union with the protracted illness and subsequent death of the then General Secretary

of the Communist Party and Soviet President, Leonid Brezhnev. The crisis in the Kremlin's upper echelons kept the Soviet Union from playing an effective role in the course of the Syrian-Israeli confrontation in Lebanon in June 1982. The same was true later, when Syria found itself engaged in a conflict with the United States in Lebanon in 1983.[27]

*Fears about the United States.* Asad also did not discount the possibility of a direct American assault. This concern arose from serious accusations directed at Syria, namely that Damascus was involved in the bombing of the Pan Am jet over Lockerbie; that Syria sponsored terrorist organizations; and even that highly-placed Syrian officials had a hand in the cultivation of and trade in illicit drugs. Such an attack became, in Asad's mind at least, a distinct scenario since his view of the United States at that time was not much better than his view of Israel. US policy in the region had contributed to this poor image during the Republican administrations of Reagan and Bush in the 1980s. Specifically, this policy had included US involvement in Lebanon, leading to a direct US Syrian confrontation in the summer of 1983, the air assault on Libya in April 1986 and the American effort since the mid-1980s to advance the Israeli-Palestinian-Jordanian peace process without Syria's participation. Nor did American military involvement in Grenada and Panama escape Asad's attention. He viewed it as a dangerous precedent with ominous implications for Syria.

## Soviet Jewish immigration to Israel

One consequence of the demise of the Soviet Union, as noted above, was the wave of Jewish immigration from Russia to Israel. More than half a million Russian Jews entered Israel within less than two years (1989-91). Asad perceived this as a factor likely to strengthen Israel even further and encourage it to proceed with new acts of aggression against the Arabs. In his 8 March 1990 address to commemorate Ba'th Revolution Day, he commented on this issue:

"Let us look at the intensive Jewish immigration to the land of Palestine. Did we ever anticipate that such a thing would take place? For the moment, it is not relevant that it is based on a lie and a fraud and that, in fact, Israel forced it upon the world, as no one argues with Israel. All support it and praise it under the slogan of man's freedom to migrate, and in the name of the right of the Jew to return to his homeland – the promised land, the land of Israel that God promised them according to their holy books. However, let us ask ourselves: in the name of what freedom of immigration are they speaking? Does no one see that the word freedom in practice means aggression? For the freedom to immigrate is in practice (in the case

before us) the freedom to conquer another's land and evict him from his home. The Jewish immigrant does not come in search of work or a place to live, he believes he is returning to the land of his forefathers given to him by God. He also believes that this homeland is his property and that of his descendants, thus he believes in his right to return to it in order to rule it and evict its local inhabitants. He returns to it in order to fight the Arabs, since Palestine is part of the Arab homeland. Thus the freedom of man to migrate from place to place becomes a false slogan, for its meaning is in fact the right to conquer another's land and evict the other from his home and from his land."[28]

The collapse of the Soviet Union thus generated both an internal crisis and an ideological split within Syrian society and among the ruling regime as well. The USSR and the socialist states of Eastern Europe had been for the Syrian regime a source of inspiration and a role model, and their collapse was emblematic of the disintegration of the Damascus regime's professed outlook. Indeed, from many points of view the collapse of the socialist regimes in Eastern Europe made the Syrian regime irrelevant and anachronistic. This came nearly twenty years after a similar process had taken place in Egypt, though against a different background, and led to the end of the Nasser era.

Naturally, the Syrian regime rushed to launch a propaganda campaign designed to emphasize its own pluralistic nature and the dramatic difference between it and the Soviet and East European regimes. "The collapse of the East European regimes that called themselves socialist", said an editorial in *Tishrin* dated 2 October 1991, "does not mean the end of socialism or the collapse of the socialist method. This development expresses the collapse of one socialist method, and only history will decide. Against this background the importance of the Corrective Movement [of 16 November 1970] under the leadership of the warrior Hafiz al-Asad is clear. This revolution predated the principle of economic and political pluralism by some two decades, and took the steps necessary to reach the goal of bringing about the development of a political and social system that can withstand the most difficult external pressures."[29]

Nonetheless, the circumstances that gripped Syria from the late 1980s, in the shadow of the Soviet collapse, would one day force the regime effectively to abandon its ideological commitment to its fundamental concepts of socialism, Arab unity and the struggle against imperialism and Zionism. In the past, this commitment had been its life-blood and source of legitimacy. The end of Ba'thist ideology was of course liable to rouse from hibernation some of the regime's traditional enemies at home, chief among them being the Islamic

circles, but also including the Sunni urban middle class. Indeed, after the fall of Ceauşescu's regime in Romania in December 1989, printed circulars and graffiti appeared in Damascus which indicated that at least some Syrian citizens made a connection between events in Eastern Europe and current events in Syria. Their content ("Every Ceauşescu has his day" [*kull ceauescu biyaji yumh*] or "Asadcescu"[30]) was, in this perspective, a warning sign to the rulers of Syria. The end of Ba'thist ideology was also liable to undermine several sources of power and strength on which the regime relied. Most important of these were the weak strata of society and citizens from rural areas, and the support of the party and government bureaucracy that had managed the Syrian economy hitherto.

The regime's characteristic passivity and propensity for defensive tactics since Asad's rise to power had virtually frozen all foreign, social and economic policy, as well as the roster of personnel in the upper echelons of politics, security and finance in Syria. Mounting difficulties now exacerbated the cumulative effect of this long freeze. Inertia made it all the more difficult for the regime to demonstrate the initiative, openness and creativity necessary to deal with the problem. One could, of course, argue that the crisis was one of perception, stemming from the way the regime had concepualized the circumstances that had prevailed since the late 1980s. But in that case, Damascus could only see itself as even more under threat.

Seen from the standpoint of the 1990s, the Syrian regime's achievements over the first half of the 1980s thus appear minimal. The regime had indeed proved remarkably adept at the art of survival over the years, but its policy of a determinedly defensive posture – successful as it may have been – did not look likely to help it achieve a breakthrough either at home or abroad. In any case it became clear that such a breakthrough was not anywhere on the regime's agenda. All its thoughts centered, as has been said, on holding firm to preserve the *status quo* – especially where Israel and the West were concerned. It slowly became clear, however, that standing on the spot in a changing world was tantamount to moving backwards.

This sense of real danger spurred the Syrian regime to acknowledge the need to adopt a new path and institute real changes in its policy. The regime could not, however, ignore the possibility that such changes might exacerbate rather than resolve the crisis, for a number of reasons. First, it feared a loss of control over these processes of change; once they were set in motion, halting them would be impossible, as the fate of the Soviet communist regime under Gorbachev made clear. Second, at least some of these changes involved abandoning the worldview to which the regime had clung and for which no suitable substitute had yet appeared. They were

also liable to arouse uncertainty within Syria regarding the relevance and right to exist of a dictatorial regime of sectarian cast such as the Syrian Ba'th regime. Lastly, given the growing movement toward democratization and globalization in wide areas of the world, and faced with an increasing openness toward the West as a necessary outgrowth of the changes in Syrian foreign policy, an undesirable Syrian dependence on the West was liable to develop. This, then, is the essence of the dilemma that faced the Syrian regime throughout much of the 1990s. On the one hand, there was the pressing need for a real change in its policy and, on the other, its tendency to confine such changes to the absolute minimum. In practice, the regime's steps lacked determination and were hesitant and slow, always responding to events and never pre-empting them.

Yet from the late 1980s Syria had begun to strike out along a new path. Certain economic and social changes took place, which were meant to improve the economic situation and thereby assure continued political stability, even without starting any real changes in the political system (see Chapter 9). Thus the major change of direction in Syria was in foreign policy. This was because of the prevailing assessment in Damascus that regional and international developments were what posed an immediate threat to Syria's stability and existence, and what determined its fate. In its new policy at that time Syria's sought to come to terms with the challenge presented to it by the rise of the United States to the status of the only world superpower. It set itself a primary strategic objective: to seek dialogue and an understanding with the United States with the aim of finding a place in the new world and regional order that was taking shape under US leadership.

In June 1990 Syria and the United States restored full diplomatic relations for the first time since 1987, when Washington recalled its ambassador over the Hindawi affair (see above, p.42). However, the objective was essentially defensive. The understanding that the Syrians sought to establish with the United States was intended to protect the regime against an American threat as well as against the need to institute dramatic domestic changes. So this foreign policy aim did not rest on a vision of a "new Syrian order" at home, or of a new regional or world order. On the contrary, it aimed to prevent these from ever coming into being (see Ch. 5).

In conjunction with this objective the Syrian regime acted to improve relations with the Arab countries, especially Egypt and the Gulf states. Its aim was partly to strengthen its regional standing with Israel and Iraq, but it mainly wanted to improve its potential bargaining position in the dialogue it sought with the United States. In the late 1980s Damascus hoped to establish a channel of commu-

nication with Washington via its Arab friends, and the first step on
its new path was the renewal of relations with Egypt in December
1989. This was significant because of President Asad's past declarations that he would never re-open relations with Egypt as long as
Cairo upheld its peace treaty with Israel. In July 1990 Asad visited
Egypt, and President Mubarak escorted him on a tour of Sharm al-
Shaykh, an area returned to Egypt in the framework of the peace
accord it had signed with Israel. Meanwhile, the Syrian effort to
establish a dialogue with Western countries, chiefly the United States,
gathered momentum.[31] However, in the wake of the Iraqi invasion
of Kuwait on 2 August 1990, it was clearly this event that extricated
Syria from its troubles and vastly improved its regional and international standing.

## NOTES

[1] *Tishrin*, 14 March 1985.
[2] Daniel Pipes, *Syria beyond the Peace Process*, pp. 6-8.
[3] See Efraim Karsh, *The Soviet Union and Syria: The Asad years* (London: Royal Institute of International Affairs, 1988), pp. 73-93.
[4] Efraim Karsh, *The Soviet Union and Syria: The Asad Years* (London: Routledge, 1988),
pp. 73-85; Helena Cobban, *The Superpowers and the Syrian-Israeli Conflict*
(New York: Praeger, 1991), pp. 50-8.
[5] Moshe Maoz, *Asad*, pp. 100-18; see also Henry Kissinger, *Years of Upheaval*, pp. 1065-
1109.
[6] Ze'ev Eitan, "Tsva Surya" (The Syrian Army) in Moshe Maoz, Avner Yaniv and Avi
Kover (eds), *Syria and Israel's Security*, pp. 155-70.
[7] See Volker Perthes, *The Political Economy of Syria under Asad*.
[8] Yosef Olmert, "Syria" in Itamar Rabinovich and Haim Shaked (eds), MECS, vol. X
(1986), pp. 610-11.
[9] *Ibid.*, pp. 608-9.
[10] See Moshe Maoz, *Syria and Israel: From War to Peace-Making*, pp. 168-70.
[11] *Tishrin*, 9 March 1986.
[12] See Itamar Rabinovich, "The Changing Prism: Syrian Policy in Lebanon as a Mir-
ror, an Issue and an Instrument" in Moshe Maoz and Avner Yaniv (eds), *Syria under
Assad*, pp. 179-90.
[13] Patrick Seale, *Asad of Syria*, pp. 461-95.
[14] See, for example, Maoz, *Asad*, pp. 179-85; see also Middle East Watch, *Syria Unmasked*, pp. 153-65.
[15] See Patrick Seale, *Asad of Syria*, pp. 474-82.
[16] *Ibid.*, p. 481-82.
[17] See Eyal Zisser, *Decision Making in Asad's Syria*, pp. 29-37.
[18] Yosef Olmert, "Syria" in Itamar Rabinovich and Haim Shaked (eds), MECS, vol. X
(1986), pp. 619-20.
[19] Eyal Zisser, "Armed Operations" in Ami Ayalon (ed.), MECS, vol. XIII (1989), pp.
112-13.
[20] See *NYT*, 24 December 1992.
[21] *Tishrin*, 13 March 1992.

[21] *Tishrin*, 13 March 1992.

[22] See Helena Cobban, "The Nature of the Soviet-Syrian Link under Asad and Gorbachev" in Richard T. Antoun and Donald Quatert (eds), *Syria: Society, Culture, and Polity*; Helena Cobban, *The Superpowers*, pp. 112-38.

[23] See John P. Hannah, "The Soviet Union and the Middle East" in Ami Ayalon (ed.), MECS, vol. XIII (1989), pp. 34-58.

[24] *FT*, 20 November 1989.

[25] *Tishrin*, 9 March 1990.

[26] *Tishrin*, 13 March 1992.

[27] Efraim Karsh, *The Soviet Union and Syria: The Asad Years*, pp. 54-72; Helena Cobban, *The Superpowers*, pp. 112-21.

[28] *Tishrin*, 9 March 1990.

[29] *Tishrin*, 2 October 1991.

[30] See *Davar*, 8 March 1990, and Eyal Zisser, "Syria" in Ami Ayalon (ed.), MECS, vol. XIV (1990), p. 653.

[31] See Eyal Zisser, "Syria" in Ami Ayalon (ed.), MECS, vol. XIV (1990), pp. 655-59.

# 4

## START OF THE NEW PATH – SYRIA DURING THE GULF CRISIS

Iraq's invasion of Kuwait on 2 August 1990 touched off the Gulf crisis, which culminated in the Gulf War – Operation "Desert Storm" – lasting from 17 January till 28 February 1991. This turn of events marked an important crossroads in the history of the Middle East, contributing to the shaping of a new regional order and leading to the start of the peace process between Israel and the Arab states. The peace process was thus an immediate outgrowth of the crisis and took its place as the main focus of activity in the region from the first half of 1991 onwards.

The ramifications of the crisis did not bypass Syria, which from the outset was an active member of the US-led anti-Iraq coalition. It emerged from the crisis stronger both domestically and abroad. Syria's improved status stemmed from the measures it took during the crisis, which contrasted sharply with most of the concepts to which the Syrian Ba'th regime had paid allegiance for most of its years in power. Seen in this perspective, Syria's actions were the first manifestation of the turning point in its policy, based on an attempt to form closer links with the United States and, at the very least, establish a dialogue with it that would enable Syria to find its place in the new Washington-led world order.

The Gulf crisis was not, however, the root cause of this turning-point in Syrian policy. Rather, the shift began, as has been remarked, as early as the late 1980s, as a result of the Damascus regime's need to cope with its strategic difficulties. It would nonetheless seem that this change of direction gained real momentum in the course of the crisis and in its wake. In spite of their country's improved status, the Gulf crisis made tangible to the Syrians its weakness and strategic inferiority, – factors that underlay the state's problems. The crisis was thus important for Syria in that it increased and deepened its advocacy of its newly-adopted path.

*Syria on the eve of the Gulf crisis – in the shadow of
rivalry with Iraq*

Iraq's takeover of Kuwait on 2 August 1990 found the Syrian regime embroiled in a deep and protracted conflict with the Iraqi regime, which was percieved in Damascus as an ever-increasing threat. Rivalry between the Ba'th regimes of Damascus and Baghdad had deep ideological, historical, political and personal roots. It had intensified during the 1980s over Syria's support of Iran in the latter's long-drawn-out war with Iraq (1980-8). Iraq, for its part, extended aid and succor to opponents of the Syrian regime, chief among them the Muslim Brotherhood in 1976-1982.[1]

The ending of the war between Iran and Iraq in August 1988 marked the start of a new phase in the rivalry between them. It enabled Iraq to turn its attention from its eastern border with Iran to the west. The Iraqis did not conceal their desire for vengeance against Israel for its bombing of its nuclear reactor in June 1981, and against Syria for supporting Iran during the conflict. Yet it is clear that more than the desire for vengeance alone lay behind Baghdad's hostility toward Israel and Syria. This animosity should also be understood in the broader context of Iraqi aspirations under Saddam Husayn for hegemony in the regional and inter-Arab arena. Striking a blow against Asad's regime and especially the neutralization of Israel's power were vital aims on the way to realizing these aspirations.[2]

It is thus easy to understand how Iraq's re-emergence, as victor after its war with Iran, to play an active role in the inter-Arab arena stirred great anxiety in Damascus. Would Syria have to pay the price of its former anti-Iraqi stance? The Iraqi tone toward Syria was certainly belligerent and uncompromising. The Iraqi Foreign Minister Tariq 'Aziz, when asked in June 1990 why Iraq was not making efforts toward reconciliation with Syria, replied: "As Syria was the one to act against Iraq during the last eight years, it is [Syria] who must explain its policy. Such reconciliation is impossible under the current circumstances."[3]

Syrian fears were soon realized when, in 1989-90, Iraq forced Syria into isolation in the Arab world. Moreover, Syria had to contend with a direct Iraqi threat. In February 1989 Iraq, Egypt, Jordan and North Yemen established the Arab Cooperation Council, designed to enhance economic and political coordination and cooperation between them, and Syria was directly harmed by this step economically and politically.[4] In 1989 Iraq's involvement in Lebanon also increased, as it extended aid to the Maronite General Michel 'Awn. This move was a major obstacle in Damascus's path to acquiring hegemony in Lebanon and realizing its long-term goals there. Iraq's involvement in Lebanon peaked in July 1989 following the intensification of the conflict between General 'Awn and the Syrians. It sought to supply the general with Frog-7 surface-to-surface missiles, which would have given him the capability to hit Damascus. The Syrians responded by laying siege to the shores of Lebanon and so preventing the missiles from reaching Beirut.[5]

Syria's isolation in the Arab world and the growing hostility between it and Iraq were tangibly manifest at the May 1990 Arab leaders' summit conference in Baghdad. This was convened on Iraq's initiative with the intention of assuring it of general Arab backing in the event of Israeli action against it, after Saddam Husayn's declarations regarding Iraq's nuclear capability and readiness to strike at Israel and "set fire to half of its territory" if Israel were to attack.[6] Syria ostentatiously refused to take part in this summit, defined in the Damascus press as "a game meant to serve narrow and dubious personal objectives".[7] The Iraqis did indeed send a formal invitation to Syria to participate in the conference, and in the absence of diplomatic relations between the two states, the Iraqi Minister of Justice went to Damascus especially to deliver it to President Asad.[8] However, this step was taken only after pressure from the Arab states, especially Egypt, and failed to change the Syrian position.

It was ironic that the Egyptian President Muhammad Husni Mubarak and the Libyan leader Mu'ammar Qaddafi should have assumed the role of mediators between the Syrian and Iraqi Presidents and tried to persuade the Syrians to take part in the Baghdad conference.[9] As will be recalled, in October 1978, after the signing of the Camp David Accord, Syria and Iraq established a rejectionist front intended to head the opposition in the Arab world to Egyptian policy under Sadat. The two states went so far as to sign a "Pact for Joint National Action" with the aim of bolstering cooperation between them and laying the foundations for a future unification. However, once Saddam Husayn took control in Iraq in July 1979, relations between the two states began to turn sour. At the end of that month the Iraqi President was quick to accuse Syria of involvement in the plot to bring him down, while the Syrians responded with counter-accusations that Iraq had aided the Muslim Brotherhood revolt, then at its height.[10] The atmosphere of amity and cooperation vanished as though it had never been, and vitriolic rivalry between the states began again. This intensified in the Iran-Iraq war, and did not diminish when it ended. On the eve of the Gulf crisis, Syria was thus pitted against its bitter rival Iraq, and despite all efforts at reconciliation, neither showed any desire to achieve true rapprochement.

## *From the Iraqi invasion of Kuwait to "Desert Storm"*

With the news of Iraq's invasion of Kuwait, Syria was among the first Arab states to condemn the Iraqi move publicly and absolutely, and to demand immediate and unconditional withdrawal from Kuwait.

This determined stance stood out in comparison with the public hesitancy of most Arab states in the early stages of the crisis. Alongside resolute condemnation of Iraq's takeover of Kuwait, the Syrian President quickly called on most Arab leaders to hold an Arab summit conference. He aimed to establish an Arab front to resolve the crisis to Damascus's liking, that is, to force Iraq to retreat from Kuwait.[11] The urgency the Syrians attached to the convening of such a summit meeting grew in the early days of the conference, as the possibility emerged that the crisis would be resolved on Baghdad's terms within a limited framework of Arab states, and without Syria's participation.

Resolute action on this issue by the United States also troubled the Syrians. American efforts laid the stress on the inability of the Arab world to cope with the challenge presented by the Iraqi action. The United States succeeded in getting a series of anti-Iraqi resolutions adopted in the UN Security Council, chief of which was Resolution 660 of 2 August 1990, which imposed economic sanctions against Iraq. The United States also sent troops to protect Saudi Arabia and the other Gulf states against possible Iraqi aggression.

At the Arab summit which finally met in Cairo on 10-11 August 1990, the Syrians together with Egypt, Saudi Arabia and the Gulf states again procured a series of anti-Iraq resolutions. Among them was condemnation of the invasion of Kuwait and support for the UN Security Council resolutions on it, chiefly the one imposing economic sanctions. The summit also passed a resolution to send Arab troops to the Gulf alongside the US forces.[12] In the wake of this resolution Syria also dispatched troops to Saudi Arabia. At first, during August 1990, it sent a few thousand commandos, and then in September 1990 the 9th Armored Division. This division, with 10,000 troops and 300 tanks, was transferred directly to the Gulf from the Israeli front on the Golan Heights.[13] The summit conference and the ensuing political and military preparations in the inter-Arab arena marked the consolidation of a new political axis in the Arab world: Syria, Egypt and Saudi Arabia. This axis was also to play an important role in the course of the Gulf crisis, and was the vital Arab component of the US-led anti-Iraq coalition. The consolidation of this axis was thus an important Syrian achievement, one in a series that Syria would later list to its credit during the crisis.

It seems that, knowing Saddam Husayn's regime as they did, the Syrians never doubted that a peaceable Iraqi withdrawal from Kuwait would be achieved. The establishment of an Arab anti-Iraq front was thus intended, in the Syrian view, to achieve the following objectives: (1) to prevent a resolution of the crisis within a limited Arab framework that would bring significant territorial and politi-

cal gains to Saddam Husayn; (2) to give legitimacy to more determined international activity against Saddam Husayn's regime and,
more important, to ensure Arab participation in any such activity;
and (3), perhaps most important, to enable Syria to take advantage
of the crisis to break out of its isolation in the Arab world and the
international arena, and improve its relations with the United States.

Alongside the effort to consolidate an Arab anti-Iraq front, the
Syrians rejected Iraqi signs of willingness to improve bilateral relations. According to a number of reports, the Iraqis dispatched their
oil minister to Damascus to propose that Syria break the sanctions
imposed on Iraq by the UN Security Council and open the border
between the two countries to trade. They proposed, furthermore,
that Syria allow the flow of Iraqi oil through its territory in exchange
for considerable compensation, such as the purchase of that oil at
a reduced price. The Syrians rejected this attempt at reconciliation,
not even allowing the Iraqi minister to get off the airplane at Damascus airport.[14]

Syria also played an important role in getting Iran's support for
the anti-Iraq coalition, or at the very least securing assurances from
Teheran that Iran would remain neutral and refrain from aiding
Iraq in its struggle against the United States and its Arab allies. As
already said, Iran was perceived as the weak link among Iraq's
neighbors, for two reasons. First, relations between Iran and Iraq
had dramatically improved following Saddam Husayn's peace initiative beginning on 15 August 1990. Within the framework of this
initiative, Saddam Husayn expressed his readiness to accept the 1975
Algiers Agreement as the basis for a solution to the border dispute
between the two countries. In addition, he gave notice of the withdrawl
of all Iraqi forces from Iranian territory and of the release of Iranian prisoners held in Iraq. The second reason was the dissatisfaction
that Iran expressed over increasing Western military and political
involvement in the Gulf region.[15]

Between 22 and 25 September 1990, President Asad visited Teheran. At the same time he exploited his special connections with Iran
by trying to ensure that it would not weaken the unity of the ranks
drawn up against Baghdad. Asad's visit to Teheran was a success,
although it had to be extended because of difficulty in reaching an
agreement on the question of the Western presence in the Gulf.
While Iran maintained its opposition to this presence, it promised
to comply with the UN Security Council resolutions concerning
sanctions against Iraq.[16] For the duration of the crisis, Iran did indeed keep its word.

*Improved relations with the United States and the West*

Syria's position during the Gulf crisis, especially the legitimacy it gave to the actions of the US-led international coalition against Iraq, brought about a significant improvement in relations with Washington. Progress in this area now became an interest shared by both, even though it did not lead to the breakthrough hoped for by the Syrians. On 13 September 1990 the US Secretary of State James Baker flew to Syria – the first visit by a holder of the office since mid-1970.[17] As Syria and the United States had a common interest in the issue of the Gulf crisis, Baker's visit was a success. However, Baker refrained during his talks in Damascus from raising controversial issues, most notable among which was Washington's accusations regarding Syria's involvement in terrorist activity. He went so far as to declare that there were still many problems in the relations between the two countries, but that it was crucial to find a way to deal with them.[18] On 23 November 1990 Presidents Asad and Bush met in Geneva. The meeting took place at the latter's behest, and was the first between the Presidents of the two countries since the Asad-Carter meeting in March 1977. In an effort to prove to Arab public opinion that Syria remained true to its fundamental principles, the Syrian media took care to report that at the meeting Asad had raised the issue of the Israeli-Arab conflict and also attacked the United States for the criticism it had leveled at Syria over its alleged involvement in terrorist activity, but that was not enough to conceal the fact that on the issue of the Gulf crisis the two Presidents were of like mind.[19] A similar improvement took place in Syria's relations with the West European countries. The European Union began discussing the lifting of trade sanctions imposed on Syria in the late 1980s, and in November 1990, after extended behind-the-scenes contacts, the renewal of diplomatic relations between Syria and Britain was announced. They had been severed in 1987 over the Hindawi affair.[20]

One arena in which Syria's improved regional status during the Gulf crisis made itself felt was Lebanon. On 13 October 1990 the Syrians attacked the forces of the Maronite General Michel 'Awn, their main rival in Lebanon at the time. The Syrian step apparently won tacit US approval and may even have been discussed – if only in a general and vague manner – with James Baker during his visit to Damascus a month earlier.[21] In any case, the tacit if perhaps reluctant acceptance of the Syrian action in Lebanon expressed American and, by extension, Israeli recognition of Syria's hegemony in Lebanon – a position to which Syria had aspired since it stepped in there in 1976. The liquidation of General 'Awn's force cleared away the main obstacle to implementing the Ta'if Agreement faced by the Syrians and their ally and protégé, the Lebanese President Elias al-Hirawi. This agreement paved the way for the establishment of a "new Lebanese order" based on the establishment of a central, stable Lebanese government, albeit under Syrian patronage. Syrian measures after 13 October 1990 thus led to the end of the Lebanese civil war and constituted a decisive step toward realizing Syria's long-term goals in Lebanon (see Chapter 7).

## *Syria during "Desert Storm"*

The Syrian commitment to the US-led anti-Iraq coalition reached its peak with the outbreak of the Gulf War ("Desert Storm") on 17 January 1991. The Syrians were undoubtely aware of the possible negative implications for them of American military action against Iraq since, in spite of the antagonism between Baghdad and Damascus, Iraq had in the past afforded Syria strategic depth with regard to the struggle with Israel. In the course of the October 1973 war Iraq had dispatched an expeditionary force to back the Syrian army in battles with the Israeli forces.[22] An attack on Iraq could thus deprive Syria of an important ally against Israel, which was and remained – despite the Gulf crisis – a major threat in the minds of the Syrians. Moreover, American action against Iraq was also liable to create a dangerous precedent for the use of military force against an Arab regime – perhaps even in an effort to topple it. Damascus feared that with such a precedent, similar action might at some future date be directed at Syria itself. This dilemma was, however, essentially theoretical since the Syrians were not the initiators but junior partners in the military move against Iraq, even if their participation gave it legitimacy.

On the eve of the outbreak of battle on 12 January 1991, President Asad sent Saddam Husayn an open letter calling on him to accept the UN resolutions and withdraw from Kuwait in "the interests of the Arab nation". He even committed Syria to supporting Iraq should it suffer an attack after withdrawing from Kuwait.[23] It seems that Asad wrote this letter primarily for propaganda purposes, the target being Syria's own public opinion. The Syrian regime did not expect Saddam Husayn to accept Asad's appeal. In any case it assumed that even if he were to accept the US demand for a full and unconditional withdrawl from Kuwait, such a blow to his esteem would be tantamount to military defeat on the battlefield.

Press reports did not inflate the ability or motivation demonstrated by Syrian forces during the fighting. Syrian participation in the war was at first limited to artillery exchanges, and then only in response to an Iraqi attack on Syrian positions. According to these reports, Syrian cannon deliberately missed the Iraqi targets assigned to them. Later Syrian forces did engage with retreating Iraqi forces in Kuwait but not in Iraq itself.[24] Yet despite the low profile the Syrians took care to keep, there was no escaping the fact that they had sided with the United States in a war against a sister Arab state.

## Syria and the Gulf crisis – the domestic front

*Syrian propaganda during the Gulf crisis.* The Syrian regime's policy and action during the Gulf crisis were completely at odds with the image the regime had gone to such lengths to cultivate for itself since coming to power. They were not at all in keeping with the image of the revolutionary, pioneering regime struggling against imperialism and Zionism and dedicated to achieving the goal of all-Arab unification. Thus, from the start of the crisis the Syrian regime needed propaganda to explain its policy to public opinion at home. This need increased with Saddam Husayn's initiatives, which also targeted public opinion in the Arab world. Among these was his proposal of 12 August 1990 to link a solution to the Kuwait crisis with the Arab-Israeli conflict and other regional conflicts, among them the civil war in Lebanon. In the lead-up to the outbreak of the war, Saddam Husayn also strove to give his struggle an Islamic character, and to portray himself as the loyal servant of God.[25]

The war itself, and the serious damage to the Iraqi economic infrastructure and civilian population, aggravated the propaganda problem facing the Syrian regime. Syria's involvement in the war against Iraq and the Iraqi missile attacks against Israel, which placed Israel and Syria together in the anti-Iraqi front, did not simplify matters for the Syrians. Their propaganda line was based on the following arguments: first, Iraq's conquest of Kuwait was an illegitimate maneuver in both inter-Arab and international terms, and thus it was imperative to condemn it fully. Second, Saddam Husayn's regime was one with clear negative attributes. Saddam himself did not act for the good of the Arab people or out of Islamic motivation but rather out of personal, opportunistic motives, and by adopting an irresponsible, ill-considered policy. In the words of *Al-Ba'th,* "Iraq's policy is a foolish and megalomaniac one which will bring disaster down upon it."[26] Third, Saddam Husayn's policy damaged the general Arab interest as well as that of Iraq itself. Saddam was in practice dragging Iraq toward suicide, as he left its military and industrial capability open to the risk of destruction and caused division within the Arab world. Fourth, Saddam Husayn's action had enabled the West to regain the upper hand and a position of influence in the region. In contrast, Syria had taken steps to prevent such a possibility, or reduce it to the absolute minimum. Fifth, Israel alone benefited from the crisis, and was emerging stronger in military and economic terms and with an improved international political position. The crisis even legitimized Israel's continued grip on conquered Arab territories, and would thus at some future date deal the death blow to the Palestinian problem.[27]

Asad on one occasion turned to the Syrian public in rather apologetic mode, in an address to graduates of a Syrian army paratroopers' course on 12 September 1990. He explained that Syria regarded the Iraqi invasion of Kuwait as an assault on a sister Arab state and therefore a step that dealt a blow at Arab unity and diverted efforts to solve the Palestinian problem. The conquest of Kuwait by Iraq had led to the return of foreign troops to the region. Because Syria could not, Asad said, accept a situation in which dealing with the Gulf problem remained in Western hands, it, together with other Arab states, had sent military troops to that area. He added that Syria was one of the few Arab states that had previously found itself in direct conflict with the United States, and therefore no one had anything to teach it regarding the "defense of Arab rights".[28] In another address – also rare – to the Syrian public during the war itself, the Vice President for Foreign Affairs, 'Abd al-Halim Khaddam, detailed a list of grievances against the Iraqi regime, and in effect against the rulers of Iraq from the Hashemite dynasty down to Saddam Husayn. In a speech delivered on 10 February 1991 to a gathering of senior officials of the Ba'th Party and officials from popular organisations, Khaddam laid the blame on Iraq for all the differences of opinion that had emerged between the two states throughout the 1980s. As an example he cited Iraqi support for the Muslim Brotherhood's revolt early in that decade. Khaddam reiterated that Iraq's actions ran counter to all logical grounds for opposing Israel's aggression. He went on to stress that Syria could not remain neutral in the struggle being waged in the Gulf because this struggle jeopardized the resources of the Arab people; unless there was an Arab presence in the Gulf, Western forces would take the place of the Arabs.[29]

*The Iraqi missile attacks against Israel.* Syria's dilemma at the onset of hostilities intensified after the Iraqis launched a missile attack against Israel, and Syria found itself side by side with Israel as part of a single front against Iraq. Its media reports minimized the attacks; at most, they pointed to the minimal damage caused to Israel in contrast to the benefits – economic, military and political – that it had gained. On the other hand special emphasis was given to the improved image of Israel in the world at the expense of the image of the Palestinians and their struggle against Israel (the Intifada). Thus the Syrian News Agency stated: "The Iraqi regime will not be able to deceive the Arabs by firing a few missiles in the direction of occupied territories. This ruse will not lead to the liberation of lands or the return of refugees to their land. It is designed only to widen the scope of the fighting, and to involve the Arab people in war at an inappropriate time and place. In practice, this ruse has been implemented in accordance with an Israeli demand and is intended to serve Israeli interests."[30]

Senior Syrian individuals such as Vice President 'Abd al-Halim Khaddam, the Foreign Minister Faruq al-Shar', and even the Defense Minister Mustafa Talas declared in interviews to the foreign press that they would not let Iraq involve them in a war against Israel. They said, moreover, that even if Israel retaliated against Iraq, this would not lead to a change in Syria's position.[31] The Syrians none-theless condemned the mobilization of the West on the side of Israel after the Iraqi missile attacks. Furthermore, in view of the possibility that Israel would attack Jordan as part of an attack aimed against Iraq, they swiftly declared that such an attack would lead directly to Syrian involvement on Jordan's side.[32] It would seem that the Syrians perceived an Israeli attack on Jordan as beyond the bounds of what would be a reasonable response to the Iraqi missile attacks, and as a threat vital Syrian interests.

*The domestic front – the stability of the regime.* During the Gulf crisis, calm generally prevailed on the Syrian streets. Most reports of disturbances or expressions of criticism and opposition to the regime over its policy on the Gulf question came from Iraqi sources, and sometimes from Jordanian sources that echoed them. According to these reports, a series of demonstrations and disturbances took place in the northeastern Syrian cities of Hasaka and Dayr al-Zur, near the Iraqi border, in late August 1990.[33] Damascus emphatically denied their truth.

Also from Amman came reports of the arrest in Syria of eighty writers and artists who had signed a petition expressing solidarity with Iraq and strong opposition to the war declared upon it. The Syrian authorities lost no time issuing a forceful denial of this report, as did several of the Syrian writers in question.[34] The Iraqi and Jordanian media also played up the anti-regime declarations of opposition elements acting outside Syria and known for their opposition to Asad's regime, such as the Syrian National Socialist Party or the Muslim Brotherhood. These did not stop with expressions of support for Iraq's struggle against American-Zionist aggression, but also issued a call to topple the regime of Hafiz al-Asad for "the plot against Iraq in which he is taking part and for his support of Iraq's enemies, the enemies of the Arabs".[35]

Thus it seems that despite the regime's success in preserving order on the streets, Syrian public opinion – like that of the majority of people in other Arab countries – largely sided with Iraq. However, at the same time Syrian public opinion perceived the measures adopted by the regime as unavoidable under the prevailing regional and international circumstances. After the Gulf War ended, the Syrian public came to appreciate the benefits to Syria afforded by this policy.

*The economic aspect.* One area in which Syria registered immediate gains from its involvement in the Gulf crisis was the economy. Already in late 1990 Kuwait and Saudi Arabia transferred between $2.5 and 3 billion to Syria in exchange for the transfer of Syrian forces to the Gulf, and as compensation for damage to Syria due to the crisis.[36] The Syrians claimed heavy economic damage. First, the return of Syrian workers from the Gulf countries led to a drop in cash inflows transferred by those workers, as well as to a rise in domestic unemployment. Second, the slowdown of economic activity hurt exports and tourism revenues. It seems, though, that the real damage to Syria was far less than it claimed, and was covered by the generous grants it received from Saudi Arabia and Kuwait. While these grants were largely funneled into expanding and upgrading the Syrian army, they ultimately also contributed to an improvement in Syria's economic situation.[37]

## Aftermath of the war: Syria, Iraq's future, and the security arrangements in the Gulf

Syria's involvement in the Gulf crisis enabled it to return to the center of the inter-Arab arena. With the close of the war, it took part in hammering out a security formula for the Gulf, known as the Damascus Declaration; it was published on 6 March 1991 after a round of talks held there between the foreign ministers of the Gulf states, Syria and Egypt. Primarily, it specified post-war security arrangements in the Gulf, along with guidelines for economic cooperation between the countries. In this framework it was decided that the Syrian and Egyptian troops which had participated in the war would remain as a defense force in Saudi Arabia and Kuwait.[38] But the declaration was stalled as a result of second thoughts in the Gulf countries and also, apparently, by Syrian wavering under Iranian pressure. In June 1991 the Syrians began recalling their troops from the Gulf, and plans to replace them with fresh troops were scrapped.[39]

Anticipating the collapse of Saddam Husayn's regime in early March 1991, the Syrians faced a dilemma over possible Iraqi successor regimes. All were unpalatable alternatives: Shi'i fundamentalist circles with Iranian protection might take control in Baghdad, or Iraq might turn into a US protectorate. A third possibility involved the dismantling of Iraq or a change in its borders, with annexation of parts of its territory by Turkey and Iran. Syria's dilemma over the future of Iraq increased once it became clear to the Syrians that their efforts to use exiled Iraqi opposition circles, some centered in Damascus, to tailor their own alternative to Saddam Husayn's rule had failed. These exiles lacked real support within Iraq, and could not even reach consensus among themselves about their country's future. All that remained to be done with them was to exploit them for propaganda purposes against the regime of Saddam Husayn.[40] Under these circumstances Syria began to put significant efforts into safeguarding the territorial integrity and continued existence of the Iraqi state. It seems that after the Gulf War it no longer saw Saddam Husayn's regime as presenting the same degree of menace; in the absence of an acceptable alternative to his rule, continuation of the *status quo* in Iraq seemed the best option.

The Syrian dilemma increased as the following fundamental facts became clear through the 1990s. First, Saddam's regime has held on to power, and neither inside nor outside Iraq was there any opposition element capable of proposing an alternative to his rule. Second, the United States and other Western countries were determined to prevent Saddam Husayn from regaining a position of influence or regional primacy such as he had enjoyed before the crisis. Third, Turkey – perhaps with Israeli or American backing – had moved to take over territories in northern Iraq, and in so doing might have brought about the dismantling of the Iraqi state. Syrian policy toward Iraq evolved in the 1990s against this background, and culminated in efforts toward Syrian-Iraqi rapprochement initiated by Damascus' from 1997 on (see Ch. 5).

In sum, Syria emerged stronger from the Gulf crisis, both domestically and abroad, due to its unequivocal siding with the US-led anti-Iraq coalition. This policy was a direct continuation of the political line adopted by the Syrians in the late 1980s, which was intended to cope with the regional and, in particular, the international circumstances of the time. The general sense in Damascus and beyond was that Syria's involvement in the Gulf War had improved its position in its main arenas of activity. Still, in spite of its gains during the crisis, something about the experience made tangible to Syria the limits of its power, together with several other fundamental problems: The first of these was the disappearance of the Soviet Union as a power and political force. In the crisis, it had played only a supporting role, as a junior partner seconding US initiatives. Second, the Syrians were again made aware of the position of the United States as the world's sole superpower, especially in the Middle East, intent on taking action, including forceful action, to achieve its goals. Third, the Syrians again witnessed the superiority of Western technology, which afforded the United States a relatively easy victory over an Arab army armed with East European weaponry. In Syrian eyes this had implications for the balance of power with Israel, which was equipped with the best Western weapons and technology. Fourth, a precedent was set for international, particularly American, intervention in the affairs of an Arab state, and in this case it had almost toppled the Iraqi regime. This precedent was re-enacted late in 1991 in Libya's dispute with the United States and Britain, which led to the imposition of sanctions against Libya beginning on 15 April 1992. Syria – at least publicly – sided with Libya, but refrained from violating the international sanctions imposed on it.[41] Fifth, the disunity of the Arab world had been shown yet again, especially the fact that collective Arab support in the event of a conflict with Israel or the United States was not automatic. Sixth, the crisis enhanced Israel's position. The political, military and financial advantages gained by Israel, especially after the missile attacks against it, only reinforced Syria's sense of inferiority compared to Israel. Seventh, the crisis led to the liquidation of Iraq's power. Despite its deep and enduring hostility with Iraq, Syria had hitherto viewed Iraq as a source of strategic depth and possible support in the face of a future Israeli threat.

One important lesson that Syria gleaned from the crisis – on the tactical level and in the short term – was that it had to act to achieve defensive capability against an Israeli air assault, in the event that Israel should seek to emulate the Western attack on Iraq. The aim of that attack had been to destroy Iraq's industrial and economic infrastructure, thereby fatally damaging its economy, not to mention its strength as a country. Against this background, the Syrians acquired Scud-C surface-to-surface missiles, with a range of 600 km., from North Korea.[42] These missiles enabled the Syrians to establish a balance of terror with Israel, which for the first time recognized that the Syrians could cause damage deep within its territory. At the same time, the Syrian effort to arm itself aroused a forceful American reaction – the May 1991 Bush initiative for supervision of the arms race in the Middle East and, in its wake, active American efforts to frustrate the North Korean supply of missiles to Syria. This effort ultimately failed because, with Iranian and Russian aid, the missiles eventually reached Damascus.[43] However, the American preventive effort was enough once again to underscore for the Syrians their strategic weakness compared to the United States and Israel.

The primary lesson for Syria on the long-term strategic level was therefore that it must continue to adhere to the foreign policy lines it had adopted before the crisis. These were based on the effort to reach an understanding with America, with the objective of ensuring its inclusion in the new world order headed by the United States. Syria's support for the US-led coalition against a sister Arab state represented the crossing of a divide by the rulers in Damascus. As such it foreshadowed the regime's later aims and measures – in the context of the Arab-Israeli conflict as well – as was indeed borne out when Syria joined the peace process that began in the region with the close of the Gulf War.

## NOTES

[1] For more on Syrian-Iraqi relations, see Amazia Baram, "Ideology and Power Politics in Syrian-Iraqi Relations, 1968-1990" in Moshe Maoz, Avner Yaniv, and Avi Kover (eds), *Syria under Assad*, pp. 199-214; also Eberhard Kienle, *Ba'th v Ba'th*.

[2] For more on Iraqi policy during this period, see Ofra Bengio, "Iraq" in Ami Ayalon (ed.), MECS, vol. XIII (1989), pp. 404-6.

[3] *Al-Tadammun*, 9 July 1990.

[4] Bruce Maddy-Weitzman, "Inter Arab Relations" in Ami Ayalon (ed.), MECS, vol. XIII (1989), pp. 122-9.

[5] Radio Monte Carlo, 7 July – DR, 13 July 1989.

[6] Ofra Bengio, "Iraq" in Ami Ayalon (ed.), MECS, vol. XIV (1990), pp. 393-5.

[7] Radio Damascus, 26 May – DR, 29 May 1990.

[8] Syrian Television, 21 May – DR, 26 May 1990.

[9] President Mubarak visited Damascus on 2 May 1990. This was the first visit there by an Egyptian president in thirteen years. On 24 May he sent his adviser 'Usama al-Baz and the Egyptian Foreign Minister, 'Ismat Abd al-Majid, to Damascus to try to persuade the Syrians to take part in the Baghdad summit. Mubarak went to Damascus again on 31 May to update the Syrians on the results of the summit. Radio Damascus, 2 May – DR, 3 May 1990; MENA, 24, 30 May – DR, 25, 31 May 1990.

[10] Amazia Baram, "Ideology and Power Politics", pp. 125-39; see also Avraham Sela, *Ahdut betokh Perud, Ve'idot haPisga ha'Arviyot* (Unity amidst division, the Arab Summit Conferences) ( Jerusalem: The Hebrew University/J. L. Magnes Publishers, 1983), pp. 159-210.

[11] Radio Damascus, 2, 3, 8 August – DR, 2, 3, 9 August 1990.

[12] MENA, 10 August – DR, 13 August 1990.

[13] *Ha'aretz*, 14 September; *JP*, 15 September 1990.

[14] *Ha'aretz*, 20 August 1990.

[15] *Al-Jumhuriyya* (Baghdad), 16 August 1990; see also Ofra Bengio, "Iraq" in Ami Ayalon (ed.), MECS, vol. XIV (1990), pp. 409-10.

[16] IRNA, 18 September – DR, 19 September 1990; *IHT*, 26 September 1990.

[17] Radio Damascus, 14 September – DR, 14 September 1990.

[18] Syrian Television, 14 September – DR, 17 September 1990.

[19] Radio Damascus, 15 November – DR, 27 November 1990.

[20] Radio Damascus, 28 November – DR, 29 November 1990.

[21] Thus, for example, after the Syrian attack on Michel 'Awn, the American ambassador in Syria announced that Washington supported implementation of the Ta'if Agreement, and that the Syrian step was meant to enable the Lebanese government to extend its sovereignty throughout Lebanese territory. SANA, 24 October – DR, 25 October 1990.

[22] See Amazia Baram, "Ideology and Power Politics", pp. 203-4.

[23] Radio Damascus, 12 January – DR, 14 January 1991.

[24] Radio Monte Carlo, 8 February – DR, 8 February 1991; *IHT*, 6 February 1991; *'Ukaz*, 24 February 1991.

[25] Ofra Bengio, "Iraq" in Ami Ayalon (ed.), MECS, vol. XIV (1990), pp. 410-12.

[26] *Al-Ba'th*, 18 January 1991.

[27] See the commentaries broadcast on Syrian radio, Radio Damascus, 7, 8, 9 January – DR, 8, 9 January 1991.

[28] Radio Damascus, 12 September – DR, 13 September 1990.

[29] Radio Damascus, 12 February – DR, 13 February 1991.

[30] SANA, 19 January – DR, 22 January 1991.

[31] *IHT*, 22 January 1991.

[32] SANA, 19 January – DR, 22 January 1991; AFP, 20 January – DR, 22 January 1991.

[33] AFP, 29 January; INA, 30 January – DR, 30, 31 January 1991.

[34] INA, 4 February; SANA, 4 February – DR, 5 February 1991.

[35] Radio Baghdad, 23 January – DR, 23 January 1991.

[36] *Al-Hayat*, 6 July 1991.

[37] According to Syrian sources, more than 100,000 Syrian workers returned from Kuwait because of the Gulf crisis leading to a 6% rise in the state's unemployment rate. In addition, fund transfers by Syrian workers from the Gulf countries to Syria dropped. See *CF – Syria, 1991-92* (London, 1992), p. 5.

[38] *Tishrin*, 7 March 1991.

[39] Radio Damascus, 7 March, 29 April, 2 June – DR, 7 March, 30 April, 5 June 1991.

[40] *NYT*, 17 February 1991. See also Eyal Zisser, "Syria and the Gulf Crisis: Stepping on a New Path", *Orient*, 34(3), 1993, pp. 575-6; Michael Eppel, "Syria: Iraq's Radical Nemesis", in Amatzia Baram and Barry Rubin (eds), *Iraq's Road to War* (New York: St Martin's Press, 1993), pp. 177-90.

[41] Eyal Zisser, "Syria" in Ami Ayalon (ed.), MECS, vol. XV (1991), pp. 737-8.

[42] *WP*, 28 July 1991.

[43] Radio Damascus, 12 March, 2 June – DR, 12 March, 2 June 1991; see also Eyal Zisser, "Syria" in Ami Ayalon (ed.), MECS, vol. XV (1991), pp. 685-701.

# Part III

# SYRIAN FOREIGN POLICY IN THE 1990s

# 5

## SYRIA BETWEEN EAST AND WEST

*1991 – A landmark year*

The year 1991 will be remembered as important in both Syrian and Middle Eastern history, heralding the dawn of a new era. More precisely, it ushered in a new regional order that was marked, or perhaps overshadowed, by regional and international American hegemony.

Early in 1991, Operation "Desert Storm" dealt a blow to Iraq that forced it to withdraw its troops from Kuwait and did immense damage to its military and economic strength. Toward the end of the year, in October, the United States launched the Madrid Conference and the start of peace negotiations between Israel and the Arab states. These two events, in which America played a pivotal role, eclipsed another significant event – the collapse of the Soviet Union and its dissolution into the Commonwealth of Independent States on 31 December 1991.

Fateful as these events seemed to be for the Syrian state and its regime, many months passed before President Asad shared his assessment of them with his fellow-citizens. He finally told them what he thought the regional turmoil held in store for Syria's future at his swearing-in ceremony as President for a fourth term in March 1992. This address was one his few to the Syrian people in the entire decade.

Addressing the difficulties facing Syria in the new regional and international circumstances, Asad gave a sober, even sorrowful speech; his concerns and uncertainty over the future were evident. However, he did not leave his audience without hope, and expressed his conviction that future developments would prove the correctness of the course he had steered for them since rising to power, and that it would lead Syria safely into port. He said:

"Something has happened in the world and we must not ignore it. Stability has reigned in the world for a long period, during which there was a clear system of equilibrium. But significant changes have affected that equilibrium... The world today is turbulent and it is not clear where it is heading or what its last stop will be. However, even if we do not know how long the turmoil

67

in our world will continue or how it will conclude, it is clear that it will die down, and the world will stabilize itself, at least for a time. [Only for a time,] for permanent stability is not a term with which our world is familiar, and therefore we cannot estimate how long this stability will last.... The history of mankind teaches us that the duration of such stability differs from period to period, and that means the growth of systems of equilibrium and treaties different from those that were and those that are now. Therefore, at this time it is important to be alert to the dangers that threaten us until tranquility and stability are achieved in our world."[1]

These remarks illustrate the two basic assumptions that lay at the foundation of Syrian foreign policy throughout the 1990s. One was that the regional and international circumstances facing Syria posed an immediate danger to its interests and indeed to its very security and territorial integrity (and thus to the stability and future of the regime). However, circumstances were never immutable. Syria thus faced a period of transition characterized by upheavals and a lack of stability, but this period would pass, after which circumstances in the region were likely to favor it again. The second basic assumption guiding Syrian foreign policy was that Syria, in cooperation with other Arab states, must prepare itself to confront these threatening circumstances and wage a battle for survival that would at least ensure the preservation of the *status quo* in the region. To this end certain changes in policy were necessary to restore to it the capacity for maneuver which it had lost with the disintegration of the Soviet Union. At the same time Syria did not need to overhaul its policy dramatically, or retreat from its fundamental concepts. On the contrary such a reversal would probably prove catastrophic and cause damage far more serious than that generated by circumstances.

Thus the notion that Syria's condition was difficult but not hopeless was Asad's point of departure. Sensing a need for change but not a radical upheaval, he charted a new course, to which he held through most of the 1990s. It bore the marks of contradictory impulses, of which one was Syria's readiness and desire to secure Syria a place in the new regional order that was taking shape under US leadership. Within this framework it acted to improve its relations with the United States, aiming to give them a measure of depth and closeness. At the same time the Syrians were careful to preserve maneuverability and freedom of action where Washington was concerned and so avoid undue dependence on its goodwill. This they did by establishing an all-Arab front centered around the Egypt-Syria-Saudi Arabia axis and, in tandem, by fostering contacts with Western Europe.

The second impetus to guiding Syria's new path seemed completely at odds with the first. Essentially, it required Damascus to try to curb the American-Israeli effort to establish a new regional order in the Middle East. Success in that endeavour would preserve the *status quo* that had existed in the region up till then. To this end Syria acted to maintain and improve its ties with Iran, to rebuild a close relationship with Russia and, after early 1997, to make headway in its relations with Iraq. The Syrian regime was also careful to adhere, at least publicly, to its ideological commitment to the patently anti-West worldview that had been its guiding principle since it seized power in Damascus in the early 1960s. It comes as no surprise that in in such conditions Syria failed to make real progress in its relations with the United States. In bilateral relations with the countries of Western Europe and with the Arab states it also did not gain any ground. Syrian caution, hesitation and duality of purpose, evident in Damascus's efforts to improve relations with Iran and the West simultaneously, repeatedly raised the question of the country's foreign policy aims. Did Syria in the early 1990s wish to foster ties with the East or with the West?

## Syrian foreign policy – principles and goals

Before turning to a discussion of Syria's "between East and West" foreign policy in the 1990s, we should examine further the place and function of foreign policy in the worldview and overall policy of the Syrian regime. Foreign policy was just one of the many instruments at its disposal that served to realize its goals. In this perspective, Syrian foreign policy did not exist in a vacuum, but was an integral part of the overall policy of the Damascus regime.[2] From the time Asad rose to power, it was characterized above all by *Realpolitik,* i.e. keen attention to the regional, inter-Arab and international circumstances surrounding Syria and consideration of the forces that dictate them. On the other hand, the Syrian regime aspired to anchor its foreign policy within a more rooted framework – that of the overall worldview to which it paid allegiance. This duality found its clearest expression in the policy goals laid down by the regime, which can be divided into short-term, intermediate and long-term categories as indicated below.

*Immediate.* A primary aim consisted of guaranteeing the security and territorial integrity of Syria and bolstering the efforts spearheaded by the security and military forces to cope with the challenges and external dangers confronting the state, at least in the view of the regime. These included possible threats from Israel and other regional rivals: Iraq in its time and, since the end of the Gulf War in March 1991, Turkey. The second goal was to safeguard the regime, i.e. prevent the creation of an external threat to domestic stability and hence to the stability of the regime. Coupled with this was the effort to mobilize external support – political, military and economic – for the regime and its aims. Syrian foreign policy has thus enabled the regime to maintain its domestic position in two ways: first, by making use of its achievements in this arena and second, by exploiting challenges and difficulties in the regional and international arena to mobilize support or to divert public attention from domestic problems.

*Intermediate.* The regime's third policy goal was directed at the Golan Heights, occupied by Israel since 1967. The aim was to restore this territory to Syrian hands through political means, but in the event of this not succeeding the regime sought political backing – inter-Arab and international – for a military course of action that would seek to regain the Golan Heights by force. Fourth was "Greater Syria". This was the basis of Syria's regional status, and of the extension of its influence over territory and populations immediately outside its borders, chiefly in Lebanon, but also in Jordan and among the Palestinians.

*Long-term.* The fifth goal has been Arab unity. Syria has sought the realization, or at least the advancement, of the worldview of the Syrian Ba'th regime, the foundation of which is the establishment of a united Arab world, with Syria as the designated leader.

On the face of it, there was a clear contradiction between those goals concerned with immediate threats and challenges, and those aimed at realizing a the Ba'th regime's vision of the end of days. The point of departure of the latter was not current circumstances but an ideal situation not yet in existence. It is also clear that, in order to pursue its goals for the immediate future, the Syrian regime tended to adopt a defensive and rather passive "wait and see" foreign policy. This at a time when its long-term goals called for the opposite approach, namely the adoption of an active, enterprising and offensive policy.

Despite the contradictions inherent in these goals, Damascus was determined to cobble them together to form its overall foreign policy. Its slogan in the mid-1980s pointed up the regime's effort to overcome the contradictions: "Stand firm and rise to the challenge" (*al-Sumud wal-Tasaddi*). This slogan, coined in the immediate aftermath of Operation "Peace for Galilee" to further efforts toward achieving strategic parity with Israel, reflects two levels or stages in Syria's overall policy and its foreign policy throughout the 1980s. The first was "standing firm" (*al-Sumud*) to confront present dangers, and its re-alization was to provide the basis for implementing the second, "rising to the challenge" (*wal-Tasaddi*), i.e. the challenge of realizing the regime's long-term vision.[3]

Syrian foreign policy was the natural outgrowth of the regime's character and, in particular, that of its long-time leader, President Asad. First, this policy was based on an acute understanding of the limits of Syria's power and its basic weaknesses – including its relative military weakness. On the other hand, it acknowledged that in the region the building of military muscle and its occasional flexing were a practical necessity. This applied not only in the domestic arena with opponents of the regime, but also abroad with rivals in the regional and international arenas. It should also be noted that Syria was not averse to using terror, carried out when necessary by Lebanese or Palestinian groups, to advance its political interests. Examples of this included the assassination of Bashir al-Jumayyil, the President of Lebanon and Christian Phalangist leader, in September 1982, and possibly involvement in the bombing of the American embassy and Marine headquarters in Beirut in April and October 1983.[4]

Second, Syria's foreign policy always aspired to give the decision-makers in Damascus both freedom to maneuver and independence of action. It tried to steer clear of dependence on any regional or, especially, international force. In spite of the solid relationship that Asad maintained with the Soviet Union during the 1970s and '80s, for example, he did his best to avoid a situation where he relied exclusively on it for either political or military needs. Asad's depiction as a Soviet client was thus erroneous, as is clear from Syria's steps in the inter-Arab and regional arenas (such as its involvement in Lebanon in 1976). More than once these clashed sharply with the Soviet view.[5]

Finally, although Syrian foreign policy underwent certain, mostly limited, shifts in the past, it was characterized mainly by an avoidance of change, initiative and breakthrough. Its policy of preferring the *status quo* was an outgrowth of Syrian political culture and of the personality of President Asad, both characterized by uncommunicativeness and suspicion of the outside world.

Yet beyond the inherent flaws in the nature and structure of the Syrian regime there were also clear advantages that made it easy for Asad and his colleagues in the top echelon to conduct effective foreign policy. First, Syrian foreign policy was free of the limitations of time that circumscribe most Western democracies, where the length of presidential or governmental terms dictate timetables with a set term, and policy changes followed upon changes of governments. In contrast, continuity characterized Syrian foreign policy, a result of the protracted period of Asad's rule. Second, the Syrian regime rarely had to cope with domestic political pressures regarding the administration of its foreign policy. Instead it was subject to its ideological commitment, chained to both its self-image and its public image. It therefore hesitated to adopt policies which it thought might stir up real opposition among Syrian public opinion. On the other hand, the regime was free of the burden of a political opposition, and unfettered by the institutions that characterize Western democracy – parliament, a judicial system, a free press and so on. In a number of cases Asad ignored broad opposition among Syrian public opinion to his projected measures, winning public support for them retrospectively. Among these were the decision to send troops into Lebanon in 1976 and join the anti-Iraqi coalition during the Gulf crisis. Third, the Syrian regime could afford to pay a substantial political and economic price, absorb heavy human losses and still survive, a privilege not enjoyed by most democratic governments in the West.

Turning from this general survey of Syrian foreign policy to an analysis of its manifestations in the 1990s, we see three main stages. The first, which ended in 1992, was marked by fear of the United States and the attempt to dispel this threat by establishing a dialogue. This was the period when Syria joined the US-led anti-Iraq coalition and participated in the Madrid Conference which led to the opening of Arab-Israeli peace negotiations.

The second stage, 1992-6, saw progress in the peace process. This reached the point, early in 1996, where the sense was prevalent in Damascus, Jerusalem and Washington that the achievement of a peace accord between Israel and Syria was essentially only a matter of time. Progress in the peace process brought dividends, such as a strengthening of Syria's regional and international standing and especially an improvement in its relations with the United States and Western Europe. At the same time, the peace process posed a strategic challenge to Damascus: the Syrians feared that they could become marginalized and insignificant in a Middle East ruled by a coalition of powers led by the United States that included Israel and its Arab allies, chief among them Egypt and Jordan. Indeed, the signing of the Oslo accords between the PLO and Israel in September 1993 and of course the signing of the Israeli-Jordanian peace treaty in October 1994 did not augur well for Syria's regional status. Aside from the blow to its bargaining position in negotiations with Israel, these accords heralded the end of its pretensions to regional leadership. The fear of being pushed into a corner seems to have been at the root of Asad's hesitation over progress in the negotiations for peace in which he engaged with the Israeli government between 1992 and 1996.

The third stage lasted from 1996 to1999. Benjamin Netanyahu's rise to power in Israel after the May 1996 elections led to a deadlock in the peace process, at least on the Israeli-Syrian track. Furthermore, optimistic assessments of an imminent breakthrough in the Israeli-Syrian negotiations gave way to warning signals of imminent war between the two states. The freeze in the peace process after the Israeli elections exacerbated the regional problems confronting Syria at that time. Relations with Turkey deteriorated in an unprecedented fashion and those with Jordan were fraught with tension and hostility. It is thus not surprising that in late June 1996 the Syrian Minister of Information, Muhammad Salman, hastened to warn that an imperialist-Zionist conspiracy was being hatched against Syria, aimed at harming it and its ruling regime.[6]

This suspicion had a clear and immediate influence on Syrian policy from mid-1996 on. In the first half of the 1990s the peace process and the corresponding effort toward closer ties with the United States and the West had eclipsed the alliance between Damascus and Teheran – though it was not neglected altogether. But Netanyahu's rise to power changed everything. The importance of the American connection dwindled; instead, Syria began to emphasize its ties with Iran and, from the start of 1997, with Iraq as well. It would seem that a contributing factor was the erosion of America's image as an omnipotent superpower, which stemmed from the US administration's hesitancy and ineffectiveness in its treatment of various regional and international issues. These ultimately led, in the regional context, to a standstill on the Israeli-Syrian track of the peace process, and failure of the policy of dual containment that the United States. adopted early in the 1990s towards Iran and Iraq. President Asad's participation in December 1997 in the summit of heads of Muslim states convened in Teheran, to the unconcealed dissatisfaction of Washington, and his unequivocal siding with Iraq from early 1998 in the latter's conflict with the United States on the question of international supervision of the Iraqi arms build-up, clearly expressed Syria's challenge to the role that the Americans sought to play in the region, and to the new regional order which Washington hoped to establish there.

The fourth stage began with the May 1999 election and subsequent change of government in Israel. In the wake of these elections, hope revived for a breakthrough in the Israeli-Syrian negotiations, and it seemed as if just such a breakthrough occurred in December 1999 with the summit meeting between the Israeli Prime Minister Ehud Barak and the Syrian Foreign Minister Faruq al-Shar' in Washington, which led to renewed Israeli-Syrian negotiations. Immediately after Barak's victory at the polls and, of course, after talks resumed between the two states in December 1999, the Syrians exchanged signals and goodwill messages with Israel, and took steps at the same time to warm up relations with Washington and strengthen cooperation with Jordan and, to a lesser extent, with Egypt, so as to improve their position in preparation for the anticipated negotiations with Israel. However, these negotiations produced no real progress, and the failure to bridge the gap that still existed between the two countries resulted in impasse. As a result, Syria reverted to the same positions it held before the elections in Israel in May 1999 and to same foreign policy – vacillating between East and West, and between the new and old regional orders. It was as if these elecions had not taken place and Netanyahu still held power in Israel.

Having reviewed the principal stages in the development of Syria's foreign policy during the 1990s, we should examine its system of foreign relations with some of the key states in the regional and international arena. This system, as already stated, has been marked by an effort to make serious progress in two directions – East and West – at the same time.

## Toward a new regional order

As stated above, Syria focused its efforts to assure itself a place in the new regional order – at least in 1992–6 and since 1999 – along three main vectors: one, by improving relations with the United States; two, by establishing an inter-Arab axis with Saudi Arabia, Egypt and Syria; and finally, by establishing a Syrian-European axis. Syria's fostering of relations with the moderate Arab states and Western Europe was designed mainly to reinforce its bargaining position with the United States and Israel in everything connected with the peace negotiations – and to bring it economic gains.

*Syria and the United States.* From the start of the decade, Syria and the United States worked together to improve bilateral relations. Compared to the deep rift between the two that existed for most of the 1980s, there was some visible improvement. However, it was still meager and fell short of any breakthrough that might have given US-Syrian relations any of the depth and closeness so lacking over the years.

Consequently, the Syrians did their best to establish and maintain a political dialogue with the Americans. Damascus hoped that this dialogue would prove a defense against a possible Israeli or American threat, and advance its political and economic interests. At the same time, the Syrians held back from paying the full price of deepening their relationship with the United States: a peace agreement with Israel, readiness to help the Americans establish a new regional order, and perhaps even opening Syria's doors to American political, economic and cultural influence.

For the whole of the 1990s the peace process was the focus of Syrian-US relations. It seems that an understanding was reached during 1992-6 between the US administration and the Syrian regime on a significant part of the components of the peace agreement negotiated by Israel and Syria. Thus the Americans supported the Syrian demand for complete Israeli withdrawal from the Golan Heights to the 4 June 1967 lines. When, in August 1993, the Israeli Prime Minister Yitzhak Rabin expressed to American ears his readiness to consider full withdrawal from the Golan, the Americans brought it to the Syrians' attention without Rabin's knowledge or consent.[7] However, they did not conceal their dissatisfaction with Asad's hesitation to move forward in negotiations with Israel, even after being given this information. Syrian resistance to implementing confidence-building measures directed to the Israeli public and its government particularly incensed them. In a press interview in September 1997 the Secretary of State Warren Christopher expressed this anger. In his view, Asad had missed a historic opportunity to regain the Golan during the Rabin and Peres governments.[8]

One notable obstacle in the way of improving Syrian-American relations was the fierce opposition among significant parts of the American public to any move toward reconciliation with Damascus. Supporters of Israel in the United States contributed to this, as did a deep-rooted enmity toward Syria, stemming from the Syrian regime's anti-American record, its dictatorial nature and its socioeconomic policy, all of which were in stark contrasted to the values cherished by American society. The antipathy was especially evident in Congress, which throughout the 1990s curbed any effort or initiative by the administration of President Clinton to improve relations with Syria.[9]

The US administration itself offered the clearest expression of reservations towards Syria. Other than the shuttle diplomacy of its Secretaries of State between Damascus and the other capitals in the region, there were hardly any high-level visits or meetings. Asad's meeting with President Bush in November 1990 (leading to Syria's joining the anti-Iraq coalition in the Gulf War), as well as his meeting with President Clinton in January 1994 (marking one of the high points in the still undisclosed Israeli-Syrian negotiations), both took place in Geneva because the US administration was averse to inviting Asad to Washington.[10] Furthermore, President Clinton's October 1994 visit to Damascus took place in the shadow of the peace agreement between Israel and Jordan, and was in fact undertaken because of it, being intended to placate the Syrians and en-sure that they did not try to undermine this accord. In February 1999 Asad and Clinton met again at the funeral of King Husayn in Amman.[11]

Beyond the question of Israeli-Syrian peace negotiations, there were bilateral issues that also clouded Syrian-American relations. Chief among these was Washington's accusation of Syrian involve-ment in terrorist acts. Over the decade Syria regularly appeared in State Department annual reports on world terror. Legal restrictions were consequently imposed on the economic links between the two countries: loans and grants to Syria were prohibited, as was bilateral trade. While these reports determined that since 1986 (the year of the Hindawi affair) no proof had been found of direct Syrian in-volvement in the planning or execution of terrorist acts, Syria was blamed for doing nothing to prevent terrorist attacks against Israel by Lebanese or Palestinian groups, for sponsoring and aiding these groups, and for hosting their compounds and training camps.[12]

Syria also figured for many years in the list of states involved in the drug trade. According to US reports, this was due to the involve-ment of senior Syrian officers in both cultivation and trafficking. Damascus put considerable effort into the fight against drugs, ex-tending into Lebanon, and this – together with the US administration's desire not to strain relations with Syria too far, and to maintain and improve them against the background of the deadlock in the peace process since the May 1996 Israeli elections – led in October 1997 to the removal of Syria and, incidentally, Lebanon from the list of states involved in the drug trade.[13]

A separate question was Syria's avoidance of full and binding ties with Washington – reminiscent of Egypt at an earlier time. This avoidance was conspicuous in Syria's efforts to rebuild its political and security relations with Moscow (an effort that culminated in Asad's visit to Moscow in July 1999) and, of course, to foster its alli-ance with Teheran. The position Damascus took during the US-Iraqi stand-off in late 1998 also aroused anger in Washington. In the aftermath of Operation "Desert Fox" in December 1998, mass dem-onstrations against the United States were organized in Damascus – apparently by the regime, or at least with its tacit knowledge – dur-ing which the US embassy and the ambassador's residence were attacked.[14] The Syrian Minister of Defense, Mustafa Talas, praised these demonstrations, declaring that Damascus alone knew how to preserve "the honor of Arabism" and that the demonstrator who had burst into the US embassy and lowered the flag from the mast-head had performed an act of heroism.[15] The Syrian Foreign Ministry naturally hurried to apologize for the incident, and Talas himself was forced to retract his statements and indeed deny that he had ever uttered them.[16] Neverthless, the incident is enough to prompt consideration of another complex aspect of relations between Washington and Damascus.

The US administration thus acted throughout the decade to improve bilateral relations with Syria, limited though this was by the opposition such moves aroused among friends of Israel in the United States, especially in Congress. Nonetheless, the administration was careful to link all progress in the bilateral Syrian-American relationship to parallel progress in the peace process. The Syrians, for their part, preferred spasmodic progress in their relations with the United States to making concessions in such sensitive areas as the peace process with Israel or domestic affairs. The upshot was a lack of any real progress in relations between the two countries, at least until the end of the decade.

*Relations with Europe.* From the start of the 1990s Syrian relations with the countries of the European Union showed marked improvement. This was manifested mainly on the economic level in a deepening of commercial ties and in European loans and grants to Syria. It seems that the European countries found economic relations with Syria easier to advance than political ones, chiefly because of the lack of progress in the Israeli-Syrian peace process. Another factor was the difference of opinion with Damascus in such areas as Syria's involvement in terror, its presence in Lebanon – a sensitive issue for France – and violations of human rights in Syria itself. On several occasions during the 1990s the European Parliament – as opposed to European governments – prevented the approval of loans and grants to Syria on grounds of violations of human rights.[17] The Syrians, for their part, gave priority to the advancement of economic relations with Europe, especially because of their desire to turn Europe into a bridgehead for its integration into the world economy.

The improvement in Syrian-European relations in practice began on the heels of the Soviet collapse in the late 1980s, and the Gulf crisis added momentum to the process. During this period the question of Syrian involvement in terror dropped out of the Syrian-European agenda because of Britain's decision in November 1990 to renew diplomatic ties with Syria, which had been severed in October 1987 over the Hindawi affair.[18] Syrian readiness to join the peace process also helped smooth the way to improved relations with the European countries. Moreover, the desire of the latter to join and play an active role in the political process – not welcomed by Israel and the United States – dovetailed with Syrian interests.

In the early 1990s Syria became an oil exporter, adding another dimension to its developing relations with European countries, and by the decade's end oil accounted for some two-thirds of its exports. Among its customers were Italy, France and Germany.[19] Oil and its products were not, however, the exclusive component of Syrian-European trade; Syrian economic reforms offered investors and European financial institutions ample opportunities. Over the whole decade trade with Europe constituted more than two-thirds of Syrian foreign trade (some 65% of exports and 45% of imports).[20] Since 1995 Syria has also taken steps to resolve the question of its debts to the European countries – this issue was the focus of prolonged financial litigation between the two sides and prevented the furthering of their economic relations. The question of Syria's debt to most West European countries, France in particular, has been resolved – though not, at the time of going to press, with Germany.[21]

The stabilization of European-Syrian relations led to the opening of negotiations over the signing of an association agreement between Syria and the European Union. The EU demanded of Syria, as a condition of signing such an agreement, that it institute reforms with the aim of adopting a free-market economy. However, Europe agreed to grant Syria an extended adjustment period of twelve years, which would enable it to carry out the required economic reforms gradually.[22]

Although Syria did its best to involve the European countries in the Israeli-Syrian peace negotiations, clear and unequivocal reservations on the part of the United States and Israel greatly limited the European role. Still, the voices raised in Damascus in a veritable plea to Europe "to fulfill its historic mission in the Middle East" were significant. According to an editorial in *Al-Ba'th*, the organ of the ruling Ba'th Party, in January 1995, the passivity demonstrated by the European countries toward this process, in that they did not line up in favor of the Syrian position in negotiations with Israel, was entirely at odds with Europe's historic role in the Middle East, as well as with its interests in the region. Or, in the words of the editorial, "Europe's vacillation [over taking a part in the peace process] and the powerlessness it displays in this connection give the impression that the continent lacks power and weight. However, European interests in the region call for Europe to play a significant role there because those interests are not transient but lasting."[23]

Damascus's recognition of the legitimacy of European interests in the Middle East and of historical ties binding Europe to the region, along with the call to the European states to play an active role, are noteworthy in view of the traditional animosity of the Syrian Ba'th regime to the West. It was the regime's worldview that engendered this animosity. It saw itself as the "pioneering soldier" of the Arab world in the struggle against Western imperialism in its various forms. The change in tone toward European countries thus reflected the change in Syria's approach and its desire to foster ties with them.

France led the European states in everything connected with bolstering relations with Syria. Its motivation was apparently a desire to resume its once pivotal role in the Middle East in general and in the Levant in particular. Fueling this desire were clearly the historic ties that bound it to this area. Thus, during "Operation Grapes of Wrath" in April 1996 the French invested a great deal of diplomatic effort into bringing the Israeli action to an end. The Syrians repaid this by arranging for French cooperation in the committee overseeing the understandings reached between Israel, Syria, Lebanon and Hizballah at the end of this operation.[24]

France was also the first of the European countries to reach an agreement on re-financing Syria's debt. In so doing, it incidentally split the front established by the European countries for the purpose of negotiating a plan for Damascus's repayment of its debts (the Paris Club).[25] In practice, the French wrote off a significant portion of the Syrian debt, and another portion was set aside as credit at Damascus' disposal to allow it to acquire French industrial goods, including thirty railway engines and six Airbus 300 planes, valued overall at some $310 million.[26]

No wonder, then, that Paris was selected as the destination for Asad's first visit of the decade to the West (excluding the Geneva meetings with Presidents Bush and Clinton). When he arrived there in July 1998, he was given a royal reception, and naturally praised his hosts, while taking trouble to stress the key role that Europe, led by France, needed to fill in the Middle East in the service of peace.[27] In an interview on French television he took pride in the tradition of friendship and cooperation between the two countries, noting that no hard feelings remained in Syria from the French Mandate period.[28]

*Syria in the inter-Arab arena.* Syria focused its efforts from the early 1990s on enhancing relations with Egypt and the Gulf states, especially Saudi Arabia. It also ensured that these links were presented as the strategic axis for regional and inter-Arab relations.

Syria tended to attribute special importance to ties with Egypt, its senior Arab sister. As will be recalled, after the signing of the Israeli-Egyptian peace accord in 1979 it severed relations with Egypt, and it was not until ten years later that they were resumed, in November 1989, in a step that heralded the imminent about-turn in Syria's political course. The Gulf crisis that followed led to still closer relations between them. The Syrians sought to make use of Egypt's firm ties with the United States to improve their bargaining position in negotiations with Israel, as well as in the direct Damascus-Washington dialogue. Indeed Presidents Mubarak and Asad met frequently in the 1990s to discuss regional and inter-Arab developments and try to crystallize a joint stand on developments.

It seems, then, that in spite of the clear interest of both countries in a cordial bilateral relationship, they refrained from forming a close strategic alliance based on political, military and security cooperation on the model of Syria's treaty with Iran. The reason for this lay, first of all, in the baggage of the past that continued to weigh upon their relations; examples include Syria's secession from the UAR in September 1961 and its stance on the sidelines during the Six-Day War until it was attacked by Israel. The Egyptians perceived these as a stab in the back. In return, Egypt's steps during the October 1973 war and thereafter, culminating in the signing of a separate peace agreement with Israel, were described in Damascus as a betrayal of the Arab cause. Differences of opinion – some of them fundamental – over various issues on the Egyptian-Syrian agenda also hampered efforts to turn the connection between the two into a strategic pact. The first of these was the peace process. It is true that as a rule Egypt tried to express open and clear support for the Syrian position in negotiations with Israel, and during the governments of Rabin and Peres and of course that of Netanyahu, it consistently laid the blame for the lack of progress in negotiations squarely on Israel. The situation reached a climax in the fall of 1996 when President Mubarak declared that, should war erupt between Israel and Syria, which seemed a distinct possibility at the time, Egypt would not stand aside.[29] Nevertheless, Egypt took care not to be dragged after the Syrians. As a case in point, Egypt avoided assisting Syrian efforts in the Arab League or in other inter-Arab institutions to pass extreme resolutions that called for a freeze on ties with Israel – this even after Netanyahu's rise to power, and in spite of the impasse at that time in Israeli-Syrian and Israeli-Palestinian negotiations.[30]

Second, Syria's pact with Iran was another thorn in Cairo's side. Egypt held Iran responsible for the increase of Islamic terrorism in Egypt. Syria invested considerable effort in mediating between Cairo and Teheran, but its repeated initiatives usually met with Egyptian rejection.[31]

Finally, it seems that there was latent competition over senior status in the Arab world between Egypt and Syria, at least where Arab public opinion at street level was concerned. Egypt saw itself as the senior Arab sister, while the Syrians refused to recognize it as such.

Syria consistently cast doubts on Egypt's commitment to the Arab cause in view of its firm ties with Washington and peace with Israel. Syria, incidentally, did not hesitate to use these ties to strengthen its bargaining position in negotiations with Israel and in its dialogue with the Americans.

Syria maintained a limited relationship with the Gulf states as well, on an economic basis. From the start of the 1990s this relationship stood firm against various challenges, primarily the deepening of Syria's ties with Iran, with which some of the Gulf states had long been in conflict. The United Arab Emirates (UAE), for example, have been involved in a dispute with it over control of three islands in the Gulf, and Bahrain has accused Iran of undermining its domestic stability by fomenting riots that broke out on the island early in 1996.[32] Syria tried its hand at mediating between the two sides, but in 1995 it joined Egypt and the Gulf states in condemning Iran for its takeover of islands belonging to the UAE. This step soured Damascus–Teheran relations.[33] The growing, if limited, amity that began between Syria and Iraq in 1997 also strained Syrian relations with the Gulf states.

Between 1992 to 1996 the Gulf states took measures to normalize relations with Israel. This too, disturbed the Syrians, who strongly denounced a series of states, chiefly Qatar, for their readiness to do so. In the winter of 1997 Qatar also hosted the Middle East and North African Economic Conference in Doha, to Damascus's unconcealed irritation.[34] Syria nonetheless managed to enlist the backing of Saudi Arabia and Kuwait, which felt indebted to it for support in the Gulf War. Indeed, these states made clear that normalization of relations with Israel depended on the achievement of an Israeli-Syrian peace agreement.[35] The cessation of the Israeli-Syrian peace process after May 1996, and likewise the freeze in the normalization process between Israel and the Arab states, made this issue a moot point in any case.

In the immediate aftermath of the Gulf War, Syria, Egypt and the Gulf states established a framework for political and security cooperation. The foreign ministers of these countries announced this framework in Damascus in March 1991 (the "Damascus Declaration"), but soon after the end of the Gulf War this framework for cooperation proved worthless. A clear manifestation of this was Kuwait's decision to sign a defense treaty with the United States and to station US troops on its soil, rather than calling on the support of Arab troops.[36] The signatories to the Damascus Declaration continued to convene conferences periodically, but little came of them; the agreement was essentially defunct.[37]

Syria's ties with the Gulf states undoubtedly strengthened its regional standing *vis-à-vis* the United States and Israel, but they were also significant for their economic contribution. During the 1990s more than $5 billion flowed into Syria from the Gulf states – in investments, loans and grants.[38] This was vital to the Syrian effort to preserve economic stability and develop the economic infrastructure.

*Toward an old order.* At the same time, and contrary to the Syrian inclination to integrate into the new regional order that the United States sought to establish in the region, Damascus showed a clear desire to preserve and improve its relations with forces "of the past" and to maintain "the old regional order", and this was at cross-purposes with all that the Americans were seeking to achieve. This tendency in Syrian policy was especially noticeable following Netanyahu's electoral victory in May 1996, and expressed itself in the Syrian effort to improve its relations with Iran and Russia, and even to resuscitate ties with Iraq.

*Relations with Iran.* In 1980, after the Islamic Revolution, Syria established a strategic alliance with Iran. This alliance has survived over the years despite significant pressures on the Syrians to break it (e.g. in the Iran–Iraq war when Syria was politically isolated in the Arab world for its pro-Iranian stance, or at the height of the peace process in the Middle East when it stood firm against American and Israeli pressure to cool relations with Teheran). The persistent efforts of Syria and Iran to preserve their relationship and their success in maintaining bilateral ties in spite of the difficulties gave it another and deeper dimension.[39]

Nevertheless, the alliance between Teheran and Damascus is neither natural nor self-explanatory, for Iran is not an Arab state, while Syria is ruled by a Ba'thist regime committed to an Arab national and secular worldview. So this alliance has been based primarily on political, security and economic interests which have enabled and even obliged the two countries to sustain it. Thus, for example, the Iranians have regarded Syria as a breach in the united Arab front which Iraq and, later, other Arab states sought to establish against it. The Syrians, for their part, have viewed Iran as a partner and vital ally against threats from Israel, Iraq and Turkey. Indeed, one expression of the alliance between the two countries was the military and security assistance Iran provided to Syria, e.g. in the acquisition and development of advanced weaponry such as surface-to-surface missiles and chemical and biological weapons. In late 1996 the Iranians declared that, should Israel or Turkey attack Syria, they would come to its aid.[40] This readiness on Iran's part to help Damascus was enough to turn it into a rearguard or area of strategic depth for Syria, a function which had traditionally been fulfilled by Iraq.

The peace process, which Syria joined in October 1991, and its consequent progress between 1992 and 1996 did not square with the Iranian-Syrian alliance, and cast a shadow over it. In late 1995 relations between the two states hit an unprecedented low because of Teheran's reservations and concern over Syria's enthusiasm for advancing the peace process; and Syrian support in 1994-5 for the Gulf countries, especially the UAE and Bahrain, in their prolonged dispute with Iran also called forth intense and unconcealed anger from Iran toward Syria, to the point where the Iranian press claimed that Syria had "stabbed Iran in the back".[41] Nevertheless, the Syrian leadership made it clear that Syria would do all in its power to preserve its relationship with Iran, even if it signed a peace treaty with Israel. Iran, by contrast, sent out contradictory statements regarding its possible reaction to such an eventuality. However, there was a general understanding of the pressures surrounding Damascus, and readiness to accept the possibility of a peace treaty with Israel as a necessary evil provided that, as spokesmen for Iran stressed, Iranian interests were protected (e.g. there was an assurance regarding the future of Hizballah in Lebanon).[42] The Iranian Foreign Minister, Kamal Kharrazi, announced during a visit to Damascus in the summer of 1997: "Every sovereign state has the right to act to achieve its goals, and to try and guarantee its interests, and it is not Iran's intention to subject others to its views."[43] The stalemate in the peace process and the regional challenges facing Syria from mid-1996 (the Israeli-Turkish alliance, Turkey's involvement in northern Iraq and, finally, concern that the conflict with Israel might flare up), all worked to make Syria and Iran put greater effort into shoring up their links.

In July 1997 President Asad went on a visit to Teheran, the first in seven years (his previous visit, in September 1990, had followed on the Iraqi invasion of Kuwait and was intended to mobilize Iranian support for an international coalition against Iraq). The visit took place after the presidential elections in Iran. The winning candidate, Mohammad Khatami, was described as a moderate; his radical rival Nateq Nuri, chairman of the Iranian Majlis (parliament), had been supported by the religious establishment. The election results in Iran aroused concern in Damascus since Khatami was perceived as liable to start a new phase in Iranian foreign relations, especially with the United States, perhaps at the expense of traditional ties with Syria. Nevertheless, it soon became clear that the election did not herald any real change in Iranian policy toward Syria or, in a more general sense, in Teheran's approach to the issue of the

Israeli-Arab conflict.[44] In any case, the Iranian press perceived Asad as a poor relation come knocking at Teheran's door in a time of need while not hesitating to turn his back on Iran when negotiating with Israel. The newspaper *Resalat* stated: "Iran warned the Arabs against supporting the peace process and now they are struggling to extricate themselves from the abyss into which they have fallen. Asad's visit to Iran comes very late but there is reason to be glad even for this little. One must hope that Syria's return to an understanding and recognition of reality will not be a temporary or passing measure. It is possible to save the Arab world, and Syria too, which has sunk into a less deep pit than other states."[45]

Asad visited Teheran again in December 1997 to take part in the summit conference of the Islamic states. That this summit was convened in Teheran attested to the failure of the US "dual containment" policy designed to isolate Iran and Iraq from the other states in the region, and it heralded the close of the era of "the new American Order" that had begun in the region late in the Gulf War.[46] The Syrian President was one of the only Arab leaders to participate in the summit, although before it convened he took steps to encourage others to do so.[47] He was received warmly in Teheran, since his presence at the talks gave Arab backing and legitimacy to the Iranian effort to play a leading role in both the Islamic and the Middle Eastern arenas. His arrival in Teheran was something of a defiant gesture toward the United States. He obviously chose to view his participation as an expression of the freedom of action that Syria enjoyed regionally and internationally, and a declaration of sorts that it was in no one's pocket, especially not that of the United States.

President Khatami went to Damascus in May 1999.[48] This visit, a sign of firmer ties between the two states, took place only days before the Israeli elections which caused Damascus-Teheran relations once again to blow hot and cold. Iran lost no time in expressing its dissatisfaction at the optimism and goodwill that Damascus appeared to radiate toward Israel. Nonetheless, its spokesmen made it clear that Iran was reconciled to the new reality in the region that followed in the wake of the Israeli elections, and was aware of and understood Syria's desire to renew negotiations with Israel and even to reach a peace agreement with it.[49]

The deadlock in the peace process during the period of the Netanyahu government (1996-9) had enabled the relationship between Damascus and Teheran to flourish once more. However, the ongoing American-Syrian dialogue, the revival of the peace process, and the potential achievement of a peace treaty between Israel and Syria may sorely test Iranian-Syrian friendship. As mentioned above, Israel is not the only issue to pose a possible threat to this alliance. There is also the question of Hizballah's status in Lebanon as well as other regional issues such as the conflict between Iran and some of the Gulf states, in which Syria has sided with the latter. However, experience has shown that Teheran and Damascus will do their best to preserve this alliance of interests. In the past, at least, they have succeeded in doing so.

*Relations with Russia.* Since the collapse of the Soviet Union, the Russian-Syrian relationship has been at an impasse. In the political domain Russia's limitations were clear to the Syrians, particularly its inability or lack of will to influence and contribute to strengthening Syria's regional and international status as it had done in the past. Russia had also become ever more dependent on the Americans and acted to improve relations with Israel. In the economic domain the controversy over the Syrian debt to the former USSR, estimated at $11-12 billion, remained unresolved. The Syrians refused to re-pay the debt, claiming that Russia was not the exclusive heir of the USSR. This dispute also prevented the sealing of arms deals, in which both sides had expressed great interest.[50]

In 1996 reports emerged of an arrangement on the question of the Syrian debt. It seemed that Russia and Syria had succeeded in resolving the problem, or at least arrived at an understanding that would make renewed economic and military cooperation possible, especially over arms.[51] Since then arms deals worth hundreds of millions of dollars have been reported, including some for advanced aircraft, air-defense equipment, tanks and anti-tank weaponry.[52]

In July 1999 President Asad made his first visit to Moscow since 1990. It reflected the relative improvement in bilateral relations and may even have signaled a partial solution to the debt question. Apart from a friendly and flattering exchange of declarations between President Boris Yeltsin and Asad and the support expressed by the Russians for Syria's position on the question of negotiations with Israel, it was reported that the two states agreed on a major arms deal worth some $2 billion, intended to bring the Syrian army up to date by the year 2000 with Russian aid.[53]

Russia's readiness to bolster its ties with Syria stemmed in no small measure from economic motives. However, it seemed that behind these negotiations also lay Russia's desire to play an active role in the region once again. This was especially evident after Yevgeni Primakov was appointed Russian foreign minister in January 1996 (he was appointed Prime Minister of Russia in September 1998, although Yeltsin removed him from that office within only a few months). It may be that the assessments heard at the time in US and Israeli official circles regarding Russia's anticipated resumption of its role as a regional power were exaggerated. However, there can be no doubt that, from the Syrian point of view such a predisposition on the part of the Russians was a positive and encouraging development. It could perhaps serve to balance the exclusive and decisive role which the United States played or, more precisely, had wished to play in the region until that time.[54] Against this backdrop, political backing and military cooperation with Russia, even if limited, was something of a new lease of life for the Syrians, and contributed to the sense of self-confidence and daring they have shown toward the United States since 1996.

*Relations with Iraq.* In 1997 the Syrian regime initiated a change – limited though it may have been – in its relationship with the regime of Saddam Husayn. After a fifteen-year break (see Ch. 4), it renewed economic ties with Iraq and took steps to consolidate and expand them. It made clear, however, that this was not a complete about-turn in its approach to the regime of Saddam Husayn, and that the political estrangement from Iraq continued for the time being.[55]

There were several reasons for this change of policy. The first was Syria's desire for more room to maneuver with the United States, Turkey and especially Israel, and of course the strengthened alliance between the latter two.[56] Second, the Syrians were concerned about Turkish designs on northern Iraq. They feared a Turkish takeover of the area, followed by the dismantling of the Iraqi state, all with Israeli or American backing. The fear was strong enough to overcome Syrian restraint toward the regime of Saddam Husayn, especially after the establishment of the Turkish security zone in northern Iraq in late 1995. Also, since the Gulf crisis the Iraqi ruler no longer seemed as threatening as he had before his invasion of Kuwait in August 1990. It should be noted that there had been similar fears for the integrity of Iraq among Syrians after the defection to Jordan of Husayn Kamil, Saddam's son-in-law, in the summer of 1995. Damascus, fearing a Jordanian-American attempt to take over Iraq, then hastened to call upon its allies in the Arab world, and in Iran as well.[57] Finally, it seems also that Syria sought to reap economic gains from the 1996 UN Security Council resolutions that allowed Iraq to make oil deals in exchange for food.

The practical implications of warmer relations between the two states included the opening up of a common border for the exchange of goods, the renewal of postal and telephone connections and, above all, reciprocal visits by trade delegations between Baghdad and Damascus.[58] While the Syrians initially made sure that their delegations were made up mainly of businessmen, senior government officials headed the Iraqi delegations to Syria. For example,

Iraqi's minister of trade and industry attended the August 1997 international trade fair in Damascus, and its oil minister went to Syria to conclude an agreement to renew the flow of oil through the pipeline that connected Mosul (in northern Iraq) to Banyas (on the Syrian coast).[59] An accord on renewed pipeline activity was signed in August 1998 in the course of the Syrian oil minister's visit to Baghdad.[60] The two states also acted to halt their propaganda war. In June 1997 the Iraqi authorities reportedly shut down the radio station "Arab Syria" in Baghdad which had broadcast propaganda against the Syrian regime. The Syrians responded by closing "The Voice of Iraq", which had broadcast from Syria since the 1970s. Restrictions on the activity of the Muslim Brotherhood faction led by 'Adnan Sa'd al-Din, which acted from Iraq against the Syrian regime, were also reported.[61]

In the conflict between Iraq and the Americans that erupted late in 1997 over the activity of UN supervisors in Iraq, Syria sided openly with the Iraqi position. In November 1997 the Syrians also agreed to receive the Iraqi Deputy Prime Minister, Tariq 'Aziz, who was traveling among the Arab capitals to explain the Iraqi position.[62] In February 1998, the Iraqi Foreign Minister Muhammad al-Sahhaf made a similar trip against a background threat of war between the United States and Iraq. On this occasion President Asad personally received the guest from Iraq.[63] By the time Operation "Desert Fox" began in December 1998, Syria was vigorously supporting Baghdad, and demonstrations against the American operation were being organized in Damascus.

Asad referred to the Iraqi issue in his address to the conference of Muslim countries in Teheran in December 1997. He explained: "Iraq is indeed obligated to implement the resolutions of the Security Council [regarding the supervision of the means of mass destruction in its possession], but the dispute as to how these resolutions are implemented must not lead to the use of force, as that could make the situation in the region even more dangerous." Asad added: "We must show awareness of the suffering of the Iraqi people and their pain, as the Iraqi citizen lacks the elementary means of livelihood. Such a situation does not serve security and stability in the region."[64]

## Syria in the regional arena

Alongside the problem of determining its regional and international orientation, Syria confronted a series of dilemmas over its regional status. These revolved around its closest neighbors, especially Jordan, the Palestinian Authority and of course Turkey (Lebanon and Israel are treated separately below). The Syrians perceive the immediately surrounding region as an integral part of the sphere of influence they have sought to establish since the early 1970s. However, Damascus suffered a constant series of failures in this very area. These were manifested in the tense, if not hostile relationships that Syria has maintained with Jordan and the Palestinians, as well as with Turkey.

The decision taken by Jordan and the Palestinian Authority to adopt a policy opposed to that of Syria put to the test not only the question of Syria's regional status and pretensions to leadership but also – and above all, in Damascus's view – the question of its national security. The peace process to which Jordan and the Palestinians consented – leaving Damascus far behind – led to a new set of forces in the region that threatened to marginalize Damascus. This is particularly so with regard to the growing Israeli-Turkish alliance and the Israel-Jordan-Palestine triangle that seems to be taking shape under the umbrella of the peace accords Israel signed with Jordan and with the PLO.

*Syria and the Palestinian Authority.* On 13 September 1993 in Washington, Israel and the PLO signed the framework for a peace agreement known as the Oslo Accords. Many saw this as a historic breakthrough on the road to achieving overall peace in the Middle East. The agreement received an enthusiastic reception worldwide and in much of the Arab world as well. The Syrian response was quite different. On 14 September 1993, one day after the signing, most of the Damascus press devoted significant space to the subject, taking a non-commital, informative, rather dry tone. The headline in most newspapers stated simply "The Accords Signed" – a foretaste of the lack of enthusiasm, coolness and reservation that Damascus was later to display toward this agreement.[65] Yet, seen in Syrian terms, and certainly in a historical perspective, the Syrian reaction to the signing of the Oslo Accords was far from negative. The day after the Israeli-Egyptian peace treaty was signed on 26 March 1979, the headlines in the Syrian press were sharp and to the point. That in *Al-Thawra*, for example, proclaimed: "The Accord of Submission and Humiliation has been signed – Sadat's end will be that of any traitor."[66] A comparison of the headlines illuminates the change that had taken place in the Syrian position on the Palestinian issue, which grew out of the abandonment of Syrian pretensions to absolute control of the Palestinian problem, along with a much greater Palestinian readiness than in the past to take a far-reaching, independent stand in clear opposition to Syria's position.

For many years Syria regarded the Palestinian issue as too important to leave in the hands of Arafat. According to the Lebanese Druze leader Kamal Junbalat, in 1975 Asad told Arafat: "You don't represent the Palestinians any more than we [do]."[67] Now the tone in Damascus was different. "All Syria insists on is minimal rights for the Palestinian people," wrote the Ba'th Party Regional Command member Ahmad Dighram in *Al-Thawra* as early as 15 November 1992. In so doing he expressed Syria's recognition (it had no other choice) of Palestinian independence of decision, as well as the fact that the solution to the Palestinian problem would fall short of the ideal (i.e. the liberation of all Palestine) which the Syrians had championed, at least publicly, for many years. Incidentally, Dighram's remarks intimated to Israel that in exchange for an Israeli-Syrian agreement Damascus would be prepared to compromise on the Palestinian issue and be satisfied with minimal rights for the Palestinian people.[68]

Without doubt, the signing of the Oslo Accords took Syria by surprise. A sense of outrage, insult and, not least, anxiety underlay their response to what they saw as a stab in the back by Arafat. After all, this agreement might well cause the dissolution of the united Arab front which Damascus had sought to establish for the purposes of negotiations with Israel, and which was of course designed to bolster the Syrian demand for complete Israeli withdrawal from the Golan Heights. Syrian concern over its weakened bargaining position in negotiations with Israel, coupled with the offence it felt at the challenge to its leading regional position and the role it sought to play in the Palestinian issue, henceforth dictated Syria's stand toward Arafat, the PLO and the Palestinian Authority.

The Syrians held back from any public confrontation with Arafat, due in no small measure to American pressure. They were also swift to make cynical use of the Oslo Accords to prepare the ground at home for a possible breakthrough in Israeli-Syrian negotiations (see below). However, at the same time Damascus refused to give legitimacy to the Accords, or to the Palestinian Authority that Arafat had established in the Gaza Strip and the West Bank. The Syrians went so far as to encourage Palestinian opposition groups, some of which were active in Damascus, to oppose Arafat. They also attacked him frequently and, in particular, refrained from all contact with him or his circle.[69] Arafat visited Damascus soon after the signing of the Oslo Accords to update the Syrian leadership on their details;[70] he also imposed himself on Asad in a condolence visit after the death of the President's son Basil in January 1994,[71] and was received in Damascus after the May 1996 Israeli elections against a background of anxiety there over how they would influence its regional position.[72] Asad and Arafat held a hasty meeting at the end of the summit conference of the heads of Islamic states in Teheran in December 1997.[73] Significant in this context was Asad's refusal to meet Arafat and agree to sign a joint position in the wake of the Israeli elections of May 1999 and Ehud Barak's rise to power.

There seems to have been more underlying the Syrian stance toward the Palestinian Authority than short-term considerations related to the negotiations with Israel. There were also long-term considerations over Syria's future position among the Palestinians, especially if and when a Palestinian state arose in the West Bank and the Gaza Strip. The Syrians were concerned that such a state would be ruled by Arafat, and in any case would be subject to Israeli-American decisions and so be outside the Syrian sphere of influence. However, Syria had few, if any cards to play in the matter of influencing Arafat. It was obliged, to its regret, to come to terms with Arafat's independent line.

In newspaper interviews in the late 1990's Vice-President Abd-al-Halim Khaddam revealed something of Syria's approach to the Palestinian issue in general, and to the Oslo agreement in particular. Khaddam testified:

"When Arafat came to us in Damascus after the signing of the Oslo Accords, we told him that we could not agree with him but we would not fight him. We said to him that he had taken a decision independently, Allah be with him, and that he had to resolve the problem himself. However, we warned him that the path he had chosen was a dead-end that would bring no good to him or to the Palestinian people. Were I to conduct the negotiations in Arafat's place, I would be ready to face differences of opinion with all the world, but never would I allow myself to arrive at a difference with Syria. What cards does Arafat hold? It would have been appropriate for our brothers in the PLO to have drawn on the moral, political and practical might of Syria in the negotiating arena. Furthermore, they should have understood that if there is no peace between Syria and Israel, then there will be no peace in the region at all... [The Palestinians] went to Oslo without anyone's knowledge, and therefore we cannot agree to the terms of the Oslo Accords."[74]

Elsewhere Khaddam also said:

"The Palestinian issue was what every Arab citizen lived and breathed and as important to him as daily bread, but then Arafat came and raised the banner of an independent Palestinian state and the banner of the PLO as the sole legitimate representative of the Palestinian people, and the result was that he relieved all the Arab governments of responsibility for the Palestinian issue... Everyone in the Arab world says, 'That is what the Palestinians want and we support what the PLO wants.' But if the PLO goes to hell, are we to let the Palestinian people go to hell together with it? The Palestinian issue does not touch only one people; it touches the entire Arab nation. We supported the PLO and we continue to support it. We supported the Palestinian cause because it was a national Arab cause. Were that not so, we would not have sacrificed hundreds of thousands of our countrymen and vast millions of our wealth... The only thing that will motivate Israel to change its position is to restore the Palestinian issue to the Arabs and to place the responsibility for it with the Arab nation. We must tell Arafat and his colleagues: the path that you have trodden has failed, and it should not be continued because it leads only to failure."[75]

*Syria and Jordan.* Frequent reversals characterized relations between Syria and Jordan in the 1990s. There were high points, moments of cooperation and shared positions, but these were the exception rather than the rule. From the start bilateral relations between these two countries bore the burden of historical baggage. First, there were essential differences in structure, character and worldview between the Syrian regime under Asad and the regime of Jordan's King Husayn. Second, past incidents resurfaced to blight relations between the two states, for example: Syrian involvement in Jordan's September 1970 civil war; the concentration of Syrian troops on the border with Jordan in 1980; the assistance proffered by the Jordanians to the Muslim Brotherhood during the Islamic Revolt waged against the Syrian regime in 1976-82; the Syrian-encouraged terror against Jordan in the mid-1980s; and finally Jordan's siding with Iraq in both the Gulf crisis and the clashes between Iraq and Syria throughout the 1980s.[76]

With the start of the peace process in the region the Syrians acted to coordinate positions with Jordan, but this effort was destined for total failure, ending in the signing of the Israeli-Jordanian peace agreement of October 1994. The tone in relations between the two states after that was tense, if not hostile, though both sought to avoid open confrontation and a complete break.[77] Beyond the question of the Israeli-Jordanian peace treaty, and in fact in the shadow of that agreement, new disputes sprang up between Syria and Jordan. Jordan accused Syria of involvement in terrorist activity directed against it and designed, according to the Jordanians, to undermine stability in the Hashemite kingdom;[78] Syria harshly criticized Jordan for what it saw as over-enthusiastic efforts to advance political and economic cooperation with Israel.[79] The language adopted by Syria in references to Jordan was often exceptionally virulent. For example, the Defense Minister Mustafa Talas announced in the summer of 1996: "Jordan is an artificial state established by Western imperialism in order to protect Israel."[80] The Jordanians generally refrained from responding directly to these Syrian provocations in order to prevent further deterioration in their relations with Damascus.

On 7 February 1999, King Husayn of Jordan died, and the Syrians sought to exploit his demise to open a fresh page in its relations with their southern neighbor. In a goodwill gesture President Asad attended King Husayn's funeral and held a long meeting with his successor King Abdallah.[81] He did not conceal his view that Jordan should cool its relationship with Israel and instead strengthen ties with Damascus. King Abdallah, for his part, had reasons to start a new with Damascus: he may have hoped that doing so would help him consolidate his position domestically. Abdallah visited Damascus in April 1999, and took the trouble to meet Asad's son Bashar, with whom he had begun to establish a personal relationship immediately after his own father's death.[82] Abdallah's readiness to place his confidence in Asad was put to the test after Ehud Barak's coming to power in Israel. The subsequent preparations for a renewal of the Israeli-Palestinian negotiations, and for the renewal of regional cooperation within the framework of the peace process, clearly necessitated a tightening of Amman's link, not to Syria, but to Israel. In any case, Jordan has remained a tough nut to crack in Syria's struggle for regional leadership.

*Syria and Turkey.* From the start of the decade, relations with its northern neighbor, Turkey, occupied an important place on Syria's public agenda. This relationship has always been fraught with suspicion and hostility. Disputes between the two centered on thorny bilateral problems which began to worsen in the late 1980s.

First there was the question of the waters of the Euphrates.[83] This river is one of the most important water sources in Syria, especially for its eastern region, the Jazira. The Euphrates rises in Turkey and flows through Syria and Iraq. Its importance to Syria as a water source has grown because of the higher demand for water due to its great population increase. This is especially the case in the Jazira region, to which migrants from overcrowded areas have moved in recent decades due to the government providing them with work, free land, health care etc. there. In 1987 Turkey, Syria and Iraq signed a protocol regulating temporarily the division of the Euphrates waters. Although promised two-thirds of the waters, Damascus was far from satisfied, and requested a permanent agreement that would assure it of its share of the water once and for all. This desire for a binding agreement increased along with the momentum of development projects in southern Turkey. Major development schemes, especially the Southeast Anatolia Project (GAP in its Turkish acronym), increased the acreage devoted to agriculture in southern Turkey and along with it water consumption in these areas. On at least one occasion, in 1990, Turkey temporarily cut off the flow of the river downstream to Syria, claiming that it had to divert its course while a number of dams were built in the region.[84]

Alongside the renewed dispute between Syria and Turkey over the division of the Euphrates waters – and, according to the Turks, as a consequence of it – another dispute arose. Turkey accused Syria of aiding and encouraging the terrorist activities of the Kurdish PKK organization against it. It was a fact that the PKK leader, Abdallah Ocalan, had been in Damascus till late 1998, and the organization maintained training bases in the Lebanese Biqa' Valey.[85] Turkey demanded that Syria first cease assisting the Kurdish underground, while Syria disclaimed all responsibility for PKK activity and demanded that, before the issue could be clarified this issue, the two countries should come to an agreement over the division of the Euphrates waters.

Now clearly linked, these two issues of water and terrorism overshadowed another significant issue – that of Alexandretta (the Turkish province of Hitay), regarded by the Syrians as Syrian territory but occupied by the Turks since they annexed it in 1939 under an agreement with France. It may be assumed that underlying these Syrian-Turkish disputes were also the differences in the nature of their respective regimes and in their political orientation, and also the fact that Turkey is heir, at least in part, to the Ottoman empire on whose ruins Arabism and the Syrian state arose and flourished.[86]

From the mid-1990s the question of the strengthened Turkish Israeli alliance, perceived by the Syrians as directed against them, also took its place on the Turkish-Syrian agenda. Turkish involvement in northern Iraq was also linked with this issue, since the Syrians perceived it as connected to, if not deriving from, Ankara's strengthened ties with Israel.

These problems gained momentum in the early 1990s until May-June 1996, when the deterioration of relations brought the two states to the brink of military conflict. This escalation was provoked by Turkey's sharper tone toward Damascus, which many claim was due to the domestic situation in Turkey.[87] Troop concentrations on both sides of the border accompanied the war of words.[88] At the same time, bombings in a number of Syrian cities, chiefly Damascus, were reported during May and June 1996. Turkish intelligence agents were apparently behind these bombings, which were designed to signal to Syria that its support for the PKK would henceforth be costly.[89] Military conflict between Syria and Turkey was averted at the last minute when Necmettin Erbakan, leader of the Islamic movement in Turkey known as the Refah, became prime minister. His appointment temporarily defused the Syrian-Turkish dispute, but with the fall of his government in late 1997 it again reared its head.

Turkey sharpened its anti-Syrian tone in the context of the question of terrorism, and the Syrians increased their attacks on Ankara over the strengthening of its alliance with Israel, a development that even the Erbakan government had not been able to curb. The

Syrian Minister of Information, Muhammad Salman, stated that the aim of "Netanyahu's alliance with Turkey" was "to besiege Syria and strengthen the military capability of Ankara and Tel Aviv". He added: "The ongoing Turkish aggression puts Iraq in danger of partition. Partition travels like a geographical virus. It will lead to a flare-up in the region and a change in its geographical coloring, and additionally will lead to the dismantling of Arab states and their being turned into small states."[90] Vice-President Abd al-Halim Khaddam defined the Israeli-Turkish alliance as "the greatest threat to the Arabs since 1948".[91] Elsewhere he said:

"Turkey is a Muslim country. The Islam in it is many times stronger than its secularism, therefore it must side with the Arabs. We triumphed in wars against the Crusaders because the Arabs were not alone but with the Turkomans. Since 1970 we have tried to improve relations with Turkey, but the problem is that certain institutions there think that they have an interest in ties with the West and try to distance themselves from the Arabs. Terrorism in Turkey is a great domestic problem.... We are working toward good relations with Turkey. We know that an absolute majority of the Turkish people sympathize with the Arabs in Syria. We do not want to give the ruling institutions in Turkey a reason to discourage this sympathy."[92]

By the end of 1998, relations between the two states had ratcheted back up to the brink of armed conflict. In Ankara an atmosphere of approaching war prevailed and the Turkish Prime Minister, Mesut Yilmaz, went so far as to declare that patience with Syria's support of the PKK was exhausted, and that unless it ceased aiding the PKK, Turkey would use all the measures at its disposal, including the possibility of a military strike against Syria. He also stated that this was Turkey's final warning, after previous warnings had fallen on deaf Syrian ears.[93]

Egypt and Iran both made efforts at mediation, with the result that the tension between Ankara and Damascus eased somewhat. Syria responded partly to Turkey's demands, chief of which was the deportation of the PKK leader Abdallah Ocalan from Damascus and the closing of his organization's training bases in the Biqa' Valley.[94] However, it was clear that this was just another temporary solution, not a response to the fundamental problems.


At the end of the 1980s, Syria adopted a new policy – the direct result of international and regional circumstances as perceived in Damascus. The new policy bore fruit, at least in part, but it was insufficient to lead to an essential change in political orientation – perhaps because of the political price that would have had to be paid.

Syria thus preferred to continue to waver between East and West

– between its commitment to the regional *status quo* and its readiness (since it had no choice) to integrate itself into the effort to establish a new regional order. This dilemma served the Syrian interest, and even complemented the cautious, hesitant nature of the Syrian regime and the man at its helm. Indeed, each time Syria had to make a clear-cut decision on the question of its political orientation – e.g. as dictated by the peace process – it refrained from taking such a step.

The Syrian view of regional and international circumstances did not, however, remain static. The erosion of the US position and its image as the leading superpower from the middle of the decade fed the Syrians' self-confidence and gave them more freedom to maneuver. Hence their alternate playing of the European and Arab cards, and readiness to put their trust again and again in the radical forces of the Middle East, mainly Iran but also later Iraq.

Changes in the region, especially from the mid-1990s onward, presented Damascus with new threats – at least in its own view. The freeze in the peace process after Israel's 1996 elections threatened to provoke a flare-up on the border with Israel, something that Damascus feared. The danger from Turkey increased as well, and relations with Jordan and the Palestinians deteriorated. Against this background the importance to Syria of maneuverability between East and West grew.

Toward the end of the 1990s Syria found itself, as at the start of the decade, in total isolation. It was still entangled in the struggle with Israel, its relations with Turkey were in grave crisis, and relations with the Palestinians were tense, even hostile. Mistrust characterized relations with Egypt, and dialogue with the United States remained limited and circumscribed. The only remaining ray of light, as in the past, was the alliance with Iran. Beside that, a few new glimmers of hope appeared in the form of strengthened ties with the West European countries, especially France, with Russia and even with Iraq. The political change in Israel in May 1999 awakened hopes of renewed peace negotiations and for a change of atmosphere in Damascus, but Syrian spokesmen preferred to adopt a cautious tone in everything connected with their hopes for the future.[95] The problems that had confronted Syria at the start of the decade thus persisted, yet the maneuverability that it gained gave it a better starting-point from which to deal with these problems in future. In any case, the question of its orientation between East and West remained unresolved.

## NOTES

[1] *Tishrin*, 13 March 1992.

[2] For more on Syrian foreign policy see Raymond A. Hinnebusch, "Revisionist Dreams, Realist Strategies: The Foreign Policy of Syria", in Ali T. Dessouki and Bahgat Korany (eds), *The Foreign Policies of Arab States* (Boulder, CO: Westview Press, 1985), pp. 288-321; Eyal Zisser, "Syrian Foreign Policy: The Reverse Side of the Same Coin", *JIME Review*, 10(36), 1997, pp. 73-92.

[3] See Patrick Seale, *Asad of Syria*, p. 485; Eyal Zisser, *Asad of Syria: The Leader and the Image*, pp. 258-9.

[4] See Moshe Maoz, *Asad*, pp. 181-2.

[5] For more on this issue see Ilana Kass, "Moscow and the Lebanese Triangle", *MEJ*, 33 (2) 1979, pp. 164-87; Efraim Karsh, *The Soviet Union and Syria: The Asad Years*.

[6] *Al-Sharq al-Awsat*, 6 June 1996.

[7] *Ha'aretz*, 10, 15 January, 29 August 1997.

[8] *Ibid.*, 24 October 1997.

[9] See Eyal Zisser, "Syria" in Bruce Maddy-Weitzman (ed.), MECS, vol. XIX (1997), pp. 665-8; *WP*, 10 July 1997. On the Syrian point of view, see *Syria Times*, 27 March, 23 August 1997.

[10] *Tishrin*, 24 November 1990, 17 January 1994.

[11] Radio Damascus, 27 October 1994.

[12] See United States Department of State, *Patterns of Global Terrorism – 1996; Patterns of Global Terrorism – 1997* (Washington, DC, April 1997; April 1998).

[13] *WT*, 12 November 1997; *Foreign Report*, 26 November 1997.

[14] *Al-Hayat*, 27 December 1998, *Al-Zaman*, 6 January 1999.

[15] *Tishrin*, 9 February 1998.

[16] Radio Monte Carlo, 13 February 1999.

[17] See Eyal Zisser, "Syria" in Ami Ayalon (ed.), MECS, vol. XVI (1992), p. 732, vol. XVII (1993), p. 646.

[18] Radio Damascus, 28 November – DR, 29 November 1990.

[19] *CR, Syria*, no. 4, 1992, pp. 15, 27.

[20] *CR, Syria*, no. 3, 1992, pp. 3, 4, 8.

[21] *Al-Hayat*, 18 December 1997; see also *CF, Syria – 1997-98*.

[22] *Al-Thawra*, 12 October 1997; *Al-Hayat*, 13 October 1997.

[23] *Al-Ba'th*, 11 January 1995.

[24] See Eyal Zisser, "Syria" in Bruce Maddy-Weitzman (ed.), MECS, vol. XX (1996), p. 645.

[25] *Ha'aretz*, 27 October 1996; *MM*, 19 November 1996.

[26] See *Al-Hayat*, 10 November 1997; *Al-Sharq al-Awsat*, 13, 14 January 1998.

[27] See *Tishrin*, 17 July 1998.

[28] Syrian Television, 15 July 1998.

[29] See *Ha'aretz*, 6, 13 November 1996; see also Eyal Zisser, "Syria" in Bruce Maddy-Weitzman (ed.), MECS, vol. XX (1996), p. 648.

[30] See for example *MM*, 10 June 1977.

[31] *Al-Hayat*, 4 June 1996; Eyal Zisser, "Syria" in Bruce Maddy-Weitzman (ed.), MECS, vol. XX (1996), 648.

[32] *Al-Mushahid al-Siyasi*, 8 June 1997; *Al-Ba'th*, 26 June 1997; *Tishrin*, 28 June 1997.

[33] Eyal Zisser, "Syria" in Bruce Maddy-Weitzman (ed.), MECS, vol. XIX (1995), p. 610-11.

[34] See Radio Damascus, 26 November 1997; *Al-Watan al-'Arabi*, 12 December 1997.

[35] Author's interview with a Syrian academic in Washington, 23 June 1996.

[36] For the Syrian reaction see Radio Damascus, 12 March – DR, 13 March 1992. See

also SANA, 20 December – DR, 21 December 1992.

[57] An announcement to this effect was made by the Syrian Defense Minister Mustafa Talas, see SANA, 20 December – DR, 21 December 1992.

[38] See Eyal Zisser, "Syria" in Bruce Maddy-Weitzman (ed.), MECS, vol. XXII (1997), pp. 671-2.

[39] See Yair Hirschfeld, "The Odd Couple: Ba'athist syria and Khomeini's Iran's in Moshe Maoz and Avner Yaniv (eds), *Syria under Assad*, pp. 105-24; see also Hussein J. Agha and Ahmad S. Khalidi, *Syria and Iran* (London: Royal Insitute of International Affairs, 1995).

[40] *Yedi'ot Aharonot*, 30 August 1996; *Al-Hayat*, 23 December 1996.

[41] See Eyal Zisser, "Syria" in Bruce Maddy-Weitzman (ed.), MECS, vol. XIX (1995), p. 611; vol. XX (1996), pp. 658-9.

[42] Eyal Zisser, "Syria" in Bruce Maddy-Weitzman (ed.), MECS, vol. XX (1996), pp. 658-9.

[43] *Al-Ba'th*, 24 October 1997.

[44] See *Al-Nahar*, 8 August 1997.

[45] *Resalat*, 3 August 1997.

[46] *Ha'aretz*, 11, 12 December 1997.

[47] *Tishrin*, 11 December 1997.

[48] *Al-Thawra*, 13, 14 May 1999.

[49] Radio Damascus, 9 July 1999; IRNA, 10 July 1999.

[50] *Al-Hayat*, 2 September 1997.

[51] Eyal Zisser, "Syria" in Bruce Maddy-Weitzman (ed.), MECS, vol. XX (1996), p. 646. See also an interview with the Russian ambassador in Damascus, *Tishrin*, 29 August 1997; *CR, Syria – 1998*, No. 23, p. 12.

[52] See *Ha'aretz*, 8 June 1997.

[53] Reuters, 4, 5 July 1999.

[54] See, for example, Reuters, 10 January 1996.

[55] Eyal Zisser, "Syria" in Bruce Maddy-Weitzman (ed.), MECS, vol. XXI (1997), pp. 674-6.

[56] Author's interview with a Syrian academic, Washington, DC, 11 June 1997.

[57] See Eyal Zisser, "Syria" in Bruce Maddy-Weitzman (ed.), MECS, vol. XIX (1995), pp. 606-7.

[58] Reuters, 29 October 1997; *MM*, 3 April, 8 August 1997.

[59] *Tishrin*, 19 August, 1997; *Al-Sharq al-Awsat*, 1 September 1997.

[60] *Al-Jumhuriyya (Baghdad)*, 26 August 1998; *Al-Usbu' al-'Arabi*, 31 August 1998.

[61] *Al-Watan al-'Arabi*, 18 July 1997; *Al-Wasat*, 28 July 1997.

[62] *Tishrin*, 23 November 1997.

[63] *Al-Hayat*, 15 February 1998.

[64] *Al-Sharq al-Awsat*, 2 August 1997.

[65] *Al-Thawra*, 14 September 1993.

[66] *Al-Thawra*, 27 March 1979.

[67] See Moshe Maoz, *Asad*, p. 124.

[68] *Al-Thawra*, 15 November 1992.

[69] See Eyal Zisser, "Syria" in Ami Ayalon and Bruce Maddy-Weitzman (eds), MECS, vol. XVIII (1994), pp. 618-19.

[70] Radio Damascus, 5 September 1993

[71] Radio Damascus, 23 January – DR, 24 January 1994.

[72] *Al-Hayat*, 26 July 1996.

[73] *Tishrin*, 11 December 1997.

[74] *Al-Quds al-'Arabi*, 14 June 1997.

[75] *Al-Sha'b*, 24 October 1997.

[76] See Joseph Nevo, "Syria and Jordan: The Politics of Subversion" in Moshe Maoz and Avner Yaniv (eds), *Syria under Assad*, pp. 140-56.

[77] Eyal Zisser, "Syria" in Bruce Maddy-Weitzman (ed.), MECS, vol. XIX (1995), pp. 604-5, and vol. XX (1996), pp. 649-50.

[78] See *MM*, 20 June, 1997; also Eyal Zisser, "Syria" in Bruce Maddy-Weitzman (ed.), MECS, vol. XX (1996), pp. 649-50.

[79] See Eyal Zisser, "Syria" in Bruce Maddy-Weitzman (ed.), MECS, vol. XIX (1995), pp. 604-5.

[80] *Al-Hayat*, 3 June 1996.

[81] Radio Damascus, 8 February 1999; *Tishrin*, 9 February 1999.

[82] *Al-Thawra*, 26 February, 23 April 1999.

[83] On the issue of the Euphrates: Arnon Sofer, *Naharot shel Esh, hā Ma'avaq 'al hā Mayim bā Mizrah haTikhon* (Rivers of Fire, the Struggle for Water in the Middle East) (Tel Aviv: Am Oved, 1992), pp. 83-130; see also *Al-Hayat*, 10 August 1994.

[84] Arnon Sofer, *Rivers of Fire*, pp. 100-1.

[85] *Al-Hayat*, 5 June 1997.

[86] See Eyal Zisser, "Remembering the Past, Looking to the Future: Syrian-Turkish Relations and their Place in Political Discourse and in Formation of Historical Memory in Syria", paper presented at the MESA (Middle Eastern Studies Association of North America) conference held in Chicago, 4-7 December 1998.

[87] The Syrian Foreign Minister, Faruq al-Shar', in an interview with Lebanese Television (LBC), 18 August 1997.

[88] *Al-Hayat*, 20 June 1996; *Yedi'ot Aharonot*, 21 June 1996.

[89] *Al-Hayat*, 10 June, *FT*, 11 June 1997; *NYT*, 11 June 1996; *Al-Thawra*, 3 January 1997.

[90] *Al-Hayat*, 18 September 1997.

[91] *Ha'aretz*, 3 June 1997.

[92] *Al-Quds al-'Arabi*, 14 June 1967.

[93] Reuters, 6 October 1998.

[94] *Ibid.*, 7, 8 October 1998.

[95] See *Al-Thawra*, 20 May 1999.

# 6

## SYRIA AND ISRAEL – ON THE
## ROAD TO PEACE

Early in 1996 it seemed only a matter of time before Syria and Israel would sign a peace accord. Even *Tishrin*, the mouthpiece of the Syrian regime, was optimistic. On the first day of the new year it published an editorial expressing hope for a breakthrough in the Israeli-Syrian peace negotiations. It wished its readers "a year of peace" in 1996.[1] In Damascus hope was even expressed that a peace treaty with Israel, once signed, would enable the regime to turn its energies to domestic problems, generate far-reaching social and economic reforms, and by so doing extricate the state from its difficulties and set it on the path to a brighter future.[2] But hopes for peace met with disappointment. After the Israeli elections of May 1996 Israeli-Syrian negotiations entered an impasse. By the year's end an atmosphere of crisis prevailed and the specter of war cast a pall over the region. Thus it comes as no surprise that *Tishrin*'s English-language sister, *Syria Times*, announced on the last day of 1996: "By all standards, 1996 was an unhappy year: a dark year with a few faint lights here and there. The good thing about it is that it cannot be repeated, it has gone forever."[3]

Earlier, on 29 September 1996, the CNN network broadcast an extensive interview with President Asad, which had deep reverberations in Israel and the Arab countries, not only for its content but also as an event in its own right. Asad was known for his reluctance to grant interviews to the Western media, and he addressed his own countrymen only rarely. It would thus seem that he consented on this occasion in order to send a message to the Israeli and the US governments. The message related to both the past – his version of the course of Israeli-Syrian negotiations from 1992 to 1996 – and the present and future: Syria's conditions for resuming negotiations with the new Israeli government under Benjamin Netanyahu which had come to power after the May 1996 elections.

As for the past, Asad claimed that during the negotiations in 1992-6, Israel and Syria had reached an agreement (*ittifaq*) according to which Israel would withdraw from the Golan Heights to the 4 June 1967 lines in the framework of a peace settlement. Asad claimed further that in early 1996, subject to this agreement and on its basis, both sides had turned their attention to the other components of an Israeli-Syrian peace accord, but that the approaching Israeli elections had interrupted this discussion and it had not been renewed since. In another part of the interview, regarding the present and future, Asad detailed his conditions for renewing negotiations with Israel. They centered on the demand to begin at the point where they had left off in March 1996 during the period of Shimon Peres's government. He warned that attempts by the Netanyahu government to renege on its predecessor's commitment to an Israeli withdrawal from the Golan Heights were liable to bring bilateral negotiations to a grinding halt. Asad added that Syria was still committed to its strategic choice of peace, but cautioned that it would be a mistake to think that a nation whose territory, or any part of it, remained under prolonged occupation would be prepared to wait patiently till the end of time for its return.[4]

President Asad's remarks on the issue of Israeli withdrawal from the Golan Heights gave the green light to a Syrian propaganda campaign designed to mobilize international support for the Damascus version of events, according to which Israel and Syria had agreed on full Israeli withdrawal to the 4 June 1967 borders.[5] For a long time the issue was the focus of Syrian-Israeli discussions and of public debate in both countries. It gained renewed attention after the May 1999 Israeli elections, when the two states began deliberating the renewal of negotiations. A clear and comprehensive version of the Syrian claim appeared in a series of articles by Patrick Seale, published in *Al-Hayat* in November 1999. These articles maintained that not only did Israel commit itself to a withdrawal to the 4 June 1967 borders, but that the Syrians had in their possession an American commitment to such a withdrawal.[6] The Netanyahu government and later the Barak government and, in particular, the Israeli negotiators who had met the Syrians during the Rabin and Peres governments, led by the former ambassador to Washington and chairman of the Israeli delegation to the negotiations with the Syrians, Professor Itamar Rabinovich, hastened to present their version of events. According to the latter, Prime Minister Yitzhak Rabin had indeed expressed, in talks with the United States, his readiness to consider the possibility of a full Israeli withdrawal from the Golan Heights. Washington then passed on the gist of these remarks to Damascus. However, this was a theoretical readiness – intended to push negotiations forward by raising hypotheses. Most important, it depended on the fulfilment of all Israel's demands in the negotiations, chiefly on issues of security and normalization. This Israeli condition was not, as we know, satisfied owing to

Damascus's hesitation to respond to Israeli demands on these issues.[7]

Rabin's talks with US Secretary of State Warren Christopher shed light on this question. Sections of the protocols were leaked and published by the journalist Ze'ev Schiff in the Israeli daily *Ha'aretz* in September 1997. According to these published sections, Yitzhak Rabin told Warren Christopher in August 1993:

"I don't want to take the chance of committing to the Golan Heights [i.e. committing to withdrawal], only to have Asad say he'll fulfill his part only after the Palestinians agree [i.e. only after a full Israeli-Palestinian peace accord is reached]...Is Syria prepared to sign a peace accord with Israel on the assumption that its demands for full withdrawal will be realized?... We will hand over the concrete things [full withdrawal from the Golan Heights] as in the Egyptian case. There are elements of peace that must be given to us before the implementation of withdrawal, such as embassies and open borders.... Apart from this, we need five years to complete a withdrawal."[8]

A year later, in July 1994, when Israeli-Syrian negotiations resumed after a prolonged break, Warren Christopher explained to Rabin: "I must be able to tell [Asad] things clearly in case he responds favorably to your conditions. In other words, is it [a proposed full Israeli withdrawal from the Golan] really being presented to him?" Rabin's response was: "You can tell him that he has every reason to believe that that will be the result, but the Israelis won't say so explicitly before their demands are met." Warren Christopher answered: "This [commitment] will be in my pocket, but won't be put on the table."[9]

The Israeli-Syrian negotiations did not achieve their ultimate goal – a signed peace accord – between 1992 and 1996. Published revelations on the matter offered an instructive glimpse of the vast progress which was achieved during those years, and of how close the two countries came to signing a peace treaty. So why, in spite of the significant advances, did they not reach the longed-for peace agreement?

After the failure to establish peace between Israel and Syria during the period of the Rabin and Peres governments, the claim was made repeatedly that Syria did not truly want peace with Israel and that it was survival tactics rather than a strategy of peace that guided President Asad's steps. This approach was most pronounced in the studies of the American scholar Daniel Pipes. For example, he claims in *Syria Beyond the Peace Process* that Asad is not at all interested in a peace treaty with Israel and moreover that he cannot allow himself to sign such a treaty because of the apparent threat it represents to the domestic stability of his regime.[10] Administration and government officials in Israel and the United States backed up this assessment. Thus the Israeli Mossad chief, Shabtai Shavit, declared in a newspaper interview published on his retirement in the summer of 1996 that he was not at all convinced that President Asad had indeed taken the strategic decision to establish peace with Israel.[11]

The moves Damascus made from 1992 to 1996 showed all the signs of foot-dragging in thought and in action – hesitation, caution, deep suspicion and a lack of enthusiasm over signing a peace treaty with Israel. Nonetheless, taken as a whole, these measures do not seem to support the claim that Syria had no interest at all in achieving such a treaty. It had internalized the necessity of "making peace" with Israel, stepped on to that road, and been prepared to move forward along it – albeit haltingly and hesitantly – until it reached this goal. Syria was thus ready to conclude a "peace deal". Such a deal was perhaps limited compared to the treaties Israel had signed with Egypt in 1979 and with Jordan in 1994, yet it was broader and more encompassing than any understanding that the Syrian President had been prepared to reach with Israel only a few years earlier. This conclusion is important against the background of the Israeli election results of May 1999, and the appointment of Bashar al-Asad as his father's heir. These developments breathed fresh hope into the prospect of renewed Israeli-Syrian negotiations and ultimately, a bilateral peace treaty.

## *The protracted struggle 1970-91*[12]

From the time Asad seized power in Syria in November 1970, his policy toward Israel oscillated between two extremes that reflected the two sides of his own personality and his apparently contradictory goals regarding the conflict with Israel. One approach was tough, ideological and even emotional: its practical expression was Asad's long-standing refusal to recognize Israel and its right to exist in the region, or to conduct peace negotiations with it. This approach reflected the desire to liquidate Israel as the sole solution to the Arab-Israeli conflict – a goal that did not necessarily have to be regarded as urgent.

The second approach was pragmatic and moderate, even rational. Its practical expression was Asad's readiness to reach tacit understandings with Israel (as in Lebanon), to preserve calm along the Syrian-Israeli border on the Golan Heights, and even to discuss the possibility of reaching an accommodation, the details of which he did not spell out. In part, at least, this approach reflected the immediate and pressing goal of restoring the Golan Heights fully to Syria's hands, if possible while Asad himself still lived.

The bedrock of Asad's ideological, tough and emotional approach toward Israel was his basic and authentic commitment to the Arab cause, as he perceived it. It was this commitment that for many years dictated his absolute rejection of Israel. Another important component of this repudiatory approach was Asad's obsessive fear of Israel and this was equally authentic. It seems that he saw Israel as a concrete, existential threat to his regime, to Syria, and to the entire Arab nation; Israel was a regional power with a clear superiority – political, military, economic and technological – over all the Arab states, including Syria. Furthermore, in Asad's eyes Israel was an aggressive entity that aspired to expand and take over Arab lands in order to realize the "divine promise". In his address to mark Ba'th Revolution Day on 8 March 1989, he expressed this perception in a characteristic way: "Israel captured Palestine and it wants to capture as many Arab lands as it can in order to establish a 'Greater Israel', stretching from the Nile to the Euphrates. We must not forget this fact just because of Israel's false claims about its desire for peace. When Israel speaks with moderation, its goal is to deceive world public opinion. It acts with moderation but its leaders want to establish a 'greater Israel', as this is a sacred goal for them."[13]

Still, Asad showed himself to be a realistic and pragmatic leader, who knew how to distinguish between vision and reality. In practice, his policy toward Israel was not divorced from the domestic reality in Syria, or from the regional and international circumstances surrounding it. On the contrary, it was anchored in this reality. Thus, the Syrians made certain to keep the peace along the border between the two states on the Golan Heights since the signing of the disengagement agreement on 31 May 1974 – the agreement that ended the October 1973 war and the war of attrition that followed it on the Heights. The Syrians even blocked terrorist action against Israel in this region. Later Israel and Syria reached a series of tacit understandings on Lebanon, which included Syria's consent to refrain from deploying its air force over Lebanese territory, thus leaving the Israeli air force in full control of its skies. In exchange, Israel was prepared to reconcile itself in practice to Syrian military involvement in Lebanon (excluding the south). These understandings held from the start of Syrian involvement in Lebanon in 1976 until the outbreak of the "missile crisis" between the two countries in 1981. Understandings were then implemented again from 1985 onward.[14]

Throughout the 1970s and '80s, Asad remained averse to joining the political process that might have led to the signing of a peace treaty with Israel. In so doing he clearly delineated the limits of his pragmatism and moderation on the question of the conflict with

Israel. Asad's refusal to adopt a more pragmatic and moderate approach on this issue stemmed from commitment to his worldview and consideration for governmental imperatives. In his assessment, conditions in Syria, the Arab world and Israel were not yet ripe for such a process, and therefore any profit he might reap from it was not worth the price he would have to pay. Over the years Asad apparently felt there to be insufficient support in the Arab world, especially in Syria, for a political process leading to recognition of Israel and the signing of a peace accord with it. He also reckoned the chances that Israel would return the Golan Heights, in full or in part, to be nil. The October 1973 war made clear to him that he lacked the military might to force Israel to do so, and he apparently doubted the power of the political process – and by extension that of Washington – to make Israel give up the Golan. Finally, for the whole of these two decades Asad did not feel pressured by social, economic and political circumstances at home, or by regional and international ones, to adopt a more pragmatic approach toward Israel, that is to join it in the quest to peace.[15]

## The peace negotiations, 1991-96

When the Gulf War ended in March 1991, the United States took up the cause of starting a political process in the region. It sought to exploit to this end convenient regional and international circumstances or, in the words of the American Secretary of State at the time, James Baker, the "window of opportunity" for peace in the Middle East. Syria and Israel – under the leadership of the then Prime Minister, Yitzhak Shamir – responded with reservations to the American peace initiative. Syria feared that regional and international circumstances would enable Israel and the United States to force a peace treaty upon it, a "treaty of submission" that would compel it to accept Israel's conditions and demands. Israel under Shamir, for its part, feared that the United States would put pressure on it to make significant concessions – territorial and political – to Syria and especially to the Palestinians.

However, Syria had few options. The regional and international reality of the day, and the new path it had adopted for itself since the start of the 1990s, with the goal of achieving improved relations with the United States, obliged Damascus to acquiesce in the American request. Under considerable American pressure, the Syrians made known their readiness to accept the US initiative and enter peace negotiations with Israel.[16] However, American pressure notwithstanding, Syria's entry into the political process was also the natural and inevitable result of the new political course it had charted since the start of the 1990s. The peace process was thus intended to fortify the Syrian regime and shore up its regional, inter-Arab and international position. The Syrians apparently also recognized that they could reap additional dividends from participating in this process – for example, in the form of generous financial aid from the United States. Such aid was perceived as an important part of the effort to ensure long-term economic stability in Syria and to integrate it sooner or later into the world economy.

Economic dividends and other benefits aside, Syria's readiness to join the peace process was unquestionably significant for future relations with Israel. It marked the start of a shift in the traditional Syrian approach to Israel and something of a genuine step on the road to peace with this long-time adversary. Asad had the reputation of a cautious and calculating leader who painstakingly weighed up the ramifications of his every step, and it is not inconceivable that he considered that if the United States had decided to impose a peace settlement on him – and perhaps on Israel as well – as a solution to the Arab-Israeli conflict, Syria would have found such an arrangement hard to reject. In spite of this possibility, uncomfortable and – in the Syrian view – risky as it may have been, Asad was prepared to join the peace process and open negotiations with Israel.[17]

There were, it seems, additional factors behind Asad's willingness to join the political process, and by extension to sign a peace accord with Israel. To begin with, for the first time since 1967 he felt it was truly feasible to restore the Golan Heights fully to Syrian hands. Second, he began to view the United States, and in particular the administration of George Bush, as a possible friend and ally because of its readiness to put pressure on Israel, even at the risk of an open rift with it. Third, the attitude of most Arab states, and especially of Arab public opinion, on the question of the Arab-Israeli conflict had changed. Since the start of the 1990s there was recognizably more readiness in the Arab world than in the past to prefer the course of a political solution as the way to resolve this conflict.

A Syrian delegation headed by the Foreign Minister, Faruq al-Shar', attended the Madrid Conference of October 1991, which gave the green light to direct negotiations between Israel and Syria. These negotiations were fraught with difficulties and obstacles, and no real progress was made for a long time. It was the change in government in Israel in June 1992 and the establishment of a Labor government under Yitzhak Rabin that brought about the shift in orientation. Between 1992 and 1996, Israeli-Syrian negotiations did indeed progress and in relative terms even made recognizable progress. Incidentally, this development confirmed Asad's misgivings over the peace process, which he had expressed more than once during the 1970s and '80s. He explained that once he joined such a process, it was liable to trap him in a vortex, and he might ultimately find himself constrained to sign a peace treaty with Israel under inconvenient or undesirable conditions.[18]

Israel had become more flexible – a far-reaching development which unquestionably laid the foundations for progress in the Israeli-Syrian negotiations. It expressed a readiness, albeit conditional, for a full withdrawal from the whole of the Golan Heights to the 4 June 1967 lines, and also intimated that it might yield on other issues, including security arrangements and normalization. In this context, progress along the other tracks in the Arab-Israeli peace process – the Palestinian one in particular, and the expedited normalization process between Israel and the countries of the Gulf and North Africa – must also be considered. These developments exerted a latent pressure on the Syrians, who feared that they would be isolated within the region and unable ever to regain the Golan Heights. This changed situation was presumably enough to prepare the ground domestically and create a climate in which the regime could comfortably move ahead in negotiations with Israel.

Syria's gradual retreat from its commitment to the Palestinian issue manifests this distinctly. In an interview with Patrick Seale in May 1994, President Asad declared that the Palestinians were in charge of the Palestinian question. When they themselves arrived at an agreement with Israel and recognized its existence, the only thing left for the Arab world as a whole, and Syria specifically, to do would be to follow their example. These remarks contrasted starkly with Syria's former position on the Palestinian issue, whereby Damascus – and not the PLO – was in charge of solving it (see Ch. 5: "Syria – Between East and West"). In his interview with Seale, Asad added: "Israelis and Palestinians live on the land of Palestine, and Syria recognizes this reality."[19]

The change in Israel's position, and likewise the progress in the Arab-Israeli negotiations, led to gradual but cumulative erosion of the Syrian position. Unsubstantial as this change may have appeared in Israeli and Western eyes, to Syria – considering its opening positions in negotiations with Israel – it was revolutionary. First, during 1992 Syria allowed Jews who so wished to leave the country, and of a community that numbered some 4,000 in the early 1990s more than 3,500 left. Most emigrated to the United States and then continued on to Israel.[20]

Second, Syrian leaders, led by President Asad, began issuing far-reaching declarations – in their terms, at least – regarding Syria's readiness to recognize the right of the Israeli state to exist, and to sign a peace agreement with it. These came to a climax at the summit meeting between Asad and President Clinton in Geneva on 16 January 1994. During this meeting Asad declared his readiness to establish regular relations ( *alaqat 'adiyya*) with Israel.[21] At a press conference held after the summit, he went on to say:

"Syria wants a just and comprehensive peace with Israel. This desire expresses [Syria's] strategic choice, intended to ensure the rights of the Arabs and the conclusion of the Israeli occupation, so that the peoples of the region can live in peace and security and honor...We fought with honor, we are waging negotiations with honor and we will establish peace with honor...We are interested in an honorable peace for our people and for the hundreds of thousands that sacrificed their lives to protect the homeland and the rights of the nation. There is hardly a home in Syria that did not lose someone [in the effort] to protect the homeland, the nation and Arab rights. For all of these individuals and their children and families, we want a peace of the brave, a true peace, that will last and guarantee the general interest, but also one that will provide everyone with his right....If the leaders of Israel gather the necessary courage to respond to this peace, then there will be a new dawn in the region, security and stability will be assured, and we will establish regular peaceful relations among all the peoples of the region."[22]

However, Asad held back in his remarks from using the customary Arabic term – "normal" relations ( *'alaqat tabi'iyya*) to describe the future relationship between Israel and Syria once peace was established between them. By stating that Syria and Israel would establish "regular" relations ( *alaqat 'adiyya*), he perhaps sought to emphasize in these remarks the difference between an Israeli-Syrian peace accord, if signed, and the Israeli-Egyptian accord, to which Syria objected fiercely at the time, and in which the term "normalization" ( *tatbi' al-'alaqat*) expressly appeared. It is also possible that Asad sought to downplay Israeli-Syrian relations in the era of peace and lessen the significance due to them. Incidentally, the matter dovetailed with the efforts of Syrian spokesmen at that time to claim that regular relations between the two states, like those Syria maintained with dozens of countries in the world, did not necessarily entail the opening of an Israeli embassy in Damascus, bilateral trade and tourism, and implementation of the additional elements of normalization that Israel demanded.[23]

Third, in March 1994 President Asad hosted a delegation of Israeli Arabs headed by a member of the Knesset, 'Abd al-Wahhab Darawsha. The delegation came to convey to Asad the condolences of Israel's Arab population on the death of his son Basil in an automobile accident in January 1994, and received a warm reception in Damascus and broad coverage in the Syrian media.[24] This was significant because formerly the Syrians had viewed the readiness of

Israeli Arabs to integrate into the Israeli political system as collaboration with the enemy. Incidentally, another similar delegation was received in Damascus in August 1997, this time on Syria's initiative, and it included Arab Knesset members from the Zionist parties of Meretz and Labor.[25]

Finally, in October 1994 the Syrian Foreign Minister, Faruq al-Shar', granted an exclusive interview to Israeli television. In the interview itself he presented positions in an obstinate way that left a poor impression on the Israeli public. He held Israel responsible for the state of war in the region and refrained from answering questions dealing with the essence and depth of the peace that Syria would be prepared to give Israel in exchange for its complete withdrawal from the Golan Heights. Yet in the Syrian view the very fact of granting the interview was an unprecedented and major step and a clear signal of basic readiness – despite the difficulties – to move forward on the road to peace.[26]

During 1992-6 a slow but steady process was under way to prepare the Syrian public for the possible establishment of peace with Israel. The Syrian press regularly reported in detail on the progress of negotiations, and it was made clear to the public that, should Syria's demands be met, a peace treaty was a real possibility. The Damascus media also gave a lot of coverage to progress in the Israeli-Palestinian and Israeli-Jordanian peace negotiations, apparently to prepare the ground for a possible breakthrough in the Israeli-Syrian peace process as well. Thus, in October 1994 Syrian television broadcast portions of the signing ceremony of the Israeli-Jordanian peace accord, and agreements Israel signed with the Palestinians in September 1993 and September 1995 received broad, if restrained press coverage.[27]

A significant if not decisive breakthrough occurred in Israeli-Syrian negotiations in the summer of 1993 on the heels of Prime Minister Rabin's efforts to test Syrian readiness in practice to establish peace with Israel. As will be recalled, Rabin expressed to American ears his readiness to weigh up the possibility of full Israeli withdrawal from the Golan Heights if the Syrians met his demands. However, the Syrians were slow to respond, and ultimately refrained from a reply that would have enabled Rabin to oil the wheels of negotiations with Syria. It may be, incidentally, that the "short circuit" between Jerusalem and Damascus originated with the American mediators. According to the Syrians, Asad responded favorably to the message passed to him from Israel and expressed a desire to engage in serious negotiations with Rabin, but at this juncture Warren Christopher, who may not have fully grasped the momentousness of the opportunity, returned to the United States to take a vacation.

Consequently, Rabin decided to press forward at full speed on the Palestinian negotiations (the Oslo agreement), at considerable expense to the Syrian process. One way or another, the Syrians interpreted the Oslo signing as proof that Rabin was not serious, and that his sole intention was to keep them quiet while he acted behind their backs to advance negotiations with the Palestinians.[28] Later the Syrians also accused Rabin of trying to deceive them, because when he sent his offer through Christopher, he already knew about the coming breakthrough in Oslo between Israel and the Palestinians.[28a] Israeli sources argued in response that only after Rabin lost hope of achieving progress with Syria did he decide to sign an agreement with the Palestinians.

After nearly a year of delays and suspensions, due largely to Syrian fury over the peace agreements Israel had signed with the PLO and Jordan, progress in Israeli-Syrian negotiations revived. In December 1994 the Chiefs of Staff Ehud Barak and Hikmat Shihabi met in Washington, and Shihabi also met Amnon Lipkin-Shahak, Barak's successor, in June 1995. Shihabi was a member of the restricted circle of close aides surrounding Asad, and in the past Asad had entrusted him with delicate and complicated tasks, including negotiations with Israel over signing the disengagement agreement after the October 1973 war. Thus it seems that Asad's readiness to send Shihabi to talk with his Israeli counterparts expressed his sense that negotiations were proceeding satisfactorily, and that it was possible to achieve results that would require the involvement of the highest levels of the Syrian elite.[29]

Indeed, behind the scenes and with American mediators, Israel and Syria progressed – slowly – along the path of peace. The meeting between Shihabi and Shahak in June 1995 was made possible because at the close of lengthy negotiations an understanding had been reached on the essence and nature of the future security arrangements to be established between them. This understanding was concluded in a written, if non-binding document (a "Non-Paper") signed by representatives of both sides in May 1995, according to which Israel agreed that the security arrangements to be included in an Israeli-Syrian peace treaty would be equal and balanced between the two sides. In so doing it backed down from several initial demands in the negotiations, including those calling for a reduction in the Syrian army, supervision of its arms build-up, and unilateral demilitarization of the area between Damascus and the Israeli-Syrian border – all to be laid down in the peace treaty.[30]

The focusing of Israeli-Syrian negotiations on the problem of security arrangements stemmed from its importance for decision-makers in both countries, but progress on this issue was slow. In July

1995 a dispute erupted between the two over the future of the Israeli early warning stations on the Golan Heights: would Israel be
able to maintain them within the framework of a peace treaty? The
Syrians refused to recognize Israel's right to raise this subject for
discussion and declined to continue negotiations until it was struck
from the agenda. Prime Minister Rabin regarded this Syrian position as breaking the rules that had governed the negotiations hitherto and refused to yield. The result was a lengthy impasse.[31]

The assassination of Rabin on the night of 4 November 1995
struck a heavy blow to the peace process. In retrospect, it can be
seen as having thwarted the chance of achieving an Israeli-Syrian
peace treaty at the time, since only Rabin was capable of mobilizing
support for it among the Israeli public.[32] Yet the appointment of
Shimon Peres as his successor gave renewed impetus to the peace
process in the intermediate term. Peres was perceived by the Syrians as more flexible than his predecessor, *inter alia* because of his
firm support, which he stated often and publicly, for a full Israeli
withdrawal from the Golan. At the same time there was some con-
sternation, if not fear, in Damascus over Peres's vision of "a new
Middle East", and likewise his proposals for a sweeping normalization of bilateral relations. He raised these ideas to advance negotiations between the two states, but in practice they aroused dormant
Syrian fears of Israeli intentions to take economic, cultural and political control of Syria and the entire Middle East under the guise of
an Israeli-Syrian peace treaty.[33]

Israeli-Syrian negotiations quickly resumed, and this time Uri
Savir, director-general of the Israeli Foreign Ministry and a close
associate of Peres, led the Israelis. Bilateral talks moved to the Wye
Plantation near Washington, which provided an intimate atmosphere
and at the same time kept the media at a distance. The Americans
hoped this would boost the discussions, and indeed at the start of 1996
significant progress in bilateral negotiations was reported. There was
also a narrowing of the gap on everything connected with the various
elements of the peace settlement, and agréement on a series of
pending problems such as the establishment of diplomatic relations
and of an Israeli embassy in Damascus, the opening of borders between
the two countries, tourism, trade, etc.[34] According to later testimony
from several of the participants in the Wye negotiations, a first draft
of an Israeli-Syrian peace treaty was even drawn up.[35] It was this progress
that gave rise at the time to the impression that the peace process was
moving forward, and that a breakthrough was only a matter of time.

In mid-January 1996 Shimon Peres announced early elections
in Israel. This decision led to a break, which Jerusalem and Damascus wished to believe was temporary in bilateral negotiations. Later

Peres explained that he had asked Asad to step up the pace of negotiations and even – half proposal, half demand – to meet him personally to facilitate a quick conclusion to the deal being put together between Syria and Israel. Peres hoped to achieve all this before the influence of the general election (due to be held in Israel in November 1996, at the same time as the US presidential election) could be felt. Asad's reply, however, was far from satisfying Peres. While he expressed readiness in principle to meet the Israeli Prime Minister, he refused to commit himself in advance to a date for such a summit.[36] Peres had no choice but to announce an early general election in Israel, a step that cost him the premiership. Some of his partners in the negotiations, chiefly Uri Savir, whom he had appointed to chair the Israeli delegation to the peace talks, and his counterpart Walid Mu'allim, the Syrian ambassador in Washington, later claimed that an Israeli-Syrian peace agreement had been within reach at the time, and that a conclusion and even a signing might have occurred before the Israeli elections (at the originally scheduled date of November 1996). Thus the decision by Shimon Peres to bring forward the elections, according to this version, undermined a historic opportunity to establish peace with Syria.[37]

In his book *The Brink of Peace* Itamar Rabinovich offers a more realistic and balanced evaluation of what was achieved during the Israeli-Syrian negotiations. According to Rabinovich, Damascus was not yet quite ready and lacked the political will to sign a peace treaty with Israel just then. He also states, however, that the achievement of a peace agreement between Israel and Syria was basically a question of time, noting the progress that had begun to be made in the bilateral negotiations of 1992-6.[38]

One way or another, the effort to bring about a positive conclusion to the Israeli-Syrian negotiations before the Israeli elections in 1996 failed. The defeat suffered by the Peres government in those elections bore witness to the basic lack of faith among the Israeli public in this policy of the government, and in the political process under its leadership. The election results were also indicative of the Israeli voters' lack of faith in Syria's sincerity and desire for peace. The steps forward made by Damascus, revolutionary as they may have been, were shown to be insufficient. Against the background of the election results and the earlier failure of the Rabin and Peres governments to mobilize broad public support for their positions, it became clear that Asad's reluctance to adopt confidence-building measures directed at the Israeli public and its government had squandered a historic opportunity.

If the Syrians were indeed interested in reaching a peace accord with Israel between 1992 and 1996, or if at least they did not totally rule out such a possibility, why then did they hesitate and ultimately reject the hand Israel held out to them? The answer to this is complex. It stems partly from the tactics chosen by the Syrians for conducting negotiations with Israel, and partly from the worldview and nature of both the Syrian regime and its leader.

However, the Syrians were not solely responsible for the failure of the effort to achieve peace. They had partners in these negotiations – Israel and the United States – and in the opinion of the Syrians and of others, these two negotiating partners also bore responsibility for the failure of the years 1992-6. As for Israel, one argument is that its readiness to relinquish the Golan Heights, though far-reaching, was not unequivocal. The Syrians knew of it only indirectly, via the Americans. Moreover, it was conditional not only on the Syrian response to Israel's demands on the questions of normalization and security arrangements but also, and most important, on the holding of a referendum in Israel, i.e. the mustering of a majority of Israeli public opinion in favor of withdrawal. There is no doubt that Asad found it difficult to comprehend this condition, because when the regime organizes referendums in Syria its victory is assured. He may also have felt this to be an Israeli tactic to gain Syrian concessions but ultimately leave the Golan in Israel's hands,[39] and indeed at no time did Asad conceal his concern that Israel's true objective in the negotiations was to assure his tacit support for the peace accords it had established with the Palestinian Authority and Jordan, and its normalization process with its Arab neighbors. Asad feared that at the decisive moment Israel would refuse to sign a peace agreement that required the full return of the Golan Heights to Syria. This is the background to the Syrians' claim that, had the Israeli position on this question been firmer and clearer to them in the early stages of the negotiations, they might have responded more willingly and enthusiastically to Israel's outstretched hand and acted to move the negotiations forward.

As for the United States, given the significance that both the Syrians and Israelis attributed to the US position, at least early in the negotiations, Washington might have been expected to support the talks and carry them forward. After all, Syria had joined the peace process under heavy American pressure, while deeply fearful of Washington. Nor did Syria conceal its expectation that in return for its readiness to reach a peace agreement with Israel it would gain ground in the area of bilateral relations with the United States. For example, it counted on being taken off the list of states that support terrorism and on receiving American economic aid. Washington's centrality was inevitable given the lack of direct contact between Jerusalem and Damascus, not to mention their mutual suspicion and lack of faith, and Syria's confidence that it was within Washington's power to influence Israel to change its policy.

From the start, however, the Clinton administration limited the US role to that of a passive mediator in the negotiations, relaying messages back and forth between Israel and Syria. The United States refrained from putting pressure on either side to be more flexible. It also neglected to motivate the Syrians to adopt "public diplomacy", i.e. to make gestures that would help the Israeli government enlist public support for the peace process and for the concessions it required. The US Secretary of State during the four years of negotiations, 1992-6, Warren Christopher, visited the region twenty-three times, but the desired results were not forthcoming. Christopher's reluctance to follow in the footsteps of his predecessor James Baker, who had brought Asad to the Madrid conference – in conjunction with other, deeper reasons – led to a gradual erosion of US status in Syrian eyes and, more important, of the intimidating image it had once had in the region. It was that image which had spurred the Syrians to begin negotiating with Israel in the first place.

*The brake on progress.* Syria was the main wrecker of the negotiations. Its top echelon lacked sufficient desire or determination to press forward negotiations with Israel. Perhaps Asad was dissatisfied with the stipulations of the developing accord with Israel, and he may have feared the risks to the stability of the regime and to Syria's regional standing that would be inherent in signing a peace accord. It seems that he also found difficulty in to abandoning the commitment to his worldview.

Finally, there is no doubt that the nature and essence of the Syrian regime and the personality of its leader were a brake on progress in the peace process. First, we must reiterate that Syria had joined the peace process not out of a desire to establish peace with Israel but rather in the hope of improving its relations with the United States – a prime strategic objective in the Syrian view since the start of the 1990s. Negotiations with Israel, and perhaps even a peace agreement between the two countries, were considered by the Syrians as a necessary evil to this end, and presented by them as such. Throughout the 1990s President Asad often declared that peace was Syria's "strategic choice". In other words Syria had decided to adopt the path of peace as a means of resolving the Arab-Israeli conflict.[40] The media and spokesmen for the regime naturally echoed their President. However, Syria's attempt to claim that it had resolved to adopt the path of peace at any price, without conditions, is misleading, or at least, needs to be clarified. In truth, its joining of the Middle East peace process and readiness to open negotiations with Israel constituted, as we have noted repeatedly, an important turning-point in Damascus policy, but it was limited in scope, with reservations and conditions. It did not manifest an unequivocal desire to establish peace with Israel, like the decision of Egypt's late leader, Anwar al-Sadat, after which he made his historic visit to Jerusalem in November 1977. At most, the Syrian measure meant that the regime had decided to put the possibility of establishing a peace agreement with Israel on the country's public agenda, and to consider and examine this possibility seriously, but without committing itself from the start to such an agreement through any irreversible action or decision.

This, it seems, was the profound historical difference between Sadat and Asad. In coming to Jerusalem, Sadat burnt all his bridges behind him, and expressed a strategic and irreversible decision to start out on the road to peace and forge a peaceful solution to the conflict with Israel. He had decided "to make peace", and all that was left for him and his Israeli interlocutors was to hammer out the precise details of an agreement. Asad, by contrast, had decided to consider the possibility of establishing peace with Israel and to have discussions on the details of a peace accord, but without binding himself in advance to conclude such an accord. The decision would only be taken – if at all – after lengthy, exhaustive and private deliberations over the details and conclusions, which had to satisfy the Syrians.

Throughout all the stages of the Israeli-Egyptian negotiations Sadat took pains to make clear that the October war was to be the last war. However, Asad and other Syrian spokesmen defined peace as a "strategic option", and by extension one of many at Syria's disposal. It was indeed an option that Syria could back, in that it was, as Syrian spokesmen said, a "strategic choice", but it did not preclude other options.[41] This approach intensified in the wake of the May 1996 Israeli elections. Thus, for example, the Syrian Chief of Staff, Hikmat Shihabi, in an interview given on 1 August 1996, Syrian Army Day, alluded to the military option (*al-khiyar al-qitali al-musallah*) Syria had taken in the past and which it still kept open.[42]

Against this background Asad was equivocal in his attitude toward the issue of terror. While declaring his commitment to refrain from international terrorism or direct involvement in such actions against Israel, he sponsored Lebanese and Palestinian terrorist organizations and, by extension, encouraged and supported their activity, which was usually described as legitimate resistance to occupation. The Syrians held back, *inter alia*, from condemning a series of terrorist attacks in Israeli cities in February-March 1996, and refused to take part in the Sharm al-Shaykh conference for the war against terrorism that met in the wake of these attacks.[43] This policy of straddling the fence between the permitted and the forbidden was designed to put pressure on Syria's interlocutors and give the advantage to the Damascus regime in deliberations with them, but it encroached on the overall message of commitment to the peace process that the Syrian regime wanted to send out.

Moreover, even when the Syrian commitment to the peace process deepened, there was a real gap between Syrian and Israeli notions of peace. The Israeli public expected an agreement that would lead to peace with all the attributes of normalization. In Syria, however, the expectation was of a political "deal" that the regime had no choice but to conclude. There was no need, nor was it necessarily even desirable, that friendship and warmth would accompany or characterize an accord. The Syrian media take care to explain to their public that a peace agreement between Israel and Syria would not be the final word in this historic struggle, but at most a shift of the battleground – from the military to, for example, the economic, diplomatic or cultural arena.[44]

It should be emphasized that Syria conducted its negotiations with Israel from a relatively advantageous position, at least as viewed in Damascus. In complete contrast to Egypt two decades before, and then the PLO and Jordan, it was under no real compulsion to sign a peace accord with Israel. This was because the Syrian regime enjoyed domestic political stability and, thanks to its decision to join the peace process, it had also improved its regional and international standing. In reality a long line of severe social and economic troubles were crowding Syria's doorstep, problems that were liable to bring Syria to a state of grave crisis, but these had not yet been felt to their full extent, and therefore did not influence the decision-making of the Syrian regime while it conducted peace negotiations with Israel.

Of course it can be argued that the progress made in the Jordanian and Palestinian peace negotiations created circumstances that, in the Syrian perspective, were threatening. It seemed that Syria might be left alone at the forefront of the conflict – or in its negotiations – with Israel. As will be recalled, at the start of the peace process the Syrians aspired to stabilize a united Arab front under their own leadership and thereby connect the various lines of negotiations. However, the Oslo agreement and the Jordanian-Israeli peace accord that followed it split the Arab front, which then collapsed with the process of normalization of relations between Israel and the countries of the Gulf and North Africa. These circumstances, from the Syrians' point of view, clearly led to the weakening of their bargaining position with Israel and damaged the chances of a full restoration of the Golan Heights – under acceptable conditions. From the moment it was proved to Israel that peaceful relations were attainable with most of the Arab world without a peace agreement with Syria, it seems that Jerusalem's as well as Washington's motivation for advancing such an agreement at any cost decreased.

Yet the fact remained that the Syrians' concerns over a weakened negotiating position did not propel Damascus into pushing forward its negotiations with Israel. First, the Syrians feared that achieving peace with Israel at any cost could strengthen the trend toward division and fragmentation in the Arab world, and legitimize Israel's penetration and even takeover of it with no real return (an issue discussed below). Second, they had succeeded in reaching partial if temporary agreement on unity with the Arab states, chiefly Saudi Arabia, and in linking the conclusion of the Arab-Israeli conflict to a Syrian-Israeli peace agreement.

Progress in the Israeli-Jordanian and Israeli-Palestinian peace processes did not lessen the degree of urgency, in Israel's view, of signing a peace agreement with Syria. This was especially evident during Shimon Peres's period as Prime Minister. He repeatedly declared that Israel must not let the conflict with Syria remain an "open wound", that would have a lethal effect on the effort that Israel and the United States had led to stabilize a regional front together with the Arab world's moderate powers against the danger presented to regional stability by radical states such as Iran and Iraq, and the fundamentalist movements active in the Arab countries generally.[45] It also seems that in Israel the drive to resolve the problem of southern Lebanon influenced its considerations. This drive gathered force as Israeli losses there mounted and more Israelis became convinced that Damascus held the key to solving this problem.[46] Finally, it must also be assumed that Asad, as a seasoned negotiator, hoped that drawing out the negotiations would enable him to force his Israeli interlocutors into further concessions. Therefore, he preferred not to be in a hurry to conclude a deal. He may also have reckoned that, even in the event of a Likud victory at the polls, he would be able to achieve a peace agreement with conditions satisfactory to Syria that were essentially no different from those he might have concluded with the Labor government. Indeed, in defiance of the Labor government, the Syrians repeatedly announced that for them there was no difference between Likud and Labor. They also emphasized more than once that it had been none other than the Likud leader Menachem Begin who had handed over the Sinai peninsula to Egypt.[47] If this was Asad's intention, then his gamble failed. The delaying tactic he adopted soured the entire deal.

Thus, neither carrot nor stick could drive Syria forward in the peace negotiations; it left the dialogue with Israel to develop at a slow pace by demonstrating passivity so extreme that it bordered on apathy. This was in spite of the danger that such a policy might ultimately spoil the historic opportunity to establish peace between the two countries.

It seems, however, that the difficulty in propelling the Israeli-Syrian peace process forward lay not only in the lack of impetus from the Syrian side, but also in a series of delaying factors. These were an obstacle in Asad's path to taking the decision to accept a historic reconciliation with Israel. The crux of these factors was the nature, essence and worldview of the Syrian regime and particularly the personality of its leader. Asad was a leader with a keen sense of history and a crystallized worldview to which he had committed himself for many years. This dedication to preserving Syria's status as a "pioneer in the Arab struggle against Israel" and as guardian of "the Arab walls" was, as we have noted repeatedly, authentic – being, as it was anchored in Asad's life-history. Moreover, Asad needed this personal and political commitment as a mechanism to ensure the future of his regime. With his historical sense he understood correctly that signing a peace agreement with Israel would be like waving a white flag in the century-old battle between Zionism and the Arab nationalist movement, a struggle that originated in Arab opposition to an independent Jewish state in Palestine. Against this background Asad's difficulty was understandable. It was a deeply personal reluctance to support a step that would be perceived as giving the stamp of approval to a reality he had refused to recognize and with which he had struggled for a generation.

In this context the collapse of the Soviet Union emptied the Ba'th Party's historical slogan "Unity, Freedom, and Socialism" of its content. The peace negotiations Damascus had opened with Jerusalem also shattered the validity of another important slogan – that of the Arab struggle against Zionism under the pioneering leadership of the Syrian Ba'th regime. These slogans and, more generally, the ideological commitment they reflected were, as is known, the basis for legitimacy and support for the regime among the Syrian public, so it was clear why Asad found it difficult to part with them.

*Fear of domestic instability.* Also important was Asad's concern over the possible domestic ramifications of a peace accord with Israel, particularly over the components of normalization that Israel demanded. Syrian anxiety over the opening of borders between the two countries to tourism and cultural ties is especially noteworthy. There was fear that such a step would lead to a proliferation in Syria of Israeli tourists and investors. Moreover, it would hasten the expo-

sure of Syrian society to the West.[48] It seems, however, that there was
a tendency in Israel and the West to overestimate the weight of such
concerns and their exclusive place in Asad's thinking. Since the start
of the 1990s Syria was already undergoing the process of opening
up – politically and economically – to the world beyond its borders,
especially the West. Indeed, voices calling for further democratization and more economic and political liberalization were heard in
Syria as early as the collapse of the USSR. It is hard to imagine that a
signed peace accord with Israel could have influenced these voices.

Nonetheless, anxiety over the consequences of a peace accord
with Israel on the "domestic front" existed and reflected above all
the fear within the regime, and especially on the part of Asad himself, of "the era of peace" with Israel. There was evidence of this in
the remarks of Dr Aziz Shukri, dean of the law faculty and lecturer
in international law at Damascus University, who often took part in
meetings with Israeli academics during the years of peace negotiations. Shukri, described as having good ties with the regime's
upper echelon, explained in a newspaper interview early in 1997:

"Israel thinks it can press a button and produce a cordial peace, and move
the Syrian people from a war footing to a peace footing. This is not logical,
because there is not a family in Syria that has not lost a son on the battlefield. Israel has asked for open borders and an open economy, a request
with implications for Syria's industry and economy. After all, we do not
open our markets to other countries either. How can anyone expect us to
open our economy, where per capita income is 900 dollars, to another [i.e.
Israel's] whose per capita income is 15,000 dollars?"

Shukri also described his talks with Israeli academics, in which he
told his interlocutors:

"It is important to fly high and fast, as Shimon Peres wishes, but it is also
important to know where and when we must land, as we are charged with
persuading our countrymen to accept the peace agreement."[49]

No less important was the question of the Syrian regime's readiness
to put its best efforts into mobilizing domestic support for a peace
agreement with Israel. Since the start of the 1990s it had found
itself once again besieged by internal social and economic problems, exacerbated by the need to ensure continued political stability
in the era to follow Asad. A major issue in this context was the succession, in view of the President's emerging desire to guarantee the
position of his son Bashar as heir. Asad habitually perceived the
signing of a peace accord as likely to produce a volatile situation
and so may have backed away from it. Indeed, he more than once
accused Israel of "trying to load the peace process with more than it
could bear",[50] an allusion to its demands regarding normalization

and security arrangements which, to Asad's way of thinking, were more than he or his people could swallow. Asad also warned that these demands could spell the collapse of the process altogether.

*Concern for Syria's regional standing.* Asad also feared the possible geopolitical ramifications of a peace agreement with Israel – i.e. the imposition of Israel's will over the entire Middle East. In this perspective the peace accords Israel signed with Jordan and the PLO were something of a bad omen to Asad, and they were signed without his knowledge and against his wishes. He anticipated that Israel might exploit a peace accord with Syria to justify or entrench the peace agreements it had signed with Jordan and the PLO and advance relations with the countries of the Gulf and North Africa. Hence, Asad was liable to find himself in the untenable position of having aided Israel to realize its long-term goal in the Middle East, namely a new Middle East subject to its dictates.

One manifestation of this concern can be found in Patrick Seale's book, *Asad of Syria*, which was published in 1988 and thus before the peace process began. Seale wrote:

> The heart of [the argument between Israel and Syria] was that a genuine settlement went beyond the return of territory to a revision of the entire power relationship between Israel and the Arabs. Whose will was to prevail in the region? The Arabs might get land back only to live in fear of what Israel might do next. What was the good of Egypt regaining Sinai if the price was toothlessness and loss of regional importance, or of Jordan recovering the West Bank if it were to become an Israeli vassal, or even of Syria winning back the Golan if it meant abandoning its Arab vocation and its championship of Palestinian rights? ...any sort of Israel-Jordan deal over the West Bank...would perpetuate Israel's hegemony and put the Arabs at a permanent strategic disadvantage.[31]

Beyond all this, the lack of progress in negotiations was largely due to Asad's personality which, for both himself and Syria clearly became an obstacle in the way of achieving a peace agreement with Israel. In spite of his image as a talented, astute and omnipotent leader who also proved to be a skillful politician, a master of survival and an excellent tactician, it became obvious during the years of negotiations with Israel that he had no clear strategy. He also lacked those qualities of statesmanship and leadership that characterized a number of prominent Middle East leaders, chiefly Anwar al-Sadat and Yitzhak Rabin, and was revealed as cautious, apprehensive and suspicious, closed and introverted, and a man obsessed with minutiae who often had difficulty seeing the wood for the trees. As Patrick Seale noted more than once, Asad loved details, and his command of them was also a source of strength.[32]

In the main, however, Asad was exposed during those years as a passive leader devoted to the *status quo* and averse to taking initiatives or action, particularly any action involving a real change in the surrounding circumstances. He did not act like someone who sought to influence public opinion in his country, or even to shape it according to his own ways and beliefs. Rather, he let public opinion guide his actions, and sought to reflect and express it. This was to his relative advantage: in contrast to Sadat and Rabin, who paid for their courage and vision with their lives, Asad remained secure on his Damascus throne. But it was also his great handicap since it meant a lack of initiative and far-sightedness which prevented any breakthrough in the negotiations and in many other areas as well.

Asad's approach from the start of the political process had been defensive. He did not show the initiative required to exploit the opportunity that had fallen into his lap. He rarely raised his own ideas for pushing forward the political process and was satisfied with responding – on the whole unfavorably – to proposals raised by Israel or the United States. His responses and actions clearly showed a lack of understanding of Western political culture. He did not recognize, for example, the importance of "public diplomacy", and treated lightly the difficulties encountered by his Israeli negotiating partners. It is thus no wonder that Shimon Peres later described Asad as merely "a leader of narrow horizons without vision, with a provincial worldview", who found it difficult to comprehend fully the vision set before him by the Prime Minister of Israel, or to show any far-sightedness, initiative or creativity.[53]

In this context it is also noteworthy that Asad's schedule and his perception of the time-scale involved were entirely different from those of his negotiating partners on the Israeli or American sides. Asad stubbornly refused to accommodate US and Israeli efforts to notch up gains before the elections scheduled to take place in the United States and Israel in November 1996. Asad was free of such political pressures (the referendum to ratify his fourth term as Syrian president was to take place at the end of 1998, and it is unlikely that he was worried about the results). He also needed time to assimilate the changing circumstances, to internalize the notion of peace with Israel, and to step up the pace on the road to peace. The Israeli effort to get him to accommodate Israeli or Western timetables in terms of weeks or even months was thus a total failure.

In passing, it should also be mentioned that Asad and his regime are the definitive products of the 1950s and '60s, a period marked by Arab nationalism as a leading worldview in the Arab world in general, and in Syria in particular. These were formative years in its growth and development. Asad belongs to the generation of 1967

that endorsed uncompromising struggle against Israel and was responsible in no small measure for the outbreak of the Six-Day War. In
Egypt a new government needed to emerge before the country could
embark upon a new path, the road to peace with Israel. Abd al-
Nasir was not concerned, and was apparently unable, personally or
politically, to cut himself off from his commitment to the path he
had chosen for himself and his people through the years, the path
of struggle against Israel. During the years of negotiations between
Israel and Syria, there was a question whether Asad would follow in
Sadat's footsteps and generate a similar turn-about in his policy or
whether – as seemed to be the case in Egypt at one time – Syria
would have to wait for a new leader. During the years 1992-6 Asad
did not offer a clear answer to this question.

## *The Netanyahu period, 1996-99*

In May 1996 elections were held in Israel for the Knesset and the
office of Prime Minister. These generated an about-turn and brought
the Likud leader Benjamin Netanyahu to power. With the establishment of his government, Netanyahu declared that he did not consider
himself bound to understandings reached between Israel and Syria
on the question of full Israeli withdrawal from the Golan Heights
since no signed and binding agreement in the style of the Oslo
Accords existed. He thus called upon the Syrians to re-start negotiations from square one, without pre-existing conditions, since in his
view nothing had been achieved during the preceding four years.
He did, however, add that once negotiations were renewed within
that framework, the Syrians could raise their demand for full Israeli
withdrawal from the Golan.[54] Syria was naturally quick to reject
Netanyahu's proposal and demand that negotiations proceed from
the point where they had broken off early in 1996, i.e. based on the
understanding that Israel was prepared for a full withdrawal from
the Golan Heights.[55] Under such circumstances the negotiations
could not be renewed and soon came to a standstill.

The impasse in the Israeli-Syrian negotiations generated an atmosphere of crisis. Among experts and government officials in Israel
and the West, pessimistic assessments mushroomed, according to
which an armed clash between the two countries was a real possibility, perhaps only a matter of time.[56] Others claimed that, as both
sides had a clear interest in continuing the peace process, a military
confrontation between them was not imminent. They also recalled
that for the fifteen years before the political process began, the *status quo* had rested on the Israeli presence in the Golan Heights. The
Syrians had not then – or later, according to this view – believed

that an assault against Israel would produce the desired result of the Golan Heights being returned to their control.[57]

A more strident Syrian tone toward Israel and its government reflected the fact that relations between the two states, had not fallen so low since the political process began in October 1991. In an "Order of the Day" published in the Syrian press on 1 August 1997 (Syrian Army Day) President Asad stated: "Arab land is not no-man's land, free for the taking. Behind this land stands a people who have been living on it for thousands of years. Its fate will not be determined by an individual or group of individuals whose only tie to it is their takeover by means of aggression."[58] In an interview on the same occasion, the then Syrian Chief of Staff, Hikmat Shihabi, said:

"We are striving to restore our sacred land. Our people have placed this strategic decision in the hands of the armed forces as a sacred pledge that is like a badge of honor on our breast...Our army is determined to restore every bit of our sacred land and to force Israel to carry out a withdrawal of its forces of aggression to the June 4 boundary lines...A peaceful solution is a strategic option, but without recognition of the principle of the return of conquered territory and the restoration of stolen rights, it is not possible to create a situation of permanent peace.... If Netanyahu and his friends should create the circumstances for war – well, Syria is not afraid of a war. It is ready for it and knows how to defend itself. Israel will pay a heavy price if it takes so foolish a step as aggression against Syria."[59]

Soon after the fall of the Netanyahu government Ze'ev Schiff reported in *Ha'aretz* that late in 1998 Israel and Syria had held secret meetings mediated by the American businessman and Netanyahu confidant Ron Lauder, and by Oman as well. According to Schiff, during the course of contacts with the Syrians Netanyahu expressed his readiness for a full Israeli withdrawal from the Golan Heights, but refused to anchor this readiness in so firm a commitment as a written document or a public declaration – a refusal which led to the cessation of contacts between Israel and Syria.[60] The Syrians hastened to deny this report categorically,[61] but Netanyahu and those close to him confirmed it, while making sure to present these contacts as an Israeli achievement. According to their account, Israel was able in these meetings to win concessions from the Syrians on a series of issues, including the continued operation of the Golan early warning stations in which there would be an Israeli presence.[62]

Two important conclusions follow from the story of contacts between Damascus and Jerusalem during the Netanyahu period. First, the very existence of these contacts attested to the eagerness on both sides to renew negotiations and to reach a positive conclusion. The evidence for this is the fact that the Syrians were willing to enter into secret negotiations with Netanyahu, even though they publicly expressed reservations about his adopted course and positions, claiming that these positions were intended to perpetuate hostility between Israel and Syria. Second, Netanyahu lacked the political ability to push forward real negotiations with Syria because of his reluctance to commit himself to pay the price of peace with the Syrians – ceding the Golan Heights. It seems that he had discovered an interest in peace with Syria and was even, personally, prepared to pay its price. However, domestic political considerations prevented him from continuing down this road. In any case, these contacts were an episode that did not significantly lessen the deadlock gripping the Israeli-Syrian peace process.

Despite this impasse and Syria's harder line toward Israel's Netanyahu government, the traditional Syrian approach to Israel had visibly shifted, recalling the way the approaches of other Arab countries toward Israel had developed in the past as a direct consequence of the Arab-Israeli peace process. Behind this shift was the distinction the Syrians had begun to make between the positive "pursuer of peace" element which they thought existed among the Israeli public and which needed to be encouraged, and the government of Israel and those it represented, who in their opinion were no more than "warmongers".

The Syrians began describing the Labor governments of Peres and Rabin in positive, sympathetic terms, although they had never done so while they were in power. For instance, the Minister of Information, Muhammad Salman, declared in an October 1997 press interview: "In the past, the Labor Party adopted an approach that facilitated [advancement of the peace process] because it had a deep understanding of the significance of the peace process. This is due, among other things, to the historic suffering that its leaders, such as Rabin and Peres, experienced in the past, since they had been witnesses to the establishment of the State of Israel."[63] Even Vice-President Khaddam, known for his extreme stand on Israel, said in a newspaper interview at the end of 1997: "If Rabin had not been murdered and Peres had not called early elections, we would have reached a peace accord."[64]

Asad himself remarked to a delegation of Israeli Arabs who visited him in July 1997:

"We found that a new spirit moved through the Labor Party, and the impression was created that they desired peace. At a certain stage we arrived at an understanding on basic issues, among them the commitment to withdraw from the Golan. You may ask: why, if they acceded to this demand of Syria's, was not peace achieved? The answer to this is that there are many issues that constitute the foundations of peace, among them matters of security. The Labor Party was the absolute opposite of the current Likud government... No one wants war, war is an abhorrent thing and I hope the situation does not deteriorate further."[65]

Such is the evidence that Israeli-Syrian peace negotiations between 1992 and 1996 had a positive impact, laying the foundation of bilateral relations. It seemed like a good start for the final effort to achieve peace between the two sides.

## After the victory of Ehud Barak

The May 1999 Israeli elections resulted in the defeat of Benjamin Netanyahu and his Likud party and put the Labor leader, Ehud Barak, in power. Barak's image as a successor to Yitzhak Rabin, ready to pay a painful price to achieve peace with the Syrians, revived hopes for a renewal of negotiations and a breakthrough on the road to peace between Israel and Syria.

In July 1999 the London Arabic-language newspaper *Al-Hayat* published a series of interviews conducted by Patrick Seale with Ehud Barak and Hafiz al-Asad. Seale had visited Israel in June 1999, after the elections, and met Barak and other Israeli leaders. He then conveyed the positive impressions he gained from these meetings to Damascus.[66] The published interviews with Israeli and Syrian leaders constituted the first clear sign of readiness for peace on the part of both states. For example, Ehud Barak said: "I would like to know if it is possible to sign a peace of the brave with Syria. The only way to build a lasting and comprehensive peace in the Middle East is via an accord with Syria."[67] Asad, for his part, said: "Barak seems a strong and sincere man. As the election results attest, he enjoys significant broad support. He wants to achieve peace with Syria. He moves forward at a very controlled pace."[68] Asad's endorsement of Barak was unprecedented. He had always refrained from paying compliments "gratis" to Israeli leaders, and praised Rabin and Peres only after the Labor government fell in the May 1996 elections.

It may be, as observers in Israel and the United States noted, that the three years of frozen negotiations under Netanyahu (1996-9) impelled Asad forward on the road to peace. He understood the importance of momentum and of exploiting an opportunity when it appeared, and learned to assess Barak's positions against the background of his bitter experience with Netanyahu. In Washington at the time, the Syrian President's age and declining health, his increasing efforts to advance his son Bashar's standing, and Syria's deteriorating economic situation were indicated as factors influencing Asad – slow as the process might have been – to show greater readiness than in the past to advance the peace process with Israel.

After prolonged and exhaustive deliberations, Syria and Israel did indeed decide to renew negotiations. In mid-December 1999 the Barak and the Syrian Foreign Minister, Faruq al-Shar', met in Washington; the meeting was sponsored by President Clinton. But the meetings between Barak and al-Shar' in Washington and later at Shepherdstown did not produce any breakthrough, although some progress was achieved, and the two sides even agreed to accept in principle the line of 4 June 1967 as their future border. However, Israel rejected Syria's demand to have a presence on the eastern shore of the Sea of Galilee, which was held by the Syrians before the 1967 war. The failure to bridge the gap between the two parties on this issue brought the Sheperdstown talks to an end and resulted in an impasse, at least temporarily.[69] Indeed after the failure of an American effort to bridge the gap between Israel and Syria at the Geneva summit between Asad and Clinton held on 26 March 2000, Ehud Barak announced that the window of opportunity for peace with Syria was closed and that peace would have to wait till the next generation in both Israel and Syria.[70] However, while Israeli and even US officials blamed Syria for not showing enough flexibility at the Geneva summit and especially for not engaging in public diplomacy with Israel, blame was also placed on Barak, who was seen by some as surrendering to public pressure in Israel and over the matter of making the needed concession – the north-eastern shore of the sea of Galilee – to the Syrians.[71]

The peace process should not be viewed solely through the prism of Israeli-Syrian relations. Syria's policy and progress on the issue have ramifications which reach beyond this relationship, and which can be seen as a reflection of its overall policy on internal matters since the late 1980s. Indeed, many of the characteristics of the Syrian regime's behavior in everything connected with the political process – hesitation, suspicion and avoidance of change – were recognizable in its policy in other areas too. Patrick Seale's argument should be seen against this background. He claims, in explanation of the regime's inactivity in everything concerned with domestic problems, that it will avoid dealing with social and economic difficulties until the conflict with Israel is resolved. According to his view, the regime feared that change and reform, especially of a revolutionary kind, would be likely – in the short term at least – to undermine its position and stability. Such developments were liable to put it in a weak position at the testing moment in dealings with Israel – be it in war or in peace negotiations. Hence, according to Seale, a peace accord or, more precisely, the resolution of the conflict with Israel by political means should herald the start of a new era in Syria – one of comprehensive domestic change which will perhaps set it on a new road.[72]

But the goal of the peace process has not only been to herald a new age and face the challenges of the future. It had also to symbolize a break with the past, and contribute to overcoming the legacy of obstructionism that Syria carries from that age. With the death of Asad in June 2000, it would seem that such an effort is only beginning.

## NOTES

[1] *Tishrin*, 2 January 1996.
[2] Patrick Seale, "Asad's Regional Strategy and the Challenge from Netanyahu", *Journal of Palestinian Studies*, vol. XXVI(1) (Fall 1996), pp. 27-42. See also an interview with Patrick Seale in the context of the proceedings of the international conference on "Modern Syria" held at Haifa University, 17-18 November 1996.
[3] *Syria Times*, 31 December 1996.
[4] *Tishrin*, 29 September 1996.
[5] See, for example, *Tishrin*, 29 September, 14 October 1996.
[6] *Al-Hayat*, 21, 22, 23 November 1999, and see below.
[7] See interviews with Itamar Rabinovich in *Ha'aretz*, 22 August 1996; *Qol Yisrael* (Voice of Israel), 3 December 1996.
[8] *Ha'aretz*, 29 August 1997. (Translator's note: the talks were, of course, conducted in English, but no written record of them is available. *Ha'aretz*, the source of these excerpts, published them in Hebrew.)
[9] *Ibid.*
[10] Daniel Pipes, *Syria Beyond the Peace Process.*
[11] Reuters, 6 June 1997; *JP*, 7 June 1997.
[12] On the history of relations between Israel and Syria see Itamar Rabinovich, *The Road not Taken* (New York: Oxford University Press, 1990), and *The Brink of Peace* (Princeton University Press, 1998); both were originally published in Hebrew. See also Moshe Maoz, *Syria and Israel: From War to Peace-Making*; Aryeh Shalev, *Shituf peulah betsel 'Imut: Mishtar Shvitot haNesheq Yisrael-Surya, 1949-1955* (Cooperation in the shadow of conflict: the Israeli-Syrian Armistice Cease-fire Committee, 1949-1955), Tel Aviv: Ma'arakhot, 1989, and Fred H. Lawson, *Why Syria Goes to War: Thirty Years of Confrontation* (Ithaca, NY: Cornell University Press, 1996).
[13] *Tishrin*, 9 March 1989.
[14] See Ze'ev Schiff and Ehud Ya'ari, *Israel's Lebanon War*, pp. 40-56; Avner Yaniv, *Politica veEstrategiya be-Yisrael* (Politics and Strategy in Israel – Tel Aviv: Sifriyat Poalim, 1994), pp. 302-18; Reuven Avi-Ran, *The Syrian involvement in Lebanon* 1975-1985 pp. 64-8.
[15] Eyal Zisser, "Syria and Israel: From War to Peace", *Orient*, 3(95), pp. 482-98.
[16] See James A. Baker, III, *The Politics of Diplomacy: Revolution, War and Peace, 1989-1992* (New York: Putnam, 1995), pp. 487-513.
[17] Rabinovich, *The Brink of Peace*, pp. 55-64; and see Itamar Rabinovich's lecture "Yisrael ve-Surya – 'Avar ve-Hoveh" (Israel and Syria – past and present), delivered at a symposium in memory of Moshe Dayan held by the Dayan Center on 5 November 1992 (Moshe Dayan Center Library).
[18] See Eyal Zisser, "Syria and Israel: From War to Peace"; Itamar Rabinovich, "Ramat ha-Golan kesugiyah ba-Sikhsukh ha-'Arvi-Yisraeli" (The Golan Heights in the context of the Arab-Israeli conflict – Moshe Dayan Center Library).
[19] *Al-Wasat*, 13 May 1994.

[20] *JP*, 12 May 1992.

[21] *Tishrin*, 17 May 1994.

[22] *Tishrin*, 18 January 1994.

[23] See *Ha'aretz*, 14, 17 January 1994.

[24] See *Tishrin*, 8, 10 March 1994; and see Eyal Zisser, "Syria" in Ami Ayalon (ed.), *MECS*, vol. XVIII (1994), pp. 641-2.

[25] See *MM*, 12 August 1997; and see Rabinovich, *The Brink of Peace*, pp. 203-4.

[26] Israel Television, Channel One, 7 October 1994.

[27] See Eyal Zisser, "Asad Inches toward Peace", *MEQ*, 1(3) (September 1994), pp. 37-44; Eyal Zisser, "Syria" in Ami Ayalon (ed.), *MECS*, vol. XVIII (1994), pp. 630-1; Rabinovich, *The Brink of Peace*, pp. 152-3.

[28] Rabinovich, *The Brink of Peace*, pp. 138-57; see also the account of Uri Saguy, *Lights within the Fog*, pp. 184-95.

[28a] See *Al-Hayat*, 21 and 23 November 1999.

[29] Rabinovich, *The Brink of Peace*, pp. 208-47; Uri Sagie, *Lights within the Fog*, pp. 246-59.

[30] Rabinovich, *The Brink of Peace*, pp. 227-8; Radio Damascus, 25 May – DR, 25 May 1991; *Ha'aretz*, 27, 28 May 1995.

[31] Radio Damascus, 10 July 1995; Rabinovich, *The Brink of Peace*, pp. 233-5.

[32] See the account of Itamar Rabinovich, *Ha'aretz*, 22 August 1996; Rabinovich, *The Brink of Peace*, pp. 248-50.

[33] Rabinovich, *The Brink of Peace*, pp. 248-93; and see *Al-Wasat*, 3 February 1997.

[34] Israel Television, Channel One, 5, 7 January 1996.

[35] *Ma'ariv*, 12 December 1997; and see Uri Savir, *HaTahalikh* (The Process – Tel Aviv: Yedi'ot Aharonot, 1998), pp. 307-8.

[36] See interview with Shimon Peres, Israel Defense Forces Radio, 20 June – DR, 21 June 1996.

[37] Uri Savir, *The Process*, pp. 298-326; and see interview with the Syrian ambassador to Washington, Walid Mu'allim, *Journal of Palestinian Studies*, XXVI(2) (winter 1997), pp. 401-12.

[38] Rabinovich, *The Brink of Peace*, pp. 305-27.

[39] See *ibid.*, pp. 169-170.

[40] *Tishrin*, 17 January 1994.

[41] See *Al-Ba'th*, 1 August 1997.

[42] *Ibid.*

[43] Uri Savir, *The Process*, pp. 318-20; see also Radio Damascus, 12, 13 May – DR 13 May 1996; *Ha'aretz*, 22 August 1996.

[44] Author's interview with a Syrian academic, Washington, 23 June 1996.

[45] Israel Defense Forces Radio, 20 June – DR, 21 June 1996.

[46] Rabinovich, *The Brink of Peace*, pp. 199-200; Uri Savir, *The Process*, p. 326.

[47] See Eyal Zisser, "Syria" in Bruce Maddy-Weitzman (ed.), *MECS*, vol. XX (1996), p. 662; and see Tishrin, 28 May 1996.

[48] See, for example, the interview with the Chief of Military Intelligence Uri Saguy, *Yedi'ot Aharonot*, 25 March 1994; and see *Ha'aretz*, 14 July 1994; *Yedi'ot Aharonot*, 21 July 1994; and see Uri Saguy, *Lights within the Fog*, p. 296.

[49] *Al-Wasat*, 3 February 1997.

[50] See *Al-Hayat*, 4 September 1995.

[51] Seale, *Asad of Syria*, pp. 347-8.

[52] *Ibid.*, pp. 340-2.

[53] *Ma'ariv*, 13 November 1996; author's interview with Shimon Peres, Jerusalem, 25 April 1995.

[54] *Ha'aretz*, 16 August 1996, 20 January 1997; *Ma'ariv*, 28 June 1996.

[55] See *Tishrin*, 29 September 1996, 11, 19 September 1997.

[56] *Ha'aretz*, 18 August 1996; see also *Ha'aretz*, 4 May, 28 May 1997.

[57] *Ibid.*, 22 August 1997.

[58] *Tishrin*, 1 August 1997.

[59] *Al-Ba'th*, 1 August 1997.

[60] *Ha'aretz*, 29 May 1999.

[61] Radio Damascus, 25 June 1999.

[62] *Al-Thawra*, 23 June 1999; *Ma'ariv*, 25 June 1999.

[63] SANA, 23 September 1997.

[64] MBC TV, 9 February 1997.

[65] *MM*, 12 August 1997.

[66] Author's interview with Patrick Seale, Tel Aviv, 10 June 1999; and see the BBC interview with Patrick Seale, 23 June 1999.

[67] *Al-Hayat*, 23 June 1996.

[68] *Ibid.*

[69] Al-Hayat, 20 March; *Yedi'ot Aharonot*, 23 March; *Ha'aretz*, 21 March 2000.

[70] *Ma'ariv*, 14 April 2000.

[71] *Ha'aretz*, 7 April; *Ma'ariv*, 31 March 2000.

[72] See *MEED*, 24 May 1996; see also the interview with Patrick Seale in the context of the proceedings of the international conference on "Modern Syria" held at Haifa University, 17–18 November 1996.

# 7

## SYRIA IN LEBANON

A brilliant if solitary achievement of President Asad in the 1990s was his establishment of a "Syrian order" in Lebanon. The Syrians brought to a close the bloody civil war that had raged there since 1975 and re-established the government institutions that had been paralysed for the duration of the war. Thanks to these achievements, the Syrians were able to turn Lebanon into a protectorate under their complete control.

The 22 May 1991 Treaty of Brotherhood, Cooperation and Coordination between Syria and Lebanon gave symbolic expression to Syria's position of seniority in Lebanon. This agreement, signed by the Presidents of the two countries, was designed to anchor and institutionalize the special senior status that Syria enjoys today in Lebanon. Although the agreement did not generate any changes, it formally validated the already existing state of affairs in Lebanon. The Syrians regarded it as highly important, because with this treaty their prolonged involvement in Lebanon (since 1976) had come full circle. That involvement was considered a devastating failure in its first years, but ultimately it brought Syria the realization of its long-term goals in Lebanon.

Asad's speech delivered at the signing of the accord expressed a sense of satisfaction and relief, and revealed his view of Lebanon, particularly over Syria's interests and goals there:

"We [the Syrians] did not create [that which binds] us to Lebanon. [This bond] is God's handiwork. We all share a common history, a common geography, and [ties of] blood. Therefore, the ties we establish today between the two countries are a reflection of our common heritage. This heritage cannot be erased, nor will it disappear with the passage of time, for brothers are brothers, whether or not they live in the same house. We are one people, even if we live in two separate states. This is the truth, and no one can ignore it. Turning away from this truth does not serve the interests of either of the two independent states, or of the people who live in them."[1]

In this address Asad emphasized a principal characteristic of his policy – the continuity of Syrian goals, interests and actions in Lebanon. He set out four basic assumptions that had guided his policy from the beginning of his involvement. First, Syria has vital interests in Lebanon – political, economic, and security-related – and is closely bound to Lebanon ideologically and historically. In order to promote and protect these interests, it needs to show active involvement in Lebanon and to achieve a position of influence and control over its affairs. Second, the annexation of Lebanon to Syria – *de facto* or *de jure* – is not a realistic goal for the near future. Such a step would be likely to arouse fierce opposition within Lebanon itself, in the Arab world, and in the international arena. Third, Syrian interests in Lebanon would therefore be best served by the establishment of a (relatively) centralized and stable Lebanese regime under Syrian patronage and influence. Only such a regime could legitimize active Syrian involvement in Lebanese affairs in the eyes of the Arab world and the international community. Moreover, it would free the Syrians of the need to maintain direct and continuous involvement in the quagmire of Lebanon's domestic problems. Fourth, the crystallization of a new order in Lebanon, based on an agreement between the various communities who live there, is a prerequisite for the establishment of a stable regime there. This is because the country is a mosaic of communities which have coexisted for centuries – a coexistence made possible in the past by the agreement reached among the communities on a formula which gave them all a share of the "national pie" – economic resources and positions of political power. This formula, known as the National Pact of 1943, served as the basis for political life in independent Lebanon until it collapsed in April 1975 with the outbreak of civil war. Syria then had to establish a new formula, acceptable to all the communities in the state; this would assure them of their share of the country's resources and enable them to coexist peacefully again. These basic assumptions, according to which Syrian policy in Lebanon was formulated and put into practice, showed Asad's acute insight into the Lebanese reality. They also demonstrated his ability to formulate and conduct realistic, pragmatic policy. These traits were a recognized source of his strength and his accomplishments as Syria's President and, in this case, Syria's successes in Lebanon.

In many ways the Lebanese-Syrian agreement of 22 May 1991 marked the close of a crucial chapter in the history of the countries' relationship. During this period Syria succeeded in implementing its strategic – and historical – goals in Lebanon, at the core of which was the acquisition of a position of influence and indeed full control over Lebanese affairs. Nevertheless, an examination of Syrian-Lebanese relations in a historical perspective is likely to show Syria's conduct in Lebanon, and especially its greatest achievement with regard to Lebanon in recent years, in a slightly different light from the prevailing view.

It is true that the Lebanon of the mid-1990s was a Syrian protectorate. However, Syria's role was essentially no different from that of France and Britain between the two World Wars and afterwards, or from the role Israel sought to play there in the early 1980s. The existence of some patron power is a permanent feature of Lebanese history, and has sometimes been crucial to enable the various communities to continue to coexist and, by extension, to make the state itself viable. Consequently, nothing in its special relationship with Syria threatens Lebanon's independent existence, nor does it necessarily presage an imminent dissolution of the state or its annexation to Syria. This explains the apparently inherent contradiction in Syria's Lebanese policy. While indeed seeking hegemony in Lebanon and thus, it would seem, encroaching on its independence and sovereignty, this policy at the same time – in the interests of the convenience and effectiveness of Syrian control over the country – has aimed to rehabilitate the Lebanese polity. One way or another, Syria's rise to ascendancy in Lebanon marked the end of a chapter in that country's history and in its relations with Syria.

## Syrian-Lebanese relations: the historical background

While it may have been stretching things for Asad to call the bond between the two states "God's handiwork", he did not overstate the truth of their closeness and common sense of identity.[2] There have in fact been long intervals during which the two comprised a single region.

The French Mandatory government established two separate states in the territory it controlled, Syria and Lebanon, yet in many ways the area remained unified. France maintained a unified economic and political policy in both these states, distinguishing them from the areas under British Mandate, which included territories once an integral part of Greater Syria: Transjordan and northern Palestine. This state of affairs led to the most pronounced characteristic of the Syrian-Lebanese relationship from its inception: on the one hand, the shared desire of both countries, or more specifically their ruling elites, to maintain their independence as distinct entities, and on the other the recognition by Syrian and Lebanese leaders of the common destiny both states share and of the practical need to maintain firm ties.[3]

In their first years of independence, the two states functioned as a single economic entity. They maintained an open border; travelers between them did not have to pass through customs, and trade was conducted freely across the border. They maintained a unified economic policy in the areas of customs, taxation and currency. The leaders of both states were careful to coordinate foreign policy positions on such regional and international questions as their future relations with Britain and France, the establishment of the Arab League; and the 1948 war in Palestine.[4] Such coordination, particularly in the inter-Arab arena, was perceived as vital in view of the two states' weakness at home and abroad – which, for example, encouraged King 'Abdallah to come up with the "Greater Syria" plan, and Nuri al-Sa'id to advance his plan for the "Fertile Crescent". These plans were viewed by the leaders of Syria and Lebanon as a real threat to the independence of both states, and they accordingly felt compelled to take a joint stand against them.[5]

This coordination of positions illustrates the "almost equal" nature of the Syrian-Lebanese relationship of that time – in spite of Syria's seemingly more advantageous position owing to its greater size and population, its location as Lebanon's gateway to the Arab world, and especially the influence of its leaders over Lebanon's Sunni Muslim community. These advantages were largely neutralized by the Syrian state's internal weakness and instability, as well as its economic difficulties. Against this background Lebanon's relative independence during those years stood out since it enjoyed greater political stability and impressive economic prosperity. Gradually, when Syria had become entangled in domestic difficulties, a prolonged break took place between the two states that lasted until the early 1970s.[6]

*Syria under Asad – first steps.* For a number of reasons, Hafiz al-Asad's rise to power in Syria on 16 November 1970 brought to an end the long period of alienation between Syria and Lebanon. Asad was successful in establishing a strong, stable regime in Damascus, which enabled him to work at strengthening Syria's regional status, with special attention to Lebanon. Notably, he profited from his familiarity with this arena, maintaining personal and political ties with some of that country's most powerful figures, chiefly the Faranjiyya family, prominent Maronites from the northern Zagharta region. (The patriarch of the family, Sulayman Faranjiyya, an old friend of Asad from the 1950s and '60s, was elected President of Lebanon in June 1970.) Asad's rise to power and subsequent entrenchment brought Syria and Lebanon closer, and the civil war that erupted in 1975 should thus be seen as a factor which speeded up this process and took it to new lengths.

In the early 1970s the Lebanese political and social system could no longer withstand the mounting pressures upon it – the changing demographic balance between Christians and Muslims; domestic social and economic difficulties; the PLO's entrenchment in Lebanon's refugee camps to the point where these became "a state within a state"; and the PLO's campaign against Israel from southern Lebanon, which turned the south of the country into a battlefield. These led to the breakdown of the existing Lebanese order and the outbreak of civil war in April 1975.[7]

The collapse of the state in Lebanon forced Syria to re-evaluate its policy and redefine its interests there. Some of these were traditional, unchanged since Syria became independent, and some were new. Its military-security interests were especially pressing since Lebanon had served for many years as an ideal arena for the activity of Syrian opposition elements which enjoyed the encouragement and patronage of the regime's rivals in the Arab world. In the 1950s and '60s, this activity patently contributed to Syria's internal destabilization, hence the importance to the Syrian regime of its ability to influence and control what happened in Lebanon and thereby block the activities of these opposition elements.[8] Added to these security considerations were Syria's national security needs over the years: since Israel's invasion of Lebanon in 1982, and to a certain extent before that, Lebanon became another front in the struggle with Israel. Its strategic importance, especially in the Biq'a Valley, was made clear to the Syrians when, during the course of the war, Israel came within artillery range of Damascus.[9]

The new reality created in Lebanon from the mid-1970s onward thus gave Syria an opening to renew and extend its involvement there. Syrian policy in Lebanon during the civil war passed through several stages.

*Syrian policy in Lebanon during the civil war*

(1) *Direct involvement alongside the Christian-Maronite camp, June 1976-November 1977.* In early February 1976 Syria was instrumental in producing the "Constitutional Document" which defined a new formula for coexistence in Lebanon. This included limited concessions by the Christians where their supremacy in Lebanon was concerned, but it also required the Muslims to give up their demand for an equal division of government positions. The Syrians hoped the implementation of this document would facilitate an end to the civil war and boost Syria's position as mediator and arbitrator between the various Lebanese communities. The Christian leadership agreed to accept the document, but the leftist camp and its Palestinian allies (the PLO) rejected the proposal, mainly because for the moment they had the upper hand in the fighting in and around Beirut.[10]

The Left's refusal to accept the Constitutional Document was a slap in the face for the Syrians. President Asad interpreted it as a personal blow to his honor and a challenge to Syria's status in Lebanon. It should be noted that the Syrians had no interest in seeing a victory for the Left, sections of which enjoyed the support of their rivals in the Arab world. Moreover, Damascus feared that the downfall of the Christians would push them into the arms of Israel or the West. It may also be said that Damascus viewed unfavorably the strengthening of the power and position of Arafat who, taking advantage of the protection he gained from the civil war, had turned West Beirut and South Lebanon into an independent territorial base.

Consequently, when the Maronite leadership sought Syrian assistance early in 1976, Damascus leapt to exploit the opportunity. In June of that year Syrian troops penetrated into Lebanon with the goal of striking a blow at the leftist camp and the PLO and forcing them to comply with the dictates of Damascus. However, the stubborn resistance encountered by the Syrian troops, together with sharp criticism of the invasion at home and abroad, halted the offensive before it could prevail on the battlefield.[11]

(2) *The struggle with Israel for control (1977-85).* From 1977, following the victory of Likud in Israel, ties between Israel and the Lebanese Maronite community were strengthened. This was a result of interests that Israel shared with the Maronite leadership, headed by Bashir al-Jumayyil. At that time Jumayyil had completed his takeover of the Maronite leadership and sought Israel's assistance in his efforts to guarantee the hegemony in Lebanon as a whole of his community, and in practice of himself and his family. Israel for its part sought Jumayyil's help in establishing a new order in Lebanon that would guarantee Israel a sympathetic regime or at least an ally on its northern border.[12] The Syrians – who had entered Lebanon, as will be recalled, to aid the Maronites in their struggle against the leftist Muslim camp – had meanwhile changed their minds. One main reason for this was the peace initiative of Egypt's President Sadat, which obliged them to make their peace with the PLO to keep it from joining this initiative.

The confrontation between Israel and Syria in Lebanon reached its peak in the Israeli invasion of Lebanon in June 1982. During the course of the invasion Israeli forces reached the Beirut-Damascus road. This precipitated the election of Bashir al-Jumayyil as President of Lebanon on 23 August 1982 and the forced evacuation of PLO and Syrian troops from Beirut on 31 August. Thus the beginning of September 1982 saw Syrian intervention in Lebanon at its lowest ebb.[13] On 14 September, just when it seemed as though Syria's position in Lebanon could not be restored, a car bomb exploded near the Phalangist headquarters in Beirut. It had been planted by a Syrian intelligence agent, the Syrian Social Nationalist

Party (PPS) member Habib Tanyus Shartuni. The building caved in and crushed everyone inside, including Bashir al-Jumayyil.[14] The new order Israel had sought to establish in Lebanon died with him. On 17 May 1983 the governments of Israel and Lebanon did indeed sign a peace agreement, but the Lebanese Parliament never ratified it and it soon became a dead letter.[15] Israel began to withdraw from Lebanon under the pressure of a wave of Palestinian and Shi'i (Hizballah) guerrilla attacks. The latter continued to attack Israeli troops as they withdrew. Israel completed the withdrawal in September 1985, except for the South Lebanon security zone over which it retained control.

(3) *Syria in Lebanon – on the road of return.* The evacuation of foreign troops from Lebanon paved the way for Syria's return to the dominant position it had lost during the course of the Lebanon war ( June 1982). On 8 December 1985, the tripartite Damascus Agreement was signed. It was based on the Constitutional Document, drafted by the Syrians before their invasion of Lebanon in 1976. This agreement called for the establishment of a parliament based on parity between Christians and Muslims, a reduction in the authority of the Maronite President, an end to the system of confessionalism, the dissolution of the militias, and strengthened cooperation with Syria. Signatories to the agreement were Nabih Barri, leader of Amal, on behalf of the Shi'is; Elie Hubayka, who headed the Lebanese Forces, on behalf of the Maronite camp; and Walid Junbalat on behalf of the Druze community.[16] Manifest in the Damascus Agreement was Syria's success in at least partly overcoming the factionalism in the leftist Muslim camp, and in making allies of parts of the Maronite camp, who now recognized that Israel could not advance or protect Maronite interests in Lebanon. The Christian camp, however, was not uniformly ready for this agreement, which required concessions on rights which they had historically enjoyed in Lebanon. Indeed Elie Hubayka was ousted from his position as commander of the Lebanese forces, and had to seek refuge with the Syrians.[17] The latter thus had to bide their time for a few years more before they could get significant Maronite-Christian backing for their maneuvers.

In July 1986 a small-scale Syrian force entered West Beirut to enforce a cease-fire on the Shi'i, Druze and Palestinian militias, and in February 1987 it was increased to 7,500 troops. The Syrian return to Beirut, less than five years after departing, came at the request of the Sunni leadership in the city, who wanted an end to the fighting there.[18]

Toward 1988 Syrian efforts revolved around the election of a new Lebanese President to replace Amin al-Jumayyil, whose six-year term was due to end in September 1988. The Syrians wanted to exploit this opportunity to break through the deadlock in the political system in Lebanon and to extricate their involvement in the country from the quagmire into which it had sunk. At first they failed to get a pro-Syrian candidate elected. The stalemate in the battle for the Lebanese presidency provided the background for the rise to prominence of the Maronite General Michel 'Awn, commander of the Lebanese army. 'Awn accepted the reins of government from Amin al-Jumayyil when the latter's term ended.

(4) *Michel 'Awn and his anti-Syrian campaign, 1988-90.* During his short period in power 'Awn won broad-based popular support which transcended ethnic boundaries; for example, although most of his backing came from the Maronite community, many Shi'is supported him. Support for 'Awn stemmed from a sense of desperation in the face of the political and military bankruptcy of the Lebanese Maronite community, added to the socio-economic crisis that threatened the livelihood of hundreds of thousands of Lebanese citizens. Finally, disappointment with the traditional communal leadership and the militia commanders who had led the Maronite community during the war and were perceived as responsible for the deterioration in its condition also contributed to 'Awn's support.[19]

Many Lebanese from across the whole political spectrum perceived General 'Awn as representing Lebanese legitimacy in that he was the commander of the army. However, he squandered his credit with the public. He set out to fight a lost cause against most of the political and military forces in Lebanon, among them the "Lebanese Forces". Furthermore, in March 1989 he declared a "war for the liberation of Lebanon" from the Syrians, whom he defined as the principal enemy of Lebanon and the Lebanese.[20] 'Awn had not taken the trouble to assure for himself significant regional or international support, and the only country to side with him was Iraq. However, Iraqi support was marginal and, if anything, it goaded the Syrians to redouble their efforts against the Maronite general.[21]

It seems that all 'Awn wanted to do was start a new conflagration in Lebanon, worse than the previous one, which would draw international attention to what was happening in his country and force the great powers to intervene, and so bring the prolonged civil war to an end. However, the price for 'Awn's tactic was to be paid by hundreds of thousands of Lebanese, most of them in the Maronite-Christian camp. The situation in Lebanon now seemed desperate, and against this background Syria came to be seen by many both inside and outside the country as the only player that could extricate it from the civil war which threatened, now more than ever, to devastate the Lebanese state.[22]

(5) *The Ta'if Accord.* On 22 October 1989 representatives of the Lebanese communities signed an agreement of national reconciliation in Ta'if, Saudi Arabia. The Ta'if Accord was an updated and expanded version of the National Pact of 1943, yet unlike its precursor it was set down in writing and signed. It aimed to lay the foundations for the establishment of a new Lebanese order by introducing a series of reforms to the structure of government. These included reducing the Maronite president's authority and placing him on an equal footing with the Sunni prime minister and Shi'i speaker of parliament, expanding parliament, and establishing parity between the numbers of Christian and Muslim deputies.

The Ta'if Accord called for the disarming of the militias and restoration of the authority of the central government in Beirut and over all Lebanon, including the south. The Accord also resolved that the number of Syrian troops remaining in Lebanon would be determined by the two states jointly, and that within two years at most from the implementation of constitutional reforms, these forces would leave Beirut and be redeployed in the Lebanese Biqa' Valley. Finally, the Accord called for Israel's withdrawal from South Lebanon in accordance with UN Security Council Resolution 425 and other UN resolutions.[23]

At the core of the Ta'if Accord was the recognition by Lebanese leaders, especially those of the Sunni and Maronite communities, that continuing the civil war was not only against their sectarian and personal interests but would threaten those interests was to altogether. At the start of the civil war the Maronites had put their faith in the Syrians, then later asked for Israel's help, and finally turned to the United States and France. However, after the withdrawal of Israel, the United States and France from Lebanon, they were left standing alone in the fray. The Sunnis' situation was bleak too. Their leadership had not succeeded in establishing a militia either before the war or during its course, and in the early 1970s, had relied on the power of the PLO. After the PLO were ousted, the Sunnis were forced to look on from the sidelines as Shi'i and Druze militia took control of West Beirut, the most important Sunni center in Lebanon.

Second, the threat facing Maronites and Sunnis from the Shi'is increased as a result not only of the Shi'i militia's military strength, but also, and especially, because this community, with its high rate of natural increase, had become the largest in the country. Various estimates of the Shi'i population in the mid 1990s set it at around 40% or of the overall population, compared to some 18% when the last census was taken in Lebanon in 1932.[24] Third, the civil war damaged the position and strength of the country's traditional leadership.

The Sunni community saw a gradual erosion of the status of its notables and their families, who were held responsible for its loss of political power. In the Maronite community the leading families such as the Chamouns and Jumayyils lost their power, and Christian military commanders – the Phalanges movement and subsequently the Lebanese Forces – began to take their place. It seems, nevertheless, that at the end of the 1980s these military leaders – Elie Hubayka and Samir Ja'ja', for instance – also ran into a dead-end.[25] Fourth, since the mid-1980s the Lebanese economy and, along with it, the country's social fabric had steadily deteriorated. Hundreds of thousands of middle-class people from all the communities, including many Christians, fell below the poverty line.

Sunni and Maronite leaders, and traditional Shi'i leaders as well, thus felt pressed to bring about a swift conclusion to the civil war before it was too late. The question was: who would be given the responsibility for doing it? The lack of trust between members of the various communities, the collapse of Lebanon's structure of authority (the military, government, parliament and the judicial system), and the bloody militia fighting throughout the country made imperative the presence of an effective agency capable of enforcing a peace agreement on all the political and military forces. In the absence of any practical alternative, Syria became the natural choice of many Lebanese, as well as of external players such as the United States. It had the strength, the determination and especially the military capability to do the job.

In truth, Syria was not responsible for the signing of the Ta'if Accord, which was drawn up in the framework of an Arab League initiative by Saudi Arabia, Morocco and Algeria, and signed in Ta'if, not Damascus. Syria also opposed portions of the Accord, such as that calling for its withdrawal from Beirut, and expressed dissatisfaction that the Accord did not recognize its special status in Lebanon.[26] Yet it was clear to all that without Syria's goodwill and, more important, its readiness to back it, the Accord would remain a dead letter. Not long after its signing and initial implementation, Syria made itself the standard-bearer of the Accord, while at the same time interpreting and implementing it as it wished and in keeping with Syrian interests.

(6) *Syria and Lebanon after Ta'if, 1991-99.* After the signing of the Ta'if Accord in October 1989, Syria and its allies in Lebanon began working energetically to implement it. This effort comprised several stages.

First came rehabilitation of the institutions of the Lebanese government in accordance with the content and spirit of the Accord:

the institution of the presidency, the government, parliament, the army and other governmental systems. Second was the strengthening of the legitimacy of these institutions and, by extension of the Accord as well, e.g. by holding presidential and parliamentary elections. Third, the authority of the Lebanese government throughout the country would be expanded by, *inter alia*, suppressing potential centers of opposition, disarming the militias, and imprisoning or eliminating the Lebanese regime's political rivals. Fourth, the social and economic systems of Lebanon would be rehabilitated with the goal of restoring life to normal. Fifth was the consolidation of ties and cooperation between Syria and Lebanon. This meant, in practice, reinforcing Lebanese dependence on Syria.

(7) *The election of a new president in Lebanon 1989.* The election of a new Lebanese President on 5 November 1989 ended the constitutional crisis that had erupted in September 1988 with the end of Amin al-Jumayyil's term of office. After a considerable scramble, René Mu'awwad, a Maronite notable from Zagharta, home also to Sulayman Faranjiyya, was elected. Mu'awwad was perceived as a strong, independent personality, and was accepted by wide sectors of the Maronite public.[27]

But less than a month into his term of office, on Lebanon's Independence Day, 22 November 1989, he was killed by a car bomb in West Beirut on his way to a parade. To date, the identity of the assassins has remained unknown: They may have been Iranians or Hizballah, seeking to express their opposition to the Ta'if Accord, which they viewed as injurious to the standing of the Shi'ite community and as a threat to Hizballah's future.[28] However, the finger of accusation also pointed at the Syrians who, it was claimed, were troubled by Mu'awwad's over-independent nature and therefore quickly eliminated him.[29]

Resistance to the Ta'if Accord from the Shi'i community in general and from Hizballah and its Iranian masters in particular, stemmed from their concern lest it should benefit the Maronites and Sunnis and create a threat to their own gains made during the protracted civil war. They perceived the compensation granted to the Shi'i community – an increase in the power of the Shi'i speaker of parliament and his being placed, at least formally, on an equal footing with the Maronite president and Sunni prime minister – as grossly inadequate in view of the fact that the Shi'i community had become the largest in the country and, by virtue of its militia, the strongest as well.

Furthermore, the process of rehabilitating the Lebanese state necessitated a return to the corridors of political power, and their transformation into the principal sphere in which struggles would thenceforth take place. Here, however, the Shiʻis had traditionally been at a disadvantage because, among other things, they had difficulty filling the political offices and positions of power allocated to them with educated members of their community. As a result, they were handicapped in the competition for a share of the national pie.[30]

Beyond weakening the Shiʻi community's position, the Ta'if Accord carried the seeds of a real threat to Hizballah since it claimed to breathe new life into the Lebanese polity, and to a significant extent succeeded in living up to this claim. Thus the vacuum exploited for years by Hizballah was being filled. Before the Accord, the lack of a living, breathing Lebanese entity had enabled that organization to propose its own alternative to the privations suffered by the members of Lebanon's Shiʻi community – the Islamic alternative. The Ta'if Accord gave a clear advantage to Hizballah's rival organization "Amal", which was prepared to reconcile itself to the existence of a Lebanese framework and hence was more capable of gaining a foothold within it.[31]

In the presidential elections of 24 November 1989, immediately after the death of René Muʻawwad, Ilyas al-Hirawi emerged the victor. Hirawi, son of a Maronite notable family of secondary importance, was known to be in league with the Syrians; still, he had maintained good relations for many years with Maronite leaders, even those known to be opponents of Damascus.[32] Promptly after his election he gave ʻUmar Karami, a Muslim notable from Tripoli and a member of the old Sunni elite, the responsibility of forming a new government in which Christian representatives would also take part. In addition, the number of seats in parliament was once again brought up to its proper total of ninety-nine (by appointing delegates to replace those who had died over the years).[33] Thus the rehabilitation of Lebanon's governmental institutions – the presidency, the government and the parliament – was complete. This was a necessary pre-requisite for laying down the legal infrastructure for future measures by the Syrians and their allies in Lebanon, beginning with the offensive against General Awn.

## *The takeover of General ʻAwn's enclave*

After the signing of the Ta'if Accord, General ʻAwn remained the Syrians' last significant opponent in Lebanon. He opposed the Accord, and in fact obstructed its implementation, at least in the territory under his control. The Syrians exercised restraint for a long period out of concern that direct Syrian action against ʻAwn might cause a bloodbath and arouse opposition within Lebanon and, more important, in the Arab and international arena. Only at the end of 1990 were conditions ripe for the Syrians to make a military move against 'Awn. First, by that time they had successfully won the support of most of the political and military forces in Lebanon for the Ta'if Accord, including Hizballah and even the "Lebanese Forces" under Samir Ja'ja', and the Maronite religious establishment in Bkerki (the seat of the Maronite patriarch). At the beginning of October President Hirawi officially requested Syrian assistance to rid them of the Maronite general.[34] Second, during 1990 and particularly after the outbreak of the Gulf crisis in August that year, Syria improved its image in the inter-Arab and international arenas. Its joining the US-led anti-Iraq coalition led to warmer ties with Western countries, especially the United States. The Syrians apparently received the green light to move against 'Awn during James Baker's visit to Damascus in September 1990.[35]

On 13 October 1990 Syrian troops attacked 'Awn's enclave around the Ba'abda presidential palace in Beirut and after capturing it took over all of East Beirut.[36] 'Awn himself took refuge in the French embassy, and later went into exile in France. Eight days after the capture of 'Awn's enclave, Dani Chamoun, the son of Camille Chamoun, fell to the hand of an assassin, apparently sent by Syrian intelligence. Dani Chamoun was a leading supporter of 'Awn and hence one of Syria's principal remaining enemies in Lebanon.[37] His assassination was a clear signal from Damascus that it was intractable on the issue of implementing the Ta'if Accord and would tolerate no resistance either to the Accord or to Syria's own presence and influence in Lebanon.

*Disarming the militias.* During 1991 the Lebanese government, with Syrian backing, called for the disarming of the various militias, which did not oppose this move by the central government in Beirut, and even began transferring most of their activity from the military to the political sphere. Hizballah received permission to continue to bear arms in South Lebanon for the purpose of carrying on the struggle against Israel, but in the rest of the country its members were prevented from carrying arms.[38] In a parallel development the Lebanese army began to deploy troops throughout the country, for example in the southern region, as an additional step in restoring the sovereignty and authority of the central government. The campaign of the Lebanese security forces, backed by Syria, against illegal drug growers and smugglers, along with the Beirut government's energetic activity against political opponents and opposition elements, illustrated the determination the Lebanese government to impose its authority throughout the country,[39] and its success at least in part.

*Elections to parliament.* In the summer of 1992 and four years later in the summer of 1996, parliamentary elections were held in Lebanon. Most of the Maronite population – estimated at more than 90% of the voters – boycotted the 1992 elections, claiming that Syrian intervention in the country made fair elections impossible. As on so many occasions in the past, the boycott backfired: its organizers were unable to prevent the elections, and parliament, with its 128 members including Maronites who had not joined the boycott, was soon functioning normally.[40] Hizballah's participation in the elections deserves special consideration. As will be recalled, it initially opposed the Ta'if Accord, but it now decided to participate in the elections, rather successfully as it turned out: the list it supported – Loyalty to the Resistance (*al-wafa lil-muqawama*) – won eight parliamentary seats in 1992 and seven in 1996.[41]

In November 1995 President Hirawi's first six-year term of office ended, but in order to prevent any shift in the Lebanese political system that would undermine the hard-won political stability, the Syrians arranged to extend his term by three years. This was in complete opposition to the letter and spirit of the Lebanese constitution, which prohibits a president from serving in that office for more than six successive years.[42] Hirawi was not, however, the only power in Lebanon to contribute to the rehabilitation of the Lebanese state. In 1992 Rafiq al-Hariri was appointed Prime Minister, with Syrian consent. This Sunni businessman was the first Lebanese prime minister not appointed by the Sunni families of notables who had controlled the post since the independent Lebanese state was first established. However, he was a businessman of vast wealth – estimated at some $3 billion – and enjoyed Saudi backing thanks to commercial and political links.[43]

With the final close of Hirawi's term of office in November 1998, the Syrians acted to have the Lebanese army commander Emile Lahhud elected as Lebanon's eleventh president. To this end they forced members of parliament to vote on changing paragraph 49 of the Lebanese Constitution which required senior members of the army and the administration – such as Lahhud – seeking presidential office to have retired from their posts at least two years before participating in a presidential election. The election of Lahhud, Damascus's loyalist and confidant in Lebanon in recent years, was also accompanied by a change of personnel in the office of the prime minister. Salim al-Huss took Hariri's place.[44]

## Resumption of normal life in Lebanon

The political stability achieved in Lebanon made possible the gradual restoration of Lebanese life to its normal course and, in particular, the rehabilitation of the country's economic infrastructure. Economic statistics for the 1990s indicate a steady improvement in the performance of the economy. The annual inflation rate was lowered to less than 10%, the exchange rate of the Lebanese lira was stabilized, and gross domestic product statistics indicated an impressive growth of some 7% annually in the middle of the decade. Lebanese citizens who had fled during the civil war began to return, and an inflow of foreign investment began, helping to finance ambitious development and reconstruction projects, mostly in the Beirut area, worth billions of dollars.[45]

The Syrians' success in rehabilitating Lebanon led to an overhaul in the approach of most Western countries to the role they had played there. From the mid-1990s Western pressure on Syria to redeploy its forces in Lebanon in accordance with the Ta'if Accord decreased. The United States and the countries of Western Europe did not repeat this demand, and hinted at increased readiness to recognize Syria's status in Lebanon in line with progress in the peace process.[46]

And so, after achieving its objective – the establishment of a new Lebanese order and a stable central government – Syria turned to the business of formally anchoring and institutionalizing its presence and hegemony in the country. On 22 May 1991, it signed with Lebanon a "Treaty of Brotherhood, Cooperation and Coordination". A string of additional agreements on domestic, economic and security affairs were signed during the years that followed, and attached to this treaty. These agreements were intended to translate the principal agreement into action, and did in fact anchor and institutionalize Syrian involvement in Lebanon and lay the foundations for continuing and enhanced cooperation and coordination between the two states.[47]

## Syrian involvement in Lebanon, 2000

Syria's involvement was not intended to bring about its annexation of Lebanon and no such annexation has taken place. Such a goal was not apparently in Hafiz al Asad's sights since in his view it was unrealistic and unattainable. All that Syria wanted was to establish a stable authority on the ground by means of which it could maintain its influence and power in Lebanon. The Syrians therefore did not work for a real transformation of the structure of Lebanon's political, social and economic systems – such a transformation would necessarily have had to precede its annexation to Syria. The presence of between half a million and a million Syrian workers in Lebanon was not enough to skew the demographic balance; they were not entitled to gain Lebanese citizenship and did not attempt to do so; non, as far as is known, did they not settle in Lebanon and bring their families over.[48]

All that the Syrians did was define the political rules of the game for the Lebanese players and, more precisely, lay down the boundaries that could not be crossed. The main thrust of these was acceptance of Syrian hegemony in Lebanon and agreement to subordinate Lebanese foreign policy interests to Syria's. The Syrians had engineered the assassination of Dani Chamoun, the man who ousted Michel 'Awn from Lebanon, and the incarceration of Samir Ja'ja' together with the dismantling of his "Lebanese Forces".[49] These targets had all refused to recognize the position Syria had gained for itself in Lebanon, or else had fought Damascus in the past by openly cooperating with Israel. In contrast, most of the other forces operating in Lebanon are in the Muslim camp: the Shi'i, Druze and Sunni organizations which, in addition to the Christian camp, continued to function freely, while expressing their support for Syria's role in Lebanon.

Lebanon's political system was still characterized at the end of the 1990s, as in the past, by power struggles for positions of strength and influence in the country on a personal, family–regional and sectarian basis. The Ta'if Accord seemed to exacerbate or reawaken these struggles because it created the first opening since the 1943 pact for real changes to be made in the division of national resources among the political forces in Lebanon – between the different communities and between the various powers within each community. The background to the power struggles played out in Lebanon was variegated and offered ample illustration of the continuity, rather than transformation or reversal, of Lebanon's distant as well as recent past. Some of these struggles were waged against a traditional background, i.e. they are *inter-communal* – between representatives of the different communities seeking to strengthen the respective positions of those communities. Examples were the struggle of the Shi'i and Druze against the Maronite-Sunni establishment, and that between Maronites and Sunnis. Then there were *intra-communal* struggles – between the various forces within each community that wished to strengthen their own position as a basis for their claim to a share of the nation's resources (e.g. the struggle within the Shi'i community between Amal and Hizballah). In addition there were struggles *within the executive authority, and between it and the institutions of the legislative authority*; these were waged between the president and the prime minister, and between the two together against parliament as representative of the legislative authority (it is also the body whose speaker was defined by the Ta'if Accord as equal to the president and the prime minister).

And there were the struggles that arose following the Accord. The older generation – in particular veteran members of the Lebanese elite, the notable families of all the communities – wanted to maintain their traditional privileges in the political, social and economic life of Lebanon *vis-à-vis* the younger generation of educated professionals, businessmen and other up-and-coming elements in soceity who wanted a share of the spoils. The former Sunni Prime Minister, Rafiq al-Hariri, belonged to the latter category and effectively represented its members. A significant portion of the power struggles waged in Lebanon was brought for arbitration or final decision to Damascus, and one cannot avoid the impression that it was often the Lebanese politicians who involved the Syrians in their power struggles in order to win their backing and thereby improve their own positions. This was a recognized and accepted *modus operandi* in Lebanon, used successfully in the past with the British and the French, and later with the United States and Israel.

Syria's involvement in Lebanon after 1975 continued along two main tracks. First, its military and security presence there was centralized at the time of President Asad's death in the hands of Lt. Gen. Ghazi Kan'an, of military security, which was headed for many years up till February 2000 by Ali Duba. Kan'an was Damascus's senior representative in Lebanon and, in the absence of a Syrian ambassador in Beirut, handled the day-to-day problems caused by Syria's military presence in Lebanon and the domestic Lebanese problems – primarily inter-communal and intra-communal power struggles – brought to him for resolution. Second, the more complex and fundamental problems were usually transferred to Damascus to be handled by Vice President 'Abd al-Halim Khaddam, who has for many years controlled the Lebanese file. From the start of the 1990s Asad delegated part of the handling of the Lebanese situation to his son Basil and, after Basil's death in January 1994, to Bashar, who began making periodic visits to Lebanon, where be established ties with various politicians.[50] One obvious manifestation of Bashar's strengthened position in the Lebanese arena was the replacement of the Prime Minister in Beirut in December 1998 after the election of Emile Lahhud as President. Rafiq al-Hariri, who was known to have a close relationship with Khaddam, was succeeded as Prime Minister by Salim al-Hus as a result of Bashar's direct involvement.[51]

*Damascus and the Israeli presence in Southern Lebanon*

In September 1985 Israel withdrew from Lebanon, while keeping control over a security strip in the south. A local militia, the SLA (South Lebanese Army), was left there under the command of the Maronite General Antoine Lahad. This strip was designed to serve as a buffer zone in case of terrorist attacks against Israeli settlements in the northern Galilee, and Israel also saw it as a card it could play in future negotiations with the Syrians and with the Lebanese government. Israel therefore gave notice that it was prepared to withdraw from southern Lebanon immediately after reaching a peace agreement with Lebanon that would include satisfactory security arrangements to guarantee Israel's northern border.[52]

In the course of the 1992-6 peace talks, Israel and Syria reached an understanding on an arrangement for South Lebanon. This would be subject to the achievement of an Israeli-Syrian peace agreement[53] – which the impasse in the peace process prevented from being implemented. Shortly after beginning his term of office in the summer of 1996, the Israeli Prime Minister Benjamin Netanyahu, proposed advancing the notion of "Lebanon first", of which the main plank was a Lebanese-Israeli arrangement that could serve in future as the basis for a dialogue between Israel and Syria.[54] This was rejected by the Syrians and, following them, by Lebanon as well. "Syria says Lebanon *and* Syria first," responded President Asad to Netanyahu's proposal, and official spokesmen for Syria hastened to follow suit and explain that Netanyahu's proposal was no more than an attempt to drive a wedge between Syria and Lebanon.[55]

At the start of 1998, Israel announced its readiness to accept the UN Security Council Resolution 425, passed in 1978, which called for its withdrawal from South Lebanon. At the same time it demanded that Lebanon should guarantee calm on their shared border.[56] In so doing, it lowered the price it was demanding in exchange for withdrawing from South Lebanon to unsubstantial agreements and understandings, instead of demanding an overall peace accord with Lebanon, as it had done in the past. The Syrians rejected this proposal too. The Lebanese, having no choice in the matter, also rejected it, though with less enthusiasm. Nonetheless, it seems that the countdown to Israel's full withdrawal from Lebanon began with the coming to power in Israel of Ehud Barak in the Knesset elections of May 1999. Barak announced on the eve of the elections that he intended to pull the Israel Defense Forces out of Lebanon within one year, and reiterated this commitment after taking office. Indeed, on 24 May 2000 the IDF was pulled out of Lebanon, and the Israeli presence there came to an end.[57]

The Israeli withdrawal from Lebanon raised anew the question of the future of Hizballah. Since the start of the 1990s the Hizballah had faced a series of challenges that threatened its continued operation and indeed its very existence. First was the Ta'if Accord, which led to the end of the civil war in which the organization had flourished. Another challenge was the Middle East peace process which at its height threatened to bring Hizballah's campaign against Israel to a halt and thereby damage one of its sources of legitimacy and power. Finally, it was weakened by political and economic difficulties. Faced with this threatening reality, it showed itself to be pragmatic and with a will to survive, and thus appeared ready to abandon its ideological aims or at least to see their realization postponed to the distant future. The organization took part in the Lebanese parliamentary elections in the summers of 1992 and 1996, and acted to expand its activity into the social and economic domains. In so doing it laid the basis for its transformation into a social and political movement that would form part of the existing Lebanese political order.[58]

In this context it should be noted that Syria had a clear interest in reining in Hizballah activity, partly because of its own commitment to the peace process but mainly because of internal Lebanese considerations. Hizballah's military and political activity threatened stability in Lebanon and thwarted the Syrian effort to establish a stable central regime there. Iran's involvement in Lebanon and the backing it gave to Hizballah only increased this threat to Syrian interests there. However, since the Syrians understood clearly that Israel stood to profit most from their move against Hizballah, they acted to link a solution to the problem of South Lebanon and Hizballah activity in the region to an overall solution of the Arab-Israeli conflict and, included in this, a solution to the Golan Heights question to the satisfaction of Damascus.

The impasse in Israeli-Syrian negotiations between 1996 and 1999 gave Hizballah a valuable respite. Nonetheless, the cloud hanging over its future did not dissipate. Even after the Israeli elections of May 1999, the challenges facing it still loomed large. Abandonment of the struggle against Israel in the wake of the Israel Defense Forces evacuating Lebanon, and the achievement of peace between Israel and Syria should it come to pass, will inevitably change the face of Hizballah. Without the struggle against Israel, and in the light of its integration into the Lebanese political system, it is likely to lose its uniqueness, and hence its vitality and power to attract followers. In such an event, the line dividing it from the "Amal" organization would blur. Amal is Hizballah's rival in the struggle for control within the Shi'i community: it advocates the integration of the community into the existing Lebanese order, with all the reforms that that entails.

On the face of it more than twenty years of Syrian involvement in Lebanon had come full circle and brought about the realization there of the long-term goals of "Asad's Syria". With the aid of Syrian arms, a central and stable Lebanese regime was established, given over completely to Syria's influence. Nonetheless, the process of Lebanon's rehabilitation, on the basis of a renewed understanding between all the communities in the country, was not entirely in response to Syria's dictates. It arose also from shared interests, at least in the interim, among the traditional communal leadership in Lebanon and among the new business elite – and between them and the Syrian regime. While this deepened dependence apparently increased the danger of a Syrian takeover of Lebanon, many Lebanese – Sunnis and Maronites alike – have seen cooperation with Syria as being in their country's best interests. They have gone so far as to claim that their country and countrymen were taking advantage of Syria, as they exploited the deployment of its troops – and, by extension, its money and blood – in order to further the sectarian and personal interests which were, and continue to be, the only truly significant interests in Lebanon. One Maronite personality even stated that "Syria is Asad" and that, once he was out of the picture, Syria would be so weakened that it would no longer be able to impose its control and influence in Lebanon. But until that time the continued Syrian presence assures Lebanon's return to the high road of political stability and economic achievement, after which it will be able, by exploiting convenient regional and international circumstances, to break away from the embrace of the Syrian giant.[59]

One can of course disagree with the underlying logic of this perception or heartfelt hope, but it cannot be entirely discounted. It is a fact that the development of relations between Syria and Lebanon has not yet brought about a union between the two states, or Lebanon's annexation to Syria, but rather the reverse. Syrian involvement has restored and strengthened the ability of the various powers in Lebanon to coexist under a stable and strong regime.

On the other hand, in the many years since the establishment of "Greater Lebanon" in 1920, broad swathes of the Lebanese Sunni population sought to unite the two countries, and a similar demand was voiced in Damascus. Yet Syrian involvement in Lebanon since 1975 not lead to anyone in Lebanon or Syria attempting to realize this ambition from the past now when it had apparently come within reach. On the contrary, most Lebanese from all communities have continued to adhere more forcefully than before to the independent existence of their state.

It also seems that the challenge facing Lebanon from the start of the 1990s was not so much the Syrian presence in the country as the rising power of the Shi'i community, which the signatories of the Ta'if Accords – both Sunni and Maronite – ignored in their desire to maintain their control in the state. In addition, there were of course other challenges, particularly in the social and economic spheres. In any case, Syrian involvement in Lebanon has constituted an important chapter in the country's modern history. But like its predecessors – the French Mandate and joint-control by Britain and France during the Second World War – it is by no means the final chapter.

## NOTES

[1] Tishrin, 23 May 1991.
[2] *Ibid.*
[3] For more on French policy in the Levant, see Philip S. Khouri, *Syria and the French Mandate*, pp. 27-71; Kamal Salibi, *The Modern History of Lebanon* (Delmar, NY: Caravan Books, 1977), pp. 151-204; *A House of Many Mansions*, pp. 200-34.
[4] For more on this issue see Eyal Zisser, *Lebanon: The Challenge of Independence* (London: I.B. Tauris, 2000); also Bishara al-Khuri, *Haqa'iq Lubnaniyya* (Lebanese truths – Beirut: Manshurat Awraq Lubnaniyya, 1960); Hassan Halak, *al-Tiyyarat al-Siyasiyya fi Lubnan 1943-52* (Political trends in Lebanon, 1943-1952 – Beirut: Ma'had al-Inma' al-'Arabi, no date).
[5] See Patrick Seale, *The Struggle for Syria*, pp. 16-30.
[6] Patrick Seale and Michael C. Hudson, *The Precarious Republic: Political Modernization in Lebanon* (New York: Random House, 1968); Itamar Rabinovich, *The War for Lebanon*, pp. 17-33.
[7] For more on the background to the outbreak of civil war in Lebanon, see Rabinovich, *The War for Lebanon*, pp. 34-88; Roger Owen (ed.), *Essays on the Conflict in Lebanon* (London: Ithaca Press, 1976); Kamal Salibi, *Crossroads to Civil War: Lebanon, 1958-1976* (Delmar, NY: Caravan Books, 1976).
[8] See Seale, *The Struggle for Syria*, pp. 210-360; Andrew Rathmall, *Secret War in the Middle East*, pp. 22-144.
[9] See Reuven Avi-Ran, *The Syrian Involvement in Lebanon*, pp. 9-24.
[10] See Rabinovich, *The War for Lebanon*, pp. 17-33; Walid Khalidi, *Conflict and Violence in Lebanon: Confrontation in the Middle East* (Cambridge, MA: Center for International Affairs and Harvard University Press, 1979).
[11] *Ibid.*, and Reuven Avi-Ran, *The Syrian Involvement in Lebanon*, pp. 9-24.
[12] Jack Reinich, "Bashir Jumayyil uTequfato" (Bashir Jumayyil and his time) Ph.D. thesis, Tel Aviv University, 1988; see also Ze'ev Schiff and Ehud Ya'ari, *Israel's Lebanon War*, pp. 21-124.
[13] On the course of the Lebanon War, see Ze'ev Schiff and Ehud Ya'ari, *Israel's Lebanon War*, pp. 163-357; and see Mustafa Talas, *al-Ghazw al-Isra'ili liLubnan* (The Israeli invasion of Lebanon – Damascus: Mu'assasat Tishrin Lil-Sahafa wal-Nashr, 1983).
[14] Ze'ev Schiff and Ehud Ya'ari, *Israel's Lebanon War*, pp. 308-10.

[15] See Yosef Olmert, "Lebanon", in Itamar Rabinovich and Haim Shaked (eds), MECS, vol. IX (1984-5), pp. 533-7; and see David Kimche, *HaOptsia haAahrona, haMa'avaq leShalom baMizrah haTichon* (The last option, the struggle for peace in the Middle East – Tel Aviv: 'Idanim, 1992), pp. 133-93; Richard B. Parker, *The Politics of Miscalculation in the Middle East* (Bloomington: Indiana University Press, 1993), pp. 167-223.

[16] See Yosef Olmert, "Lebanon," in Itamar Rabinovich and Haim Shaked (eds), *MECS*, vol. IX (1984-85), pp. 533-7.

[17] Ibid., p. 537.

[18] Olmert, "Lebanon", pp. 642-5.

[19] On this see Salim Nasr, "Lebanon's War: Is the End in Sight", *MERIP* report, vol. 20, no. 1 (January-February 1990), pp. 4-9; Harris, "Lebanon" in MECS, vol. XIII (1989), pp. 499-533; MECS, vol. XIV (1990), pp. 526-50; William B. Harris, *Faces of Lebanon* (Princeton, NJ: Marcus Wiener, 1997), pp. 243-78.

[20] William B. Harris, "Lebanon", pp. 505-19.

[21] *Ibid.*, pp. 499-533.

[22] Salim Nasr, "Lebanon's War: Is the End in Sight?", pp. 4-9.

[23] For the text of the Accord see *Al-Nahar*, 22 October 1989. For more on the Accord, see William B. Harris, *Faces of Lebanon*, pp. 279-322.

[24] On demographic aspects of Lebanon, see Arnon Soffer, "Lebanon – Where Demography is the Care of Politics and Life", *MES*, 18, 1982, pp. 197-205.

[25] For more on this see Wade R. Goria, *Sovereignty and Leadership: Lebanon 1943-1976* (London: Ithaca Press, 1985).

[26] See Salim Nasr, "Lebanon's War: is the end in sight?", pp. 4-9; William B. Harris, "Lebanon" in Ami Ayalon (ed.), MECS, vol. XIV (1990), pp. 420-56.

[27] Harris, "Lebanon" in Ami Ayalon (ed.), MECS, vol. XIV (1990), pp. 534-6.

[28] *Ibid.*, pp. 522-5.

[29] *Ibid.;* author's interview with a Lebanese academic, Oxford, 22 February 1990.

[30] Harris, "Lebanon", in Ami Ayalon (ed.) *MECS*, vol. XIV (1990), pp. 522-4.

[31] For more on the Shi'is in Lebanon see Fouad Ajami, *The Vanished Imam: Musa al-Sadr and the Shi'a of Lebanon* (Ithaca, NY: Cornell University Press, 1986).

[32] Harris, "Lebanon" p. 524.

[33] *Ibid.*, p. 533.

[34] SANA, 13 October – DR, 15 October 1990.

[35] On this matter see the announcement made by the US Ambassador in Damascus following the Syrian attack on Michel 'Awn, according to which Washington supported the implementation of the Ta'if Accords and stated that the Syrian move was intended to enable the Lebanese government to extend its sovereignty over all Lebanese territory; SANA, 24 October – DR, 25 October 1990.

[36] Harris, "Lebanon," in Ami Ayalon (ed.), MECS, vol. XIV (1990), p. 533.

[37] *Le Monde*, 20 October 1990; *FT*, 22 October 1997; Harris, "Lebanon" in Ami Ayalon (ed.), MECS, vol. XIV (1990), pp. 534-6.

[38] Harris, *ibid.*, pp. 544-7.

[39] Eyal Zisser, "Syria" in Ami Ayalon (ed.), MECS, vol. XIV (1990), pp. 665-6.

[40] See Harris, "Lebanon" (1992), pp. 598-608.

[41] See *Al-Hayat*, 2 June 1996; Zisser, "Syria" in Bruce Maddy-Weitzman (ed.), MECS, vol. XX (1996), pp. 654-5.

[42] *Al-Hayat*, 20 October 1995.

[43] See the internet site of former Lebanese prime minister, Rafiq al-Hariri, http://www.haririfoundationusa.org/herafiq/htm.

[44] *Al-Hayat*, 15, 17 October 1998, 3 January 1999.

[45] *CF, Lebanon – 1998-99*, pp. 9.

[46] Zisser, "Syria" in Ami Ayalon and Bruce Maddy-Weitzman (eds), MECS, vol. XVIII (1994), pp. 636-7; Bruce Maddy-Weitzman (ed.), MECS, vol. XIX (1995), pp. 608-9.

[47] *Tishrin*, 22 May 1991; and see Harris, "Lebanon" in Ami Ayalon (ed.), MECS, vol. XV (1991), pp. 547-50.

[48] *Al-Wasat*, 7 October 1997.

[49] Harris, *Faces of Lebanon*, pp. 291-6.

[50] See, for example, reports of Bashar al-Asad's visits to Beirut in the course of which he met senior officials in the Lebanese government; *Al-Thawra*, 26 March 1997, 1 April 1997; *Tishrin*, 5 November 1997; and see Zisser, "Syria" in Bruce Maddy-Weitzman (ed.), MECS, vol. XX (1996), pp. 634, 652-5; Zisser, *Decision-Making in Asad's Syria*, pp. 25-6.

[51] *Nida al-Watan*, 30 November 1998; *Al-Hayat*, 3 January 1999.

[52] See Reuven Avi-Ran, *The Syrian Involvement in Lebanon*, pp. 211-15.

[53] *Ha'aretz*, 16, 17 January 1997.

[54] *Ha'aretz*, 25 July 1996.

[55] *Tishrin*, 5 November 1996.

[56] See *Tishrin*, 15 January 1998; *Ha'aretz*, 17 January 1998.

[57] *Ha'aretz*, 19 May, 4 July 1999.

[58] See Nizar A. Hamzeh, "Lebanon's Hizbullah: From Islamic Revolution to Parliamentary Accommodation", *Third World Quarterly*, 14(2) 1993, p. 328; Eyal Zisser, "Hizballah in Lebanon – At the Crossroads" in Bruce Maddy-Weitzman and Efraim Inbar (eds), *Religious Radicalism in the Greater Middle East* (London: Frank Cass, 1997), pp. 90-110.

[59] Author's interview with a Lebanese academic, San Francisco, 23 November 1997.

# Part IV

# INSIDE SYRIA – A COUNTRY AT A CROSSROADS

## 8

## THE STRUGGLE OVER SUCCESSION

On 10 June 2000, President Asad died at the age of sixty-nine. The Syrian media referred to his death as being "sudden, surprising and shocking" (*Tishrin*, 12 June 2000), but it was an open secret in Damascus for several years that Asad's days were numbered. Immediately following his death his son Bashar took over in what seemed to be a smooth process of transition, thus bringing to at least a temporary end the struggle for succession to Asad's throne. However, taking into consideration the history of the modern Syrian state, it seemed that Bashar's emergence as President was an end of a chapter in this struggle for power rather than the end of the struggle itself.[1]

The question of succession had first erupted in 1983-4. The deterioration of President Asad's health following a heart attack led his brother Rif'at to try to advance his position as successor, and Asad made no pretense of concealing his dissatisfaction. The brothers' struggle over the succession presented a challenge to the regime, threatening its internal solidarity and stability, and essentially jeopardizing its existence. The regime emerged intact from the crisis thanks to an improvement in the President's health, and the issue of succession became much less acute, although it remained unresolved.[2]

From the beginning of the 1990s, the question reappeared on the Syrian agenda, this time on the initiative of President Asad himself. It has been said that he sought to designate his son Basil as his successor and thereby resolve this highly charged and problematic issue while he still lived. In so doing he hoped to assure the future of his regime and the continuation of the course he had charted during his rule. On Friday, 21 January 1994, Basil al-Asad, the President's eldest son, died in an automobile accident aged thirty-two (he was born on 23 March 1962) and his death renewed the succession struggle and, at the very least, produced tension and restiveness among the political, party, military and security elite in Syria.

Asad's second son, Bashar, born on 11 September 1965, replaced Basil as his father's choice of successor. At the time of Basil's death he was an ophthalmologist at a hospital in Britain, but he returned to Syria and, with his father's encouragement, began to move forward on the same military track so successfully followed by his elder brother. He replaced Basil as brigade commander in the Republican Guard – the elite force charged with protecting the regime – and took training courses in all branches of military service, including ones for tank battalion commanders, command and staff. Completion of these last two training courses was a crucial step toward senior command in the Syrian army.[3]

No less significant was the process of building a support base for Bashar in the Syrian army. Starting in 1994, many new appointments were made in the upper echelons of the military, especially at the intermediate, divisional commander level. The extent of this round of replacements was unprecedented; a whole crop of young 'Alawite officers received promotions in rank. Most were unknown outside their immediate circle and apparently were close associates and loyal supporters of Bashar. These officers were meant one day to provide him with the necessary backing in the struggle over the succession.[4] This trend continued in the following years, reaching a peak in the pensioning-off of the Chief of Staff, Hikmat Shihabi, on 1 July 1998 and the promotion of his deputy, 'Ali Aslan, to replace him. Shihabi had been named in the past as a possible successor to President Asad, and his removal from the arena was thus another step in the establishment of Bashar as heir-apparent.[5]

President Asad's efforts to create a basis for his son's standing at first met with considerable skepticism, both within Syria and beyond. Bashar was young and lacked practical experience of managing military and state affairs. Not only that, but he was not known for either charisma, determination or the "killer instinct", all of which were essential in anyone aspiring to take up the reins of government in Syria.[6] Reservations among the Syrian public about Bashar's suitability emerged in comments – from both within the regime and outside it, and mostly not for attribution – that Syria was not a monarchy, and its people would not accept any attempt to force an unsuitable successor upon them.[7] However, it seems that as the years passed Bashar's standing as heir grew stronger, and the doubts over his ability to take over the helm receded.

Nevertheless, the question of succession thus occupied an important place on the Syrian agenda from the early 1980s onwards, and continues to do so even after Bashar al-Asad's succession. Indeed it is the key question where the country's stability, if not the very existence of the Syrian regime, is concerned.

## Roots of the succession struggle

On 13 November 1983 President Asad suffered a severe heart attack from which he nearly died. This was one more medical problem
in a long list of ailments from which the President suffered, including asthma, diabetes, cancer and kidney disease.[8] The illness in 1983
came at a difficult moment for his regime, which had to cope simultaneously with a series of problems both at home and in the regional
and international arena. There has never seemed to be quite such a
correspondence between the state of health of President Asad and
that of his regime as there was at that time.

As will be recalled, the regime was enmeshed before 1982 in a
long and difficult campaign against the Muslim Brotherhood movement, which at its high point posed a serious challenge to the regime
and was perceived as a threat to its existence. Syria was also in the
midst of a grave crisis in the regional, inter-Arab and international
arena. The Lebanon war had weakened its regional status, if only
temporarily, and in addition Damascus was completely isolated
from the rest of the Arab world and on a collision course with the
United States and the West. The President's illness exacerbated this
state of crisis and put the question of succession squarely back on
the Syrian public agenda. The regime's ability to survive seemed to
depend on a solution to this question.

On the face of it, the Syrian constitution provided such a solution, as President Asad took pains to mention on many occasions.
For example, in a newspaper interview he granted in 1984 to *Le
Monde*, he was asked if the question of who would one day take his
place ever bothered him. He replied:

"No, I have never been troubled, for the simple reason that this question
has a solution in the Syrian constitution, which was ratified twelve years
ago in a referendum. The leadership of the Ba'th Party – a body number-
ing twenty-one members elected by the party members [the Regional Command,
*al-Qiyada al-Qutriyya*] – and, in addition, the People's Assembly, which is
the supreme legislative authority in the state whose members are elected
directly by the people, are those who will choose, by vote, a candidate to
stand in a referendum. If he wins a majority he will be President, and if not
they will have to propose [another candidate]."[9]

It is nonetheless clear that this solution was a formal one, which he
had alluded to purely for the sake of appearances. Since the Ba'th
Party seized control in Syria in the 1960s, the formal governmental
system, based on the constitution and on the legislative institutions,
was a façade for another ruling system – an informal one – in which
the real power in the state resided. This system includes the military
commanders and heads of the security forces. They maintain and

protect the regime, guarantee its stability, and have the power to decide its future. The status of some of these people is nominally anchored in their membership of senior institutions of the ruling Ba'th Party such as the Central Committee (*al-Lajna al-Markaziyya*) and the Regional Command (*al-Qiyada al-Qutriyya*). However, as past experience in Syria shows, their true power and authority lie ultimately in their direct control of the military forces and the security apparatuses. They have the power to mobilize these forces in time of need to defeat all imaginable rivals to the regime or, in the case in question, to enforce their will over who will succeed to the presidency.

Over the years these individuals have demonstrated unity in the face of the challenges and threats to the Syrian regime, particularly during the Muslim Brotherhood revolt of 1976-82. This unity stemmed from a shared communal-tribal and sometimes familial loyalty and, of course, from recognition of personal and existential interests in preserving the regime. Their personal fealty to President Asad was yet another factor, and was in this factor that the difference lay between the political reality in Syria since Asad rose to power and the conditions prevailing before his time, when the political system lacked a ruling center that maintained undisputed control over the various power centers in the state. It was Asad's ability to control this system that united these forces and held them in check. Over the years it kept internal disputes from erupting within the regime's ranks.

Asad's illness and temporary absence from the scene in November 1983 thus created a vacuum that was felt predominantly within the informal governing system, and when the system temporarily lost its restraining and unifying factor, it became clear that the former unity of the forces within Syria could not prevent the outbreak of a fierce struggle over succession within the ranks of the regime. Rif'at moved quickly to exploit his brother's temporary absence from the seat of power. He served as a member of the Ba'th Party Regional Command and fulfilled a series of key roles in the top echelon of the regime, chief of which was as commander of the Defense Companies (*Saraya al-Difa'*) – an elite force of division size, deployed near Damascus and designed to protect the regime. Many, himself included, perceived Rif'at as the number-two man in Syria and as his brother's heir-apparent. Now, while President Asad lay ill, Rif'at tried to secure his position as successor.

The immediate background to the eruption of the succession struggle within the Asad family is not altogether clear. In *Asad of Syria* Patrick Seale supplied the most detailed and, to all appearances, the most reliable description of events in Damascus at that time. According to him, a group of senior 'Alawi officers turned to Rif'at, and demanded that he assume leadership in view of the possibility that his brother would not recover. These officers hoped that in this way they would be able to assure the continuity of the regime, the special status of the 'Alawi community, and their own position in the state. Among them were several pillars of the regime: Shafiq Fayyad, then commander of the Third Division; 'Ali Haydar, head of the Special Forces; 'Ali Duba, head of military security; and Muhammad al-Khuly, chief of air force security. The steps taken by this group of officers came in response to Asad's decision to establish a six-man committee to manage Syria's daily affairs in his absence. The committee included the President's Sunni friends, some of them old rivals of Rif'at, such as 'Abd al-Halim Khaddam, Mustafa Talas and Hikmat Shihabi. Seale notes, however, that once it became clear that Asad was recovering, and furthermore not concealing his rage at his brother's attempt to defy him, those same senior 'Alawi officers were quick to abandon Rif'at and line up against him. Threatened and hurt, Rif'at responded by attempting to distance his rivals from the key positions they held in the branches of the administration, the party and the army, and to appoint others loyal to him in their stead. He also deployed the military forces faithful to him around Damascus and threatened to use them unless his demand was met.[10]

For several months the conflict between the Asad brothers threatened to turn bloody. However, at the last minute President Asad succeeded in preventing this. He and Rif'at confronted each other head-on in the presence of their elderly mother, whom the President had brought to the capital for this purpose from Qurdaha, the village of their birth. The resolution favored the elder brother,[11] and Rif'at was forced gradually to give up his power centers. Although he retained his membership of the Ba'th Party Regional Command, all his supporters and confidants in this body, the highest in the Ba'th Party hierarchy in Syria, were ousted. In March 1984, in exchange for this concession, Rif'at was awarded the nominal post of Vice-President, alongside two other vice-presidents appointed at the same time: 'Abd al-Halim Khaddam and Zuhayr Mashariqa. In November that same year Rif'at was named Vice President for National Security Affairs, but it was clear that the President had no intention of creating any real content to go with the title.[12] The Eighth Regional Congress of the Ba'th Party, held in January 1985, endorsed the renewed array of powers in the top echelon of government in Syria, thus making clear its approval of Rif'at's removal from that echelon. With the close of the Congress, Rif'at left for a lengthy exile in Europe, which lasted some eight years.[13] He was given leave to return to Syria only after the death of his mother in July 1992, apparently in accordance with her will.[14]

On 10 February 1985 a referendum endorsed Asad's candidacy for a third seven-year term.[15] After that, the question of succession became less acute. During the 1980s, involvement with this question lessened both within Syria and beyond for a number of reasons: first, Asad appeared to be healthy and, therefore, no immediate naming of an heir was necessary. Second, Rif'at seemed to have dropped his claim, or at least he remained silent about it. Third, it was possible that in the President's view no suitable and mature heir had yet been found who could command the institutions of government. Therefore, he refrained – perhaps deliberately, for the sake of expediency and convenience – from dealing with the succession issue, and it remained unresolved.

In the early 1990s the President changed his mind. In contrast to his past tendency to put off dealing with the issue of succession, he decided that the time had come to resolve it. Several reasons seemed to have underliain this decision, the chief of which was the coming of age of his son Basil. The latter, who had always been regarded as the talented and preferred son, chose – or more likely was sent – to follow in his father's footsteps and build up a military career as the basis for a future role in politics. In 1990-3, Basil's military career gathered momentum, culminating in his appointment as a brigade commander in the Republican Guard.[16]

At the same time, there were increasing signals from Damascus that Asad intended to name his son as heir. These were meant in part to test public reaction, and perhaps also to prepare the ground in Syria for an official and binding declaration of Basil as the successor. First, Basil was gradually given more exposure to the broader Syrian public, most of whom had known little of him before this time. Attention was focused primarily on his athletic activity as leader of the Syrian Olympic equestrian team.[17] Second, in the course of a referendum held in December 1991 to endorse the President's candidacy for a fourth term, Basil's picture was distributed alongside ones of his father. In speeches at assemblies and demonstrations, and on placards and posters, Asad was called "Abu Basil" (Father of Basil), although he had previously been referred to as Abu Sulayman, after his grandfather.[18] Finally, the Arab press outside Syria issued numerous reports of the intention to appoint Basil as his successor,[19] some of which apparently originated in leaks emanating from Damascus.

If Asad had indeed decided on Basil as his heir, this decision was anchored in the character and nature of the regime, which was not merely a military one. It had a sectarian, tribal and familial hue, and was also identified closely with the work and image of President Asad, who had established it and maintained it for twenty-two years. Finally, as has already been noted, Asad was influenced by a number of dictatorial communist regimes with a family orientation, and maintained especially firm relations throughout the 1970s and '80s with the regimes of Kim Il Sung in North Korea and Nicolae Ceauşescu in Romania.

Nevertheless, the signals from Damascus only expressed an inclination and not yet a clear decision to name Basil as successor. It should be remembered that he was thirty-two years old at the time of his death. He was inexperienced in managing affairs of state and it is doubtful if his public image and status – compared to other personalities in the top Syrian echelon – afforded him an adequate basis for claiming the top position. It also happens that the Syrian constitution specifies that only a Syrian citizen at least forty years old may serve as president,[20] and while this is a formality and therefore subject to change, it was enough to raise the question of Basil's youth and lack of the necessary personal and political maturity. It could therefore be presumed that Asad – with his customary caution and patience – intended that the process of "building" Basil or of transferring governmental authority to his hands would be as protracted as possible. This process would begin in his own lifetime, while he was still at the height of his power and strength, in order to help his son overcome the obstacles in his path.

The question of succession was complicated in the summer of 1992 by the return, after the death of their mother Na'isa al-Asad, of Rif'at from prolonged exile in Western Europe. Rif'at's return started a wave of rumors and conjectures about its probable impact on the constellation of forces in the higher leadership of the country.[21] But Asad did not restore his brother's former authority and powers. The Syrian media did not mention his name, or even report that he had returned. Foreign media, on the other hand, reported that Rif'at was completely isolated and even under a kind of house arrest.[22] This was enough to attest to President Asad's continued distance and even hostility toward his brother, whom he clearly did not regard as a suitable and worthy successor. Patrick Seale's book, based on his interviews with Asad, offers a glimpse of this negative attitude. The descriptions of Rif'at, especially in the section of the book dealing with the power struggle between the two brothers in 1983-4, are far from complimentary. Seale paints Rif'at as unbalanced, brutal and corrupt, and hints that he was no more than a puppet in the hands of the Americans and Saudis, who tried to use him in those years to topple his brother.[23]

## After Basil's death – the rise of Bashar

The succession issue took a dramatic turn after the death of Basil al-Asad on 21 January 1994 in a car accident on his way to Damascus airport.[24] His death stunned the country, and five days of national mourning were declared. In addition to the President and his family, hundreds of thousands of Syrians took part in the funeral processions in Damascus and in Qurdaha, where Basil was buried. The President led the cortège, and some of those present described him as being in a state of shock and radiating a palpable sense of sorrow. It was also reported that his escorts physically supported him and that he burst into tears during the funeral.[25]

The grief of the Syrian public was understandable since Basil had enjoyed great popularity across the country: he was young, strong and handsome, and was often described as courteous, educated – he spoke many languages – and as manifesting honesty, diligence and humility. In contrast to other government figures and close associates of the elite, his name was never linked to corruption and he was known for the unequivocal war he waged on graft in the state's administrative apparatuses.[26]

There were other, deeper reasons for the grief over Basil's death. For members of the 'Alawi community, among them members of President Asad's tribe and family, he served as a guarantee of their continued rule over Syria. and, for many outside the 'Alawi community, as a promise of continued relative political and economic stability in the state. He may also have been perceived as certain to carry on his father's policy, which at the time was marked by improving relations with the United States and the West, as well as participation in the peace process.

On Basil's death, Asad's second son Bashar was called home from Britain where, as already mentioned, he worked as a hospital intern. His father immediately sent him on a crash course of military training, including courses for tank battalion commanders and for command and staff, which are important stepping stones in the formation of the Syrian army's senior officer corps. He succeeded Basil as a brigade commander in the Republican Guard,[27] and in July 1997 it was reported that he had been promoted to *muqaddam* (lieutenant-colonel), and in January 1999 this was followed by his further promotion, greatly accelerated, to '*aqid* (colonel).[28] This was a rapid rise indeed, considering that on his return to Syria he had held no more senior rank than *naqib* (captain). Syrian sources explain Bashar's rapid rise as due to his "overall excellence in the staff officers' course, and in the outstanding final project he submitted as part of the course for command and staff ".[29]

From the time he returned home Bashar was given extensive media coverage in Syria. During the memorial ceremonies for his brother he was hailed as Basil's successor and torchbearer. He also stepped into his brother's shoes in other activities that he had sponsored, including equestrian competitions and conferences on computer technology (he served, incidentally, as chairman of the Syrian Computer Association).[30] In articles about Bashar's effort to promote the use of computers, there was a clear effort to describe him as open-minded and enlightened, and aware of Syrian society's need to catch up with developments in computer technology in the world at large. Thus the press highlighted his efforts to promote the use of the Internet in Syria.[31] Bashar granted an interview to *Al-Hayat* in which he boasted of his mastery of the Internet and spoke of efforts to integrate Syria into the worldwide web, and "get Arab information and views on to the Internet so that it isn't dominated by the other side [Israel]."[32]

In January 1997 the newspaper *Al-Thawra*, organ of the Syrian government, published an article by Dr Bahjat Sulayaman, a close friend of Bashar, virtually crowning him as his father's successor. The article stated, *inter alia*:

Bashar has proven within a short time that he is a branch of the blessed tree. Indeed, this branch has rapidly grown into a solid trunk that answers the call of his brethren of the homeland to fulfill Basil's mission and protect the legacy of the great leader on the path to the third millennium. With Basil's departure, the hope and the dream vanished, but soon a spark of new hope appeared. The citizens of Syria loved Basil, because they regarded him as a symbol of the continuity of the Arab struggle that Asad led. They turned to Bashar because he is Asad's son and Basil's brother, and made him their new symbol; they expect him to translate their conceptions into practical language.[33]

Bashar's growing involvement in the Lebanese arena should be emphasised, especially in the light of the marginalization of Vice-President 'Abd al-Halim Khaddam, who in the past had been responsible for the "Lebanese file". Bashar was known for his contacts with such Lebanese leaders as Sulayman Tony Faranjiyya, grandson of the former Lebanese President, Sulayman Faranjiyya, and scion of a family with whom the Asad family had maintained firm ties for many years. Bashar also began to visit Beirut periodically and hold well-publicized meetings with the official Lebanese elite, members of the opposition in the Christian and Muslim camps, and even with Hizballah leaders. In December 1998 Bashar was involved in the replacement of the Prime Minister, Rafiq al-Hariri, a close associate of Khaddam, by Salim al-Huss.[34]

Apart from dealing with the Lebanese issue, Bashar now also became involved in foreign policy, although he had shied away from it when he first returned to Syria after his brother's death. In February 1999, after the death of King Husayn of Jordan, Bashar paid a condolence call on King 'Abdallah, and in April and November 1999 met the king again during the latter's visits to Damascus.[35] King ' Abdallah boasted of this tie with the son of the Syrian President as expressing the spirit of hope in relations between the two states, and praised Bashar for being "like himself, of his generation, the Internet generation".[36] In July 1999 Bashar made a visit to Saudi Arabia to consolidate links with the Saudi leadership, and in the course of it also went to Mecca.[37] The latter visit was undoubtedly intended to give his candidacy religious legitimacy and avoid any repetition of the scandal that surrounded his father's candidacy for the presidency, when it was claimed that 'Alawis were not true Muslims. As well as Saudi Arabia, Bashar visited most of the Gulf states, and in November 1999 made his first formal visit to the West, to France, where he met Jacques Chirac.[38]

Reports from Damascus relayed Bashar's growing role in the army command and other sections of the Syrian security apparatus. It became clear that he had become involved in appointments and promotions in the army, and that he was regularly present at training sessions and other military exercises.[39] Indeed, from mid-1994 President Asad made a visible effort to establish support bases for Bashar within the Syrian military. This was apparently behind a wave of new appointments – unprecedented in scope – in the upper echelons of the army command, particularly at the intermediate levels among divisional commanders. In this framework promotion was given to young 'Alawi officers, most of whom were unknown and apparently associates and supporters of Bashar.[40] One day, the Asad family hoped, these officers would give Bashar the necessary support in the struggle for the succession. Among them were *liwa'* (Major-General) 'Ali Hasan, who replaced 'Adnan Makhluf as commander of the Republican Guard. Makhluf was a nephew of the President's wife, and had served in this post since the Guard's establishment. The prelude to his dismissal was a personal quarrel between him and Bashar from which Bashar emerged with the upper hand. Alongside this, 'Asaf Shawkat, who is married to the President's daughter Bushra, established himself in military security and was mentioned as a possible successor to its head, 'Ali Duba.[41]

A high point of this process was the pensioning-off of Hikmat Shihabi, the Chief of Staff, on 1 July 1998, after twenty-four years in the post.[42] Shihabi was seen, certainly by himself, as the number-two man in Syria, second only to the President, and his name was frequently mentioned as a possible successor to him when the time came – this in spite of his Sunni extraction and having no real support base in the army and security apparatus. His removal in July 1998 thus cleared a real obstacle in Bashar's path to the top. Shihabi's place was taken by 'Ali Aslan, a career soldier, an 'Alawi, and a member of Asad's tribe, and the fact furthermore that Aslan is an 'Alawi and a military man not involved in political affairs clearly reinforces Bashar's standing further.[43] The excuse for Shihabi's ousting was that, according to the Military Service Law, an *'Imad* (General – Shihabi's rank) was supposed to retire at the age of sixty-seven (Shihabi's age). Aslan was sixty-six on his appointment and a decree was soon published in Damascus raising the age of retirement to seventy.[44]

Despite the widespread skepticism over Bashar's rise noted above, there was a recognizable acceptance, albeit without enthusiasm, of Asad's desire as a father that his son should take his place. This acceptance of the situation was basically dependent on the notion that the President would have the time needed – a few more years – to prepare his son for the job.[45] Asad was asked outright in an interview with French television in July 1998 if he viewed Bashar as his heir. Characteristically he avoided the question, answering: "I am not preparing my son to take my place, nor have I ever heard him speak of this matter. It seems to me that the fact that such a possibility is mentioned derives from his activity, which earns him the esteem and love of his colleagues, as well as respect among the residents of the country. As for the issue of succession, there is no clause whatsoever in our constitution that gives the right of succession to family members."[46] Thus Asad did not repudiate in the interview the possibility that his son would one day succeed him but, true to his cautious and hesitant nature, he made clear that he was leaving time to do its work, and that he was not leaning toward any hasty, premature steps that might cause unnecessary shocks in the leadership and among the Syrian public.

## The end of the 1990s – Asad in decline

Asad's heart attack in November 1983 was the main cause of the struggle over the succession between him and his brother Rif'at which lasted for most of 1984. Because Asad's health improved, the question was removed, at least temporarily, from the Syrian agenda from 1985 till the beginning of the 1990s. This also enabled Asad to groom his two sons – first Basil and, after his death, Bashar, – as his successors. But during the 1990s there was a clear deterioration in his health, and during his last few years he barely seemed to be functioning and his health was clearly in rapid decline.

Indeed, from the beginning of the 1990s Asad's daily schedule consisted of no real activity. He rarely left his palace and only infrequently held meetings. He had long since lost any interest in running the country's day-to-day affairs and in his last years his health prevented him from managing them efficiently. He had almost completely cut himself off from direct contact with the population. He had ceased visiting army camps, factories and agricultural projects around the country, and only travelled to Damascus airport to receive foreign dignitaries, to the Najha military cemetery outside the city to lay a wreath on the grave of the unknown soldier on Army Memorial Day (May 6) and on the anniversary of the October war (October 6), and to the grave of his son Basil on the anniversary of his death, January 21. During the last five years Asad's travels abroad were limited to one or two trips each year: he went to Iran in July and November 1997, to France in July 1998, to Russia in July 1999, and made a few short trips, mainly to Egypt, each lasting less than a day.

Asad severely limited his addresses to the Syrian public in speeches to the nation and media interviews. In the past he had addressed the country once a year on March 8, the anniversary of the Ba'th revolution, but he discontinued this ritual obligation after 1990. In December 1998 the People's Assembly met for its first session following the parliamentary elections in November that year, and Asad deviated from his practice, established over many years of appearing to address the People's Assembly at its first session following an election. The speaker of the assembly, 'Abd al-Qadir Qaddura, laconically explained that the President was absent because he was suffering from "a severe cold".[47]

During the entire decade of the 1990s Asad addressed the Syrian public just three times, the last occasion being September 1994, when he opened a session of the People's Assembly; the previous one had been in March 1992, when he began his fourth term as President. He made very few public appearances; one was before the Worker's Unions in December 1992, and another at a meeting of clerics in February 1996.[48] Asad gradually decreased his exposure to Arab and foreign media. The last full interview he granted was in July 1998 to French television during his visit to France; the previous had been in September 1996 to CNN.[49] He did, however, join in news conferences with Mubarak and Clinton.

In his last few years, Asad avoided talking to journalists in the course of visits or meetings with foreign dignitaries because of what was explained as a hearing problem – he had difficulty hearing the journalists' questions. However, even in the distant past journalists had been asked to state their questions in a loud voice. This problem was said to be the result of an injury he suffered during the failed attempt on his life in June 1980. That attack by members of the Muslim Brotherhood may partly explain why Asad closed himself off. Yet the main change in his work-patterns seems to have followed his severe heart attack in November 1983, from which he never fully recovered. His self-imposed isolation, and even his withdrawl into himself, was accelerated and even exacerbated with the death of his eldest son Basil in January 1994. In addition to everything else, there was also the simple problem of advancing age. Asad's birthday was long believed to be 6 October 1930, but Patrick Seale has suggested, following a visit to his birth town Qurdaha, that he may have been born in the mid-1920s. This would have made him some five years older than was generally supposed.

On 10 February 1999 Asad won the usual majority of 99.99 per cent of the votes at a referendum held to approve his candidacy for the presidency. On 12 March he arrived at the People's Assembly to be sworn in, more than a month after beginning his fifth presidential term. The swearing-in ceremony was shorter than usual, and in a departure from custom Asad did not then address the assembly. Later that day, the surprised deputies received copies of the address the President had prepared for them, and it was clear from its contents that it had been intended to be read from the speaker's podium.[50] Several of the deputies who were fortunate enough to shake Asad's hand immediately after he was sworn in discovered to their amazement that he found it difficult to recognize some of them or address them by name.[51]

Asad's disappearance from Syrian public life compelled one newspaper, *Al-Thawra*, to publish in January 2000 an editorial with an explanation of Asad's absences: "It is only natural that the President is not always unoccupied or in perfect health, and therefore the citizens of Syria, who love Asad and are anxious and worried because they do not see him, really have nothing to worry about in this respect."[52] But Asad's physical health, and even more his mental health, were deteriorating. The Israeli press quoted a Central Intelligence Agency (CIA) report that he suffered from dementia and did not have long to live.[53] Israeli intelligence sources tended to disagree with the report, but considered that he appeared to be "mummified" and that his death could only be a matter of "between one day and three years". His appearance had changed so that, according to some descriptions, he looked like a "walking cadaver".[54] Statesmen who met him in his last years noted a dramatic decline in his ability to function. He could no longer hold lengthy meetings, found details difficult to remember and sometimes withdrew into himself, losing contact with his interlocutor.[55]

Foreign leaders seemed to start making decisions based in part on the expectation of Asad's demise. A senior Israeli official stated early in 2000 that Israel must be quick about reaching an agreement with Damascus because "Asad will not be with us for very much longer, and in effect the window of opportunity to reach a peace agreement with him while he is still relatively able to reach this agreement and recruit the necessary support for it in Syria will be open for only a few months."[56]

## Assuring Bashar al-Asad's succession

All this propelled Asad, his son Bashar, and their close family and associates to make great efforts to ensure Bashar's succession. To this end a series of significant steps were made to ensure a smooth transition. First, as will be recalled, Asad ousted the three other potential candidates from Syrian political life, starting with his brother Rif'at who was dismissed from his position as vice president in February 1998;[57] the Chief of the General Staff, Hikmat Shihabi, was pensioned off in July 1998 after having serving in this post for twenty-four years;[58] and Vice President 'Abd al-Halim Khaddam was stripped of most of his authority in the sphere of foreign relations (this had mainly concerned the Lebanese and Iranian portfolios).[59] Shihabi and Khadam, who had been thought of as possible compromise candidates to succeed Asad, are both Sunnis, whereas most of the senior Syrian army officers who might decide the fate of the Syrian presidency are 'Alawis.

Second, Asad ousted the old guard in the army and security apparatuses whose loyalty to Bashar was in doubt, but who had filled key positions from the time the President rose to power and who had ensured the survival of his regime. In June 1999 the commander of the Air Force, Muhammad al-Khuli, was pensioned off, along with the deputy head of the general security directorate, Muhammad Nassif Khayr Bek. The head of the general security directorate is 'Ali Khuri, an Isma'ili, but Bashar's close friend Major-General Bahjat Sulayman became the strong figure there.[60] In February 2000, 'Ali Duba, the head of the military security department, was retired and replaced by Major-General Hasan Khalil, with Major-General 'Asaf Shawkat, the husband of Bashar's sister Bushra, playing a leading role in the department.[61] A host of veteran officers, mainly divisional commanders, were dismissed and replaced by relatively young men, who were considered to be close to Bashar. Bashar was undoubtedly exploiting the vacuum created by his father's absence to take over his authority in spheres of activity he had once reserved for himself.

The decision made by the Syrian authorities to take the former prime minister Mahmud az-Zu'bi to court on charges of corruption, which led to Zu'bi's suicide, was probably part of Bashar's efforts to project the image of a clean leader. At the same time, this decision was a signal to his rivals, especially the old guard, that he would not hesitate to act against them with his father's backing. However, Zu'bi was perceived as weak – which may suggest that Bashar did not feel strong enough to directly confront the old guard and so preferred to deal only with Zu'bi.[62]

Third, the decision to convene the Ba'th congress on 17 June 2000 after a break of fifteen years and to appoint Bashar as a member of the Regional Command of the party, the highest political body in Syria, should be considered proof of Asad's having decided to accelerate the process of cultivating his son as his successor.

## Smooth transition and the challenges ahead

Over the years, since the death of Basil al-Asad, various commentators and experts devoted considerable discussion to whether or not his younger brother Bashar would be able to take his father's place and be appointed president. Their question has been answered affirmatively. On 10 June 2000, the very day on which Asad died, the the Syrian parliament undertook an accelerated legislation process to amend the constitution, so as to enable Bashar, who is aged thirty-four, to become president. On 17 June the Ba'th congress appointed him general secretary of the party and a candidate for the presidency. The latter was approved by the parliament and by the Syrian people in a well-organized and state-controlled referendum.[63] Bashar became president of Syria, but the main question remains unanswered: will he succeed in stepping into his father's oversized shoes, in stabilising his rule and in surviving as his father did for thirty years?

By the time of his succession Bashar had been recognized for several years as an open-minded Western-educated young man, aware of events in the world, and especially of Syria's need to join that world after thirty years behind the wall of isolation created by Hafiz al-Asad. The Western press has written extensively of his skills as an Internet surfer,[64] but these are not the qualities he most needs. He will survive only if he shows determination, leadership capabilities, charisma and finally the necessary degree of brutality towards his enemies at home. Does he have the "killer instinct"? Only time will tell, but everything depends on it.

Indeed, the formation of the new Syrian government in March 2000 provided insight into Bashar's limitations. It was portrayed as a clear example of determination to tread a new path of reform and modernization, mainly in economic spheres, as well as being the result of Bashar al-Asad's personal choice, and thus an expression of the desire to take over the management of Syria's day-to-day affairs.[65] If that was the case, the new government raised serious questions regarding Bashar's ability to influence matters and the direction in which Syria is really going. Far from manifesting a new spirit coursing through Syria, the government expressed only the existing state of decay and stagnation.

In spite of the praise heaped upon the new prime minister, Mustafa Miru, as an unblemished individual whose appointment marked the beginning of a new era in Syrian politics, the man was in fact a second-rate party hack. Aged fifty-nine had been a member of the Ba'th party since 1966, and before his appointment as prime minister he had served as a governor for twenty years of the Dar'a district in 1980-6, of the Al-Hasaka district in 1986-93 and of the Aleppo district in 1993-2000). He was born in a village north of Damascus and represents the Sunni rural sector, which is a junior partner in the Asad coalition. He is related to other leaders: his wife is the sister of 'Abdallah al-Ahmar, assistant secretary-general of the National Command of the Ba'th Party. Miru holds a doctorate from the University of Moscow in Arabic language and literature. The conclusion to be drawn was that Bashar's man who was supposedly to revolutionize Syrian life is nothing more that a rank-and-file politician from the back benches of the Ba'th Party, and his ability to lead his government along a new path is doubtful.[66]

The media underscored the fact that twenty-two out of the thirty-four ministers in the new cabinet were new faces – among them were 'Adnan 'Umran, who replaced Muhammad Salman as minister of information and Maha Qannut, who replaced Najjah al-'Attar as minister of culture. However, two facts need to be emphasised. First, all of the ministers came from the upper or middle echelons of the Ba'th Party or the government bureaucracy; like Miru, they represent the old, discredited policies. Second, the holders of the key portfolios, especially those dealing with economic affairs, remained the same. The ministers of economy and finance, Muhammad al-'Imadi and Muhammad Khalid al-Mahayani, respectively, retained their portfolios in the new government despite a broad consensus inside and outside Syria that these men had failed in their tasks and represent a tired and ageing generation that finds new global economic realities difficult to understand.[67]

Why did this happen? It may reflect Bashar's inability to force his will on the party establishment and the government bureaucracy, who are afraid of the changes he wants to make, changes which

port in April 1986), and 'Ali Duba, as head of military security,
s involved in the suppression of the Muslim Brotherhood revolt
Hama in February 1982. This greatly hampered the regime's ef-
rts to improve Syria's image as an enlightened state, an essential
p to improved relations with the United States and the West gen-
ally.[78]

n the West and in Israel the claim was voiced that the present
litary and security elite in Syria would hinder the regime's effort
bring about a change in the country's political, social and eco-
mic orientation, fearing that such a change might weaken its position
d influence. In Israel some believe that this elite is likely to op-
se the signing of a peace accord with Israel if and when one is
nieved – due to the fear that in the "era of peace" a reduction of
ces in the Syrian army and a drop in its status are sure to follow.[79]
n if Syria's political orientation changes and it signs a peace ac-
d, the military and security force will almost certainly remain an
portant foundation for the stability and existence of the Damas-
regime. This is because the regime sees the main threat to stability
oming from within the state. Indeed, experience in other Arab
es such as Egypt suggests that this internal threat will increase
therefore the regime will continue to rely on its military and
lligence to cope with it. In this context one must mention the
e of *liwa'* (Major-General) 'Ali Haydar, commander of the Spe-
Forces. In July 1994 a report emerged from Damascus that he
been dismissed and arrested after he had criticized President
d and his policy. In addition to Haydar, several other senior of-
rs in the Special Forces, who were apparently his close associates
members of his family and tribe, were dismissed. Major-General
Habib, who led the Syrian expeditionary force during the Gulf
replaced Haydar.[80]
li Haydar had commanded the Special Forces for over two
des and was considered a pillar of the regime. The forces
er his command had played a central role in suppressing the
nic revolt of 1976-82, particularly the Hama uprising of Feb-
y 1982. He had sided with Asad during the power struggle
een the President and his brother Rif'at in late 1983 and early
and, together with several other high-ranking army officers,
the President his victory.[81] What lay behind Haydar's criticism
ad was never made clear, but it apparently grew out of personal
ration at not having been promoted in recent years in rank
osition, and perhaps also a sense that the end of his career
lose. Haydar's colleagues and peers, including Shafiq Fayyad
Ibrahim Safi, had become corps commanders, leaving him
nd.[82]

signify a deviation from the old ideological line, as well as the loss of
key positions through which these institutions and people have managed
state affairs till now. It is also possible that Asad did not give full
backing to his son, not wanting to upset the old guard and himself
apprehensive of too dramatic a change. Whatever the reasons, it
typifies both the limpness with which Syrian affairs have been managed for many years, marking time, and Bashar's vulnerability.[68]

Against this background it is well understood that in order to
survive Bashar also needs to secure, as his first mission, the support
of the Asad family, the 'Alawite community, the military and the
security forces for himself and his regime. It is within the immediate family that he does not enjoy total support. His father's brothers
Rif'at and Jamil, expressed reservations about his candidacy more
than once in the past, and Rif'at was quick to challenge his legitimacy as an heir to the succession.[69] Even the old guard in Syria, who
were gradually removed from positions of power and influence, still
maintain a considerable number of foci of power. Early in 2000,
while Asad was alive, Edward Djerejian, a former US ambassador in
Damascus, noted that Duba, Khuli and other old-guard figures –
men whose vigor is far from being diminished and who are still
smarting over their removal from positions of power – are lying in
wait for Bashar to make his first mistake to settle accounts with him.[70]

Syria's leaders, led by commanders of the military and heads of
the security services, have unquestionably learned the lessons of past
experience, especially that of Rif'at's rebellion in 1983-4. Therefore
there was nothing unexpected in their readiness to consolidate at
any price a united front of the top echelon of the regime – at least
toward the outside world – and to support Bashar al-Asad in order to
avoid arousing an internal threat to the regime's stability or to its
very existence. Had the leadership shown hesitation, weakness or
factionalism, this threat could emerge against a background of Islam,
or from the demand for more economic and political liberalization.

As far as Rif'at is concerned, there is much doubt whether he
should be considered a threat to Bashar for the time being. As has
been mentioned above, on returning to Syria in 1992 after his lengthy
exile in Europe he carefully kept a low profile, yet it seems that he
had not given up his political ambitions. He acted behind the scenes,
especially abroad, to strengthen his position as possible successor.
One important instrument at his disposal was the media. He owns
several newspapers, a radio station and a television station, through
which he took pains to remind everyone of his existence and to
strengthen his image and status. He has presented himself as a
statesman and man of the world, not only in the 'Alawi community
or even in Syria, but throughout the Arab world.

In February 1997 the establishment of the Arab People's Democratic Party (*Hizb al-Sha'b al-'Arabi al-Dimuqrati*) was publicized in London. The party's slogan was "Solidarity, Democracy, Unity and Freedom", seemingly based on the historic slogan of the Ba'th Party, "Unity, Freedom and Socialism".[71] The editor of the party organ, which made its first appearance that month in London under the banner *Al-Sha'b al-'Arabi*, is Sumar al-Asad, Rif'at's son, who also heads the board of directors of a new Arab satellite television station, the Arab News Network (ANN), which began broadcasting from London in October 1997, apparently with Saudi and Lebanese funding.[72] It will be recalled that Darid, another of Rif'at's sons, published the monthly *Al-Fursan* in Paris up till 1992. At the time he also contributed to his father's struggle to survive.

The steps that Rif'at was taking angered his brother, President Asad. On 8 February 1998, a Presidential Decree was issued in Damascus stripping Rif'at of his title of Vice-President for Security Affairs – a title without any function which he had held since late 1984. According to reports from Damascus, he was for a time placed under house arrest,[73] and at the end of 1999 he left Syria for renewed exile in Europe, and expanded his political activities (for example, holding meetings with Arab leaders). The President and his son Bashar then took further action against him. In late October 1999 security forces broke into one of Rif'at's houses and a landing-stage he kept near the Ladhiqiyya harbor, claiming that these were state lands. This was meant to make clear that Asad rejected Rif'at's assumed status of successor and that Bashar, with power enough to spare, could face up to Rif'at.[74] It will be recalled that Asad clipped the wings of another brother, Jamil, who had served in the late 1970s as the "political boss" of the 'Alawi region. The President's break with Jamil took place concurrently with the power struggle that erupted between him and Rif'at in 1983-4, and apparently stemmed from his sense that Jamil had not leapt to his side fast enough.[75]

Despite Rif'at's weakened position, he is still the most recognized and senior 'Alawi personality after his nephew Bashar, and if Bashar should prove a weak and incapable leader, the 'Alawi community, the Kalbiya tribe and the Asad family could come flocking to Rif'at's side: this is because, in the absence of an acceptable 'Alawi successor, they could lose control to the Sunni community. It will be recalled that in November 1983, when the 'Alawi officer corps realized that from his sickbed Asad had handed over the reins of practical leadership to his Sunni colleagues, led by Shihabi and Khaddam, they hastened to close ranks – even if only temporarily – around Rif'at al-Asad as the leader of the community, the tribe and the family.

Along with Rif'at, other senior 'Alawis were men[tioned] as possible contenders for the presidency – amon[g them com]mander of the Third Corps, Shafiq Fayyad, and th[e commander of] the Second Corps, Ibrahim Safi, formerly comma[nder of the Third] and First Divisions; the Chief of Staff 'Ali Aslan; [the com]mander of the Air Force, Muhammad al-Khuli, wh[o was] pensioned off in the summer of 1999; and the he[ads of] security bodies such as 'Ali Duba, former deputy [chief of the] head of military security, and 'Adnan Badr Hasa[n of the Po]litical Security Directorate.[76] Members of the you[nger] 'Alawi officers who, since the mid-1990s, have m[oved up] to senior command positions are not yet well enc[ugh known. It] is doubtful if they are ready to play a leading r[ole as a] contender from within their own ranks. It seem[s that the] young officers are close associates of Bashar or [have rela]tions to him, and are thus ready to give him their [support.]

### Syria's security and military leadership the regim[e's] asset turned liability

Against this background it is clear that the se[curity] leadership was an asset to the regime and cru[cial to] ensure its stability and its future. However, in re[cent years, indi]viduals who make up this top echelon have slow[ly become a drag] to the regime and an obstacle in its path. This [is because from the] early 1970s to the late 1990s there was no real c[hange] in many of the army and security services. The [leadership was] in place for a long time, and some of its memb[ers were] in poor health. 'Ali Duba, for example, serve[d in military] security from 1974 till 2000, and Ibrahim Saf[i and others] served as divisional commanders for mo[re than a decade] before their promotion in 1995 as corps comm[anders. This situ]ation had a patently negative effect on the e[fficiency of these] people, and fostered inefficiency and corrup[tion. It is clear] that any attempt to install Bashar, the young[er] generation, as successor to President Asad w[ould face] resistance. If they do support him, they will [consider] themselves his equals if not superiors, since i[t is thanks to them] that he rose to power and thanks to them tha[t he could] hold on to it. Finally, part of the Syrian securit[y elite is] identified with the dark and brutal side of the [regime.] Muhammad al-Khuli, who served as comma[nder of the Air Force] between 1993 and 1999, was accused of respon[sibility for the] affair (the attempt to blow up an El Al jet a[irliner).

In this context one must re-emphasise the tensions that emerged in Syria's top echelon with the replacement in recent years of many high-ranking officers. This process was designed to invigorate and pump new blood into the ranks of the military and security services, to ensure its effectiveness in the service of the regime and perhaps also its support for Bashar's standing as successor. It was natural that the rise of the young officers' corps should occasionally come at the expense of the old guard, who had to make way.

Haydar's specific case can be seen as typical, and as reflecting a general problem among the high-ranking officers of Syria's military and security services. They, like him, found themselves at the end of the road. Frustrated and despairing, and perhaps hoping to maintain their positions, they were apt to disrupt the internal cohesiveness of the Syrian leadership. When it became known that the Chief of Staff, Hikmat Shihabi, had been replaced on 1 July 1998, concern and unrest in the military leadership was anticipated, but it never happened. One reason was that, because of his Sunni origins, Shihabi lacked any real support. Moreover, he was old and in poor health and found it difficult to carry out his duties.[83] The removal of other major players in the military and the security services, like Khuli and Duba, also went ahead smoothly.

## *The next generation in the political leadership*

The issue of succession that today occupies Syria focuses on the image of Bashar and his place in the elite, but clearly he does not stand alone and uncontested. The problem is wider – extending beyond the military – and touches on the need for change in the ranks of the regime: a new generation needs to emerge, grow, and ultimately succeed the current generation of leaders not only in the military and security services, but in the civilian administration.

The old guard, members of President Asad's generation, still controls Syria. It is a generation of political and economic leaders faithful to the worldview that combines the pan-Arab nationalist concept that was current in the Arab world in the 1960s and '70s with a socio-economic derived from the former East European socialist regimes. The members of this generation have difficulty coping with the domestic, regional and international circumstances Syria faces today. They also need to find a way to integrate the state into the international political and economic system. Members of the old guard value their positions and are unlikely to give them up willingly. Bashar al-Asad's priority on stepping into his father's shoes is undoubtedly to establish for himself a loyal elite such as his father had.

*The sons of the veterans.* It should be mentioned that Bashar's emergence as his father's successor was hardly unique. Members of the Syrian elite emulated the example offered by President Asad and his sons. Sons have been fostered as heirs to the family *latifundia* founded by their fathers. Each of the current leading families of Syria seems to have established a kind of "division of labor" among its members, which incidentally resembles the custom of the notables who ruled Syria in the century before the Ba'th Party came to power in March 1963. One son might turn (or be directed) to a political or military career, another toward a business career, and sometimes one son is sent abroad to get a higher education or develop a business career and a family base beyond the state's borders against a time of need in the future. Thus Firas Talas, son of the Syrian Defense Minister Mustafa Talas, is a well-known businessman in Damascus; another son, Manaf, is an army officer and close associate of Bashar al-Asad, and Talas's daughter Nahid lives in Paris. Following the Ba'th Congress of June 2000 Manaf became a member of the Ba'th Party Central Committee. The sons of 'Abd al-Halim Khaddam, Jihad and Jamil, turned to business careers in Syria and another son lives overseas.[84] The 'Alawi military and security elite make sure to direct their sons firmly toward military careers, so that when the time comes they can succeed to their parents' positions of power. In the case of President Asad the eldest son, Basil, was groomed as heir-apparent; another, Mahir, went for a military career, and Bashar turned to medicine which he studied in Britain. Following Bashar's appointment as President, Mahir, who commands a tank battalion, became a member of the Ba'th Party Central Comittee. Another son, Majd, is incapable – apparently for medical and psychological reasons – of playing any political or military role.[85]

The sons of the elite seem not to form a cohesive group, nor do they yet play a prominent role in Syrian political life. Their rise to power arouses much criticism among the Syrian public, which was clearly expressed by the Syrian ambassador in Paris, Ilyas al-Najma, during a meeting he held with French businessmen in February 1997. Najma sharply attacked the sons of the elite for wanting to establish an economic base for themselves by exploiting their parents' status, and warned his audience against forming business liaisons with them.[86] In Damascus some accused this group of exploiting the recent Syrian policy of economic liberalization in a bid to take over the economy; this policy, it was argued, served a small group and not the broad business sector in the country.[87]

To conclude, the big question today in Syria is whether Bashar will succeed, after he has stablized his rule, in leading the people into a new path of change and openness, mainly in the economic signify a deviation from the old ideological line, as well as the loss of key positions through which these institutions and people have managed state affairs till now. It is also possible that Asad did not give full backing to his son, not wanting to upset the old guard and himself apprehensive of too dramatic a change. Whatever the reasons, it typifies both the limpness with which Syrian affairs have been managed for many years, marking time, and Bashar's vulnerability.[68]

Against this background it is well understood that in order to survive Bashar also needs to secure, as his first mission, the support of the Asad family, the 'Alawite community, the military and the security forces for himself and his regime. It is within the immediate family that he does not enjoy total support. His father's brothers Rif'at and Jamil, expressed reservations about his candidacy more than once in the past, and Rif'at was quick to challenge his legitimacy as an heir to the succession.[69] Even the old guard in Syria, who were gradually removed from positions of power and influence, still maintain a considerable number of foci of power. Early in 2000, while Asad was alive, Edward Djerejian, a former US ambassador in Damascus, noted that Duba, Khuli and other old-guard figures – men whose vigor is far from being diminished and who are still smarting over their removal from positions of power – are lying in wait for Bashar to make his first mistake to settle accounts with him.[70]

Syria's leaders, led by commanders of the military and heads of the security services, have unquestionably learned the lessons of past experience, especially that of Rif'at's rebellion in 1983-4. Therefore there was nothing unexpected in their readiness to consolidate at any price a united front of the top echelon of the regime – at least toward the outside world – and to support Bashar al-Asad in order to avoid arousing an internal threat to the regime's stability or to its very existence. Had the leadership shown hesitation, weakness or factionalism, this threat could emerge against a background of Islam, or from the demand for more economic and political liberalization.

As far as Rif'at is concerned, there is much doubt whether he should be considered a threat to Bashar for the time being. As has been mentioned above, on returning to Syria in 1992 after his lengthy exile in Europe he carefully kept a low profile, yet it seems that he had not given up his political ambitions. He acted behind the scenes, especially abroad, to strengthen his position as possible successor. One important instrument at his disposal was the media. He owns several newspapers, a radio station and a television station, through which he took pains to remind everyone of his existence and to strengthen his image and status. He has presented himself as a statesman and man of the world, not only in the 'Alawi community or even in Syria, but throughout the Arab world.

In February 1997 the establishment of the Arab People's Demo-
cratic Party (*Hizb al-Sha'b al-'Arabi al-Dimuqrati*) was publicized in
London. The party's slogan was "Solidarity, Democracy, Unity and
Freedom", seemingly based on the historic slogan of the Ba'th Party,
"Unity, Freedom and Socialism".[71] The editor of the party organ, which
made its first appearance that month in London under the banner
*Al-Sha'b al-'Arabi*, is Sumar al-Asad, Rif'at's son, who also heads the
board of directors of a new Arab satellite television station, the Arab
News Network (ANN), which began broadcasting from London in
October 1997, apparently with Saudi and Lebanese funding.[72] It will
be recalled that Darid, another of Rif'at's sons, published the monthly
*Al-Fursan* in Paris up till 1992. At the time he also contributed to his
father's struggle to survive.

The steps that Rif'at was taking angered his brother, President
Asad. On 8 February 1998, a Presidential Decree was issued in Damascus stripping Rif'at of his title of Vice-President for Security
Affairs – a title without any function which he had held since late
1984. According to reports from Damascus, he was for a time placed
under house arrest,[73] and at the end of 1999 he left Syria for renewed exile in Europe, and expanded his political activities (for
example, holding meetings with Arab leaders). The President and
his son Bashar then took further action against him. In late October 1999 security forces broke into one of Rif'at's houses and a
landing-stage he kept near the Ladhiqiyya harbor, claiming that these
were state lands. This was meant to make clear that Asad rejected
Rif'at's assumed status of successor and that Bashar, with power
enough to spare, could face up to Rif'at.[74] It will be recalled that
Asad clipped the wings of another brother, Jamil, who had served
in the late 1970s as the "political boss" of the 'Alawi region. The
President's break with Jamil took place concurrently with the power
struggle that erupted between him and Rif'at in 1983-4, and apparently stemmed from his sense that Jamil had not leapt to his side
fast enough.[75]

Despite Rif'at's weakened position, he is still the most recognized
and senior 'Alawi personality after his nephew Bashar, and if Bashar
should prove a weak and incapable leader, the 'Alawi community,
the Kalbiya tribe and the Asad family could come flocking to Rif'at's
side: this is because, in the absence of an acceptable 'Alawi successor, they could lose control to the Sunni community. It will be recalled
that in November 1983, when the 'Alawi officer corps realized that
from his sickbed Asad had handed over the reins of practical leadership to his Sunni colleagues, led by Shihabi and Khaddam, they
hastened to close ranks – even if only temporarily – around Rif'at al-
Asad as the leader of the community, the tribe and the family.

Along with Rif'at, other senior 'Alawis were mentioned in the past as possible contenders for the presidency – among them the commander of the Third Corps, Shafiq Fayyad, and the Commander of the Second Corps, Ibrahim Safi, formerly commander of the Third and First Divisions; the Chief of Staff 'Ali Aslan; the former commander of the Air Force, Muhammad al-Khuli, who was incidentally pensioned off in the summer of 1999; and the heads of the various security bodies such as 'Ali Duba, former deputy Chief of Staff and head of military security, and 'Adnan Badr Hasan, head of the Political Security Directorate.[76] Members of the young generation of 'Alawi officers who, since the mid-1990s, have moved up the ranks to senior command positions are not yet well enough known, and it is doubtful if they are ready to play a leading role in producing a contender from within their own ranks. It seems that most of the young officers are close associates of Bashar or owe their promotions to him, and are thus ready to give him their full support.

### *Syria's security and military leadership the regime's asset turned liability*

Against this background it is clear that the security and military leadership was an asset to the regime and crucial to the effort to ensure its stability and its future. However, in recent years the individuals who make up this top echelon have slowly become a liability to the regime and an obstacle in its path. This is because from the early 1970s to the late 1990s there was no real change of personnel in many of the army and security services. The leadership had been in place for a long time, and some of its members were ageing and in poor health. 'Ali Duba, for example, served as head of military security from 1974 till 2000, and Ibrahim Safi and Shafiq Fayyad served as divisional commanders for more than a decade before their promotion in 1995 as corps commanders.[77] Such a situation had a patently negative effect on the effectiveness of these people, and fostered inefficiency and corruption. It was also clear that any attempt to install Bashar, the youngest of the group by a generation, as successor to President Asad would encounter their resistance. If they do support him, they will presumably consider themselves his equals if not superiors, since it was thanks to them that he rose to power and thanks to them that he would be able to hold on to it. Finally, part of the Syrian security leadership has been identified with the dark and brutal side of the regime. For example, Muhammad al-Khuli, who served as commander of the Air Force between 1993 and 1999, was accused of responsibility for the Hindawi affair (the attempt to blow up an El Al jet at London's Heathrow airport in April 1986), and 'Ali Duba, as head of military security, was involved in the suppression of the Muslim Brotherhood revolt in Hama in February 1982. This greatly hampered the regime's efforts to improve Syria's image as an enlightened state, an essential step to improved relations with the United States and the West generally.[78]

In the West and in Israel the claim was voiced that the present military and security elite in Syria would hinder the regime's effort to bring about a change in the country's political, social and economic orientation, fearing that such a change might weaken its position and influence. In Israel some believe that this elite is likely to oppose the signing of a peace accord with Israel if and when one is achieved – due to the fear that in the "era of peace" a reduction of forces in the Syrian army and a drop in its status are sure to follow.[79] Even if Syria's political orientation changes and it signs a peace accord, the military and security force will almost certainly remain an important foundation for the stability and existence of the Damascus regime. This is because the regime sees the main threat to stability as coming from within the state. Indeed, experience in other Arab states such as Egypt suggests that this internal threat will increase and therefore the regime will continue to rely on its military and intelligence to cope with it. In this context one must mention the case of *liwa'* (Major-General) 'Ali Haydar, commander of the Special Forces. In July 1994 a report emerged from Damascus that he had been dismissed and arrested after he had criticized President Asad and his policy. In addition to Haydar, several other senior officers in the Special Forces, who were apparently his close associates or members of his family and tribe, were dismissed. Major-General 'Ali Habib, who led the Syrian expeditionary force during the Gulf War, replaced Haydar.[80]

'Ali Haydar had commanded the Special Forces for over two decades and was considered a pillar of the regime. The forces under his command had played a central role in suppressing the Islamic revolt of 1976-82, particularly the Hama uprising of February 1982. He had sided with Asad during the power struggle between the President and his brother Rif'at in late 1983 and early 1984 and, together with several other high-ranking army officers, won the President his victory.[81] What lay behind Haydar's criticism of Asad was never made clear, but it apparently grew out of personal frustration at not having been promoted in recent years in rank or position, and perhaps also a sense that the end of his career was close. Haydar's colleagues and peers, including Shafiq Fayyad and Ibrahim Safi, had become corps commanders, leaving him behind.[82]

In this context one must re-emphasise the tensions that emerged in Syria's top echelon with the replacement in recent years of many high-ranking officers. This process was designed to invigorate and pump new blood into the ranks of the military and security services, to ensure its effectiveness in the service of the regime and perhaps also its support for Bashar's standing as successor. It was natural that the rise of the young officers' corps should occasionally come at the expense of the old guard, who had to make way.

Haydar's specific case can be seen as typical, and as reflecting a general problem among the high-ranking officers of Syria's military and security services. They, like him, found themselves at the end of the road. Frustrated and despairing, and perhaps hoping to maintain their positions, they were apt to disrupt the internal cohesiveness of the Syrian leadership. When it became known that the Chief of Staff, Hikmat Shihabi, had been replaced on 1 July 1998, concern and unrest in the military leadership was anticipated, but it never happened. One reason was that, because of his Sunni origins, Shihabi lacked any real support. Moreover, he was old and in poor health and found it difficult to carry out his duties.[83] The removal of other major players in the military and the security services, like Khuli and Duba, also went ahead smoothly.

## The next generation in the political leadership

The issue of succession that today occupies Syria focuses on the image of Bashar and his place in the elite, but clearly he does not stand alone and uncontested. The problem is wider – extending beyond the military – and touches on the need for change in the ranks of the regime: a new generation needs to emerge, grow, and ultimately succeed the current generation of leaders not only in the military and security services, but in the civilian administration.

The old guard, members of President Asad's generation, still controls Syria. It is a generation of political and economic leaders faithful to the worldview that combines the pan-Arab nationalist concept that was current in the Arab world in the 1960s and '70s with a socio-economic derived from the former East European socialist regimes. The members of this generation have difficulty coping with the domestic, regional and international circumstances Syria faces today. They also need to find a way to integrate the state into the international political and economic system. Members of the old guard value their positions and are unlikely to give them up willingly. Bashar al-Asad's priority on stepping into his father's shoes is undoubtedly to establish for himself a loyal elite such as his father had.

*The sons of the veterans.* It should be mentioned that Bashar's emergence as his father's successor was hardly unique. Members of the Syrian elite emulated the example offered by President Asad and his sons. Sons have been fostered as heirs to the family *latifundia* founded by their fathers. Each of the current leading families of Syria seems to have established a kind of "division of labor" among its members, which incidentally resembles the custom of the notables who ruled Syria in the century before the Ba'th Party came to power in March 1963. One son might turn (or be directed) to a political or military career, another toward a business career, and sometimes one son is sent abroad to get a higher education or develop a business career and a family base beyond the state's borders against a time of need in the future. Thus Firas Talas, son of the Syrian Defense Minister Mustafa Talas, is a well-known businessman in Damascus; another son, Manaf, is an army officer and close associate of Bashar al-Asad, and Talas's daughter Nahid lives in Paris. Following the Ba'th Congress of June 2000 Manaf became a member of the Ba'th Party Central Committee. The sons of 'Abd al-Halim Khaddam, Jihad and Jamil, turned to business careers in Syria and another son lives overseas.[84] The 'Alawi military and security elite make sure to direct their sons firmly toward military careers, so that when the time comes they can succeed to their parents' positions of power. In the case of President Asad the eldest son, Basil, was groomed as heir-apparent; another, Mahir, went for a military career, and Bashar turned to medicine which he studied in Britain. Following Bashar's appointment as President, Mahir, who commands a tank battalion, became a member of the Ba'th Party Central Comittee. Another son, Majd, is incapable – apparently for medical and psychological reasons – of playing any political or military role.[85]

The sons of the elite seem not to form a cohesive group, nor do they yet play a prominent role in Syrian political life. Their rise to power arouses much criticism among the Syrian public, which was clearly expressed by the Syrian ambassador in Paris, Ilyas al-Najma, during a meeting he held with French businessmen in February 1997. Najma sharply attacked the sons of the elite for wanting to establish an economic base for themselves by exploiting their parents' status, and warned his audience against forming business liaisons with them.[86] In Damascus some accused this group of exploiting the recent Syrian policy of economic liberalization in a bid to take over the economy; this policy, it was argued, served a small group and not the broad business sector in the country.[87]

To conclude, the big question today in Syria is whether Bashar will succeed, after he has stablized his rule, in leading the people into a new path of change and openness, mainly in the economic

sphere. It appears, and Bashar has expressed himself on the subject before and since taking office as President, that his path will be one of change combined with continuity, since too dramatic a change, in a country that had been under iron-fisted rule for so long, is liable to cause the Syrian structure to collapse.[88] What does the future hold in store for Syria? Everything depends on Bashar al-Asad, his personality and the leadership qualities he demonstrates. Neverthless, the Asad era has ended, and the Bashar era has begun. As for how long this era will last, one can only wait and see.

Will the Syrian regime be able to hold its ground and survive under Bashar? What kind of regime will it become? There is no clear answer to these questions, which at the time of writing are all-important.

First, the regime does not today face a real threat to its stability or existence, and it is difficult to imagine such a threat – particularly an organized one – suddenly arising. For years the Islamic movement was the main focus of opposition to the regime – indeed the only one – but the regime dealt it so serious a blow that it has essentially vanished as an organized and active movement within the country. Its leadership is split and located mostly outside Syria, and in part is engaged in a search for means of reconciliation with the Damascus regime. While it should be assumed that Islamic sentiment still exists among parts of the Syrian public, and that the movement might one day revive, this is unlikely in the foreseeable future (see Ch. 9: "State, Society and Economy in the 1990s").

Second, even if an unexpected internal challenge does arise, the regime has the necessary strength to maintain its hold. It still enjoys significant support among wide segments of the Syrian population, as well as in the military and security services. The fact that members of the 'Alawi community make up the majority of the senior and junior general staff, and of the troops in the security units and some military ones, ensures that this support will continue. Moreover, it gives the regime freedom to act and make use of the army against its enemies. For example, it enjoyed that freedom of action in the course of suppressing the Islamic revolt in February 1982, when army units were sent against the civilian population in Hama.

However, alongside these two factors – military might and the ability, readiness and determination to employ it – there is another important element, and that is the unity of the Syrian leadership in the face of possible future challenges. This unity existed in the past and aided the regime in grappling with a series of challenges, but there is no guarantee that it will continue.

## NOTES

[1] See *Tishrin*, 22 January 1994; *Al-Hayat*, 22 January 1994; *Ha'aretz*, 23 January 1994.

[2] For a historical survey of the question of succession, see Alasdair Drysdale, "The Succession Question in Syria", *MEJ*, 39(2) (Spring 1985), pp. 246-57; Patrick Seale, *Asad of Syria*, pp. 421-40; Eyal Zisser, The Renewed Struggle over the Succession", *The World Today*, 50(7) ( July 1994), pp. 136-9; "The Succession Struggle in Damascus", *MEQ*, 2(3), 1995, pp. 57-64.

[3] See, for example, the report of Bashar's completion of the command and staff course in April 1997 as an outstanding graduate, *Al-Ba'th*, 17 April 1997.

[4] Eyal Zisser, "Syria" in Bruce Maddy-Weitzman (ed.), MECS, vol. XIX (1995), p. 595; vol. XX (1996), p. 634.

[5] *Ha'aretz*, 3 July 1998.

[6] Author's interviews with Syrian academics, Washington, DC, 23 June 1996, 11 June 1998.

[7] Author's interview with a Syrian academic, San Francisco, 23 November 1997.

[8] Moshe Maoz, *Asad*, p. 178.

[9] Radio Damascus, 1 August – DR, 2 August 1984.

[10] Seale, *Asad of Syria*, pp. 421-40.

[11] *Ibid.*, pp. 430-3.

[12] Itamar Rabinovich, "Syria" in Itamar Rabinovich and Haim Shaked (eds), MECS, vol. IX (1984-85), pp. 645-6.

[13] *Ibid.*, and see Seale, *Asad of Syria*, pp. 431, 433, 437.

[14] *The Independent*, 22 October 1992; *Liberation*, 23–24 January – DR, 27 January 1993.

[15] *Tishrin*, 12 February 1985.

[16] See 'Izzat al-Sa'dni, *Basil fi 'Ayun al-Misriyyin* (Basil in the eyes of the Egyptians) (Cairo: Al-Ahram, 1995).

[17] See, for example, *Al-Ba'th*, 12, 16 August 1992.

[18] On past references to Asad as Abu Sulayman, see Moshe Maoz, *Asad*, p. 34; see also *FT*, 18 March 1992.

[19] See *Al-Muharrir*, 30 March; *Akhbar al-Usbu'*, 25 June 1992.

[20] *Al-Thawra*, 1 February 1973; for the English version of the Constitution, see "The Syrian Arab Republic: The Constitution of 1973", *MEJ*, 28(1), 19XX, pp. 53-66.

[21] *The Independent*, 22 October 1992; *Liberation*, 23-24 January – DR, 27 January 1993.

[22] *Al-Sharq al-Awsat*, 10 February 1998; and see *NYT*, 10 January 1997; *Ha'aretz*, 8 February 1997.

[23] Seale, *Asad of Syria*, pp. 426-40.

[24] *Tishrin*, 22 January 1994; *Ha'aretz*, 23 January 1994.

[25] *Ha'aretz*, 23 January 1994; *Yedi'ot Aharonot*, 23 January 1994; *Al-Muharrir*, 1 February 1994.

[26] *Liberation*, 23-24 January – DR, 27 January 1993.

[27] See the report on his completion of the command and staff course as an outstanding graduate, *Al-Ba'th*, 17 April 1996.

[28] *Yedi'ot Aharonot*, 25 July 1997; *Al-Wasat*, 14 August 1997; *Al-Hayat*, 3, 5 January 1998.

[29] *Al-Wasat*, 14 August 1997.

[30] See the association's internet site: http://www.scs-syria.com

[31] See *Al-Ba'th*, 12 January 1997; *Tishrin*, 28 May, 14 July 1997; see also *Yedi'ot Aharonot*, 25 July 1997.

[32] *Al-Hayat*, 12 October 1997.

[33] *Al-Thawra*, 19 January 1997.

[34] See reports of Bashar's meetings with Tony Sulayman Faranjiyya, *Al-Watan al-'Arabi*,

23 May 1997; *Al-Bayraq,* 17 December 1997; see also *Nida' al-Watan,* 30 November 1998.

[35] *Al-Thawra,* 26 February, 23 April 1999.

[36] *Yedi'ot Aharonot,* 18 May 1999.

[37] Radio Damascus, 11, 12 July 1999.

[38] *Al-Hayat,* 8 November 1999.

[39] See, for example, Syrian Television, 15 August 1997.

[40] See Eyal Zisser, "Syria" in Bruce Maddy-Weitzman (ed.), MECS, vol. XIX (1995), p. 595.

[41] *Ibid.,* p. 595; Al-*Wasat,* 7 May 1995.

[42] *Ha'aretz,* 3 July 1997; Reuters, 3 July 1997.

[43] *Ibid.,* and see Seale, *Asad of Syria,* pp. 429-30.

[44] *Al-Hayat,* 29 January 1999.

[45] Author's interview with Syrian academics, Washington, 23 June 1996; 11 June 1998.

[46] Syrian Television, 15 July 1997.

[47] SANA, 17 December 1998.

[48] *Tishrin,* 15 December 1992; *al-Thawra,* 17 February 1996.

[49] *Tishrin,* 29 September 1996; R. Damascus, 15 July 1998.

[50] *Tishrin,* 12 March 1999 .

[51] Author's interview with a Syrian academic, New York, 13 October 1999.

[52] *Al-thawra,* 25 January 2000.

[53] *Ha'aretz,* 6 March 2000; *Daily Telegraph,* 30 April 2000.

[54] *Ha'aretz,* 6 March 2000.

[55] *Washington Post,* 6 March 2000; Israeli TV Channel 1, 20 March 2000.

[56] Interview with Uri Sagie, head of the Israeli delegation to the peace talks with Syria, Israeli TV Channel 2, 29 April 2000.

[57] SANA, 8 February 1998.

[58] *Al-Hayat,* 3, 5 July 1998.

[59] *Al-Safir,* 14 January 1999.

[60] *Al-Hayat,* 14, 29 June 1999; AP, 12, 13 June 1999.

[61] Reuter, 6 February 2000; *Al-Quds al-'Arabi,* 14 February, 25 April 2000.

[62] *Al-Hayat,* 11, 13 May 2000.

[63] SANA, 10, 17, 25 June, 10 July 2000.

[64] *Washington Post,* 24 April 2000.

[65] *Al-Hayat,* 8, 11, 13 March 2000.

[66] For Miru's biography see SANA, 7 March; *Al-Hayat* 8 March 2000.

[67] *Al-Hayat,* 16, 21 March; *Al-Quds al-'Arabi,* 16 March 2000.

[68] *Al-Quds al-'Arabi,* 16 March, 25 April 2000.

[69] ANN TV, 16 June 2000.

[70] Voice of Israel, 15 March 2000.

[71] *Al-Sha'b al-'Arabi,* 21 July, 15 September 1997.

[72] *Al-Mushahid al-Siyasi,* 7 February 1997; *Al-Ittihad* (Abu Dhabi), 21 February 1997; *MM,* 28 May 1997.

[73] *Tishrin,* 9 February 998; and see *NYT,* 10 January 1997; *Ha'aretz,* 9 February 1998.

[74] Al-Hayat, 22, 23 October 1999.

[75] *Al-Aswaq,* 12 December 1996; *NYT,* 10 January 1997.

[76] Zisser, *Decision Making,* pp. 21-5.

[77] Seale, *Asad of Syria,* pp. 429-30

[78] *Ibid.,* pp. 339-40, 475-83.

[79] See *Ha'aretz,* 22 September 1994; *Yedi'ot Aharonot,* 25 November 1994.

[80] *Al-Hayat,* 25 October 1994; *Ma'ariv,* 4 September 1995.

[81] See Zisser, "Syria" in Bruce Maddy-Weitzman (ed.), MECS, vol. XVIII (1994), p. 613.

[82] *Yedi'ot Aharonot*, 25 November 1994.

[83] *Ha'aretz*, 3 July 1998.

[54] *Al-Wasat*, 13 May 1997; and see Seale, *Asad of Syria*, pp. 429-30.

[85] Zisser, *Decision Making*, pp. 18-21.

[86] *Al-Nahar*, 30 January 1997.

[87] Zisser, "Syria", in Bruce Maddy-Weitzman (ed.), MECS, vol. XX (1996), p. 638.

[88] *Al-Wasat*, 29 August 2000..

# 9

## STATE, SOCIETY AND ECONOMY
## IN THE 1990s

From the mid-1990s onwards signs increased of a lively public debate, particularly among the political and economic elite, over Syria's future path in the areas of domestic, social and economic policy. The debate attests to the bewilderment that had swept the elite of the Damascus regime, a sense that Syria had lost its way and reached an impasse. The challenges and difficulties facing the country since the start of the 1990s stepped up the controversy. Rapid decisions are crucial to ensuring economic and political stability, and will be particularly so in the post-Asad era. The 1990s, however, saw no such decisions being taken. The regime in its then political and personal composition hardly seemed capable of making them.

Two principal camps, representing opposing worldviews, have emerged in the debate over the country's future course. One consists of proponents of the political, social and economic *status quo*, who hope to prevent any real change that might undermine the regime. On the other side of the debate are a minority who maintain that if the regime is to survive the difficulties it faces in the regional, international and, especially, the domestic arena, it needs a completely new outlook and course.[1]

In an article published late in 1996 on the Syrian-Israeli peace talks, and on several other occasions, Patrick Seale predicted that until a solution to the conflict with Israel was found, Asad would hold back from deciding between the two camps, and in practice would preserve the *status quo* in the state. This was because he feared that any change could destabilize his regime and weaken his bargaining position with Israel. However, Seale speculated that once Israel and Syria reached an accommodation, Asad would turn his attention to domestic problems and their root cause. The Syrian elite would then have the political will and energy needed to generate a transformation in the domestic, social and economic areas. But this elite, led by Asad, drew back from any such transformation.[2]

Seale's forecast that the Syrian regime was ready to introduce real

179

changes in its policy, and that it was only waiting to achieve a peace agreement with Israel in order to begin the process, seemed premature and over-optimistic. It seemed that the prevailing attitude among that elite, certainly in Asad's inner circle which still controls Syria even after his death, was that the regime would be best served by maintaining the *status quo* in the state at any price and preventing any deviation from it.

The regime had introduced certain limited changes in its policy. Since the start of the decade and in the light of favourable economic circumstances, it had shown an openness in the economic sphere and taken measures to improve the standard of living and welfare of the population. However, these measures did not amount to a general change dictated from above; there was no accompanying vision of reform or of a new "Syrian order". On the contrary, it seems that many of the measures taken were tactical, designed to maintain rather than alter the existing situation. Moreover, the regime deliberately refrained from exploiting the favourable economic circumstances that were prevailing in Syria in the first half of the 1990s to bring about a structural and conceptual change in the economy. The government maintained its level of involvement in economic life, and no steps were taken toward privatization or a shift to a market economy.

This chapter attempts to characterize some of the key political, social, and economic issues on the Syrian agenda during the 1990s and to examine the way in which the regime treated them. The first of these issues centers on how the political system responded to the demand for greater democracy and the global challenge by opening its doors to the surrounding world. The second concerns the social and economic problems which have been pounding at the doors of the state since the start of the 1990s. Finally, there is the issue of the Ba'th regime's attitude toward the Islamic movement in Syria, which in the early 1980s represented a genuine threat. Treatment of these issues illuminates the depth of the problems facing the Syrian regime domestically; the method it has chosen to cope with them, if any; and Syria's path as it emerged over the decade – a path that preserved continuity yet, in spite of everything, was leading toward change.

## *The political system in Syria – and the growing demand for more openness*

For the Syrian regime the collapse of the Soviet Union posed a grave domestic challenge. The extinguishing of this great beacon which had guided Damascus for so many years cast doubts on the regime's *raison d'être* and fundamental values. The public reaction in Syria to events in Eastern Europe was hesitant, due to the prevailing social, economic and political conditions and the experience of three decades of harsh Ba'th rule. Even so, signs of dissatisfaction were reported. For example, graffiti comparing President Asad to Ceauçescu[3] attested to an expectation among certain sectors of the Syrian public that there would be more openness in political life and, especially, economic improvements. The regime did not ignore this dissatisfaction, and it recognized the necessity of acting to improve the standard of living and welfare of the individual, and to lessen social and economic hardship. However, there is no doubt that the primary lesson President Asad learned from the collapse of the Soviet Union and the ensuing public reaction in Syria was that any demand for change within the political system had to be curbed; any such change might spiral out of control and bring down disaster on his regime.

The speeches Asad gave during the 1990s offered a clear expression the regime's concern over the possible implications of the Soviet collapse for Syria. His address on 12 March 1992, marking the start of his fourth term as President, was mostly a response to the demand that the regime demonstrate more political openness – a demand, incidentally, which was only revealed for the first time in this very address. Asad rejected it outright: Syria, he explained, had a democratic system based on the historical and cultural heritage of the Syrian people. He admitted that there was room in it for improvement, but stressed that the Western democratic system was not suited to Syria and, therefore, could not replace its existing system. In his speech Asad went on:

"The democratic system our people adopted is not a fixed and rigid framework, and it does not lead to a dead-end. It lives, develops and is renewed in accordance with the political, economic, social, and cultural changes that we undergo. This democratic system is not like merchandise imported or exported from one country to another. It is a framework in which citizens manage their lives, achieve their rights and fulfill their duties... I once said to a foreign citizen visiting our country that the average per capita income in his country was 20,000 dollars a year. I added that, only when they [helped us reach an average per capita income of] 20,000 dollars a year, only then could they speak to us in praise of their democratic system. I told him also that their problems were not the problems that we deal with. They – the affluent – want us to implement their system, but we do not intend to do so, as such a system would impoverish us, take away our security and set us back, and we want to progress. Apart from this, each nation has its own tradition – history, culture, spirit, and frame of reference; otherwise all the peoples of the world would be a single nation, and that is not the case. From this cultural legacy and history grows our democracy... There are those, even in the Arab states, who speak in praise of democracy. Each of them imagines a different kind of democracy, the one that he favors. But he does not bother to search for the one most suitable [to the prevailing conditions in his country], rather he seeks to exploit something that another has created, or to wear another's mantle, without checking whether it is his size, or if it suits him."

Asad concluded his speech with an attack on those Western states that preached to Syria about its political system. He declared:

"Democracy has many faces. There is political democracy and social democracy, there is economic democracy and also – and this is important in relation to us, the peoples of the Third World – international democracy. It is therefore appropriate that the states waving the banner of democracy implement it in practice, especially when they engage in dialogue with other peoples, as happens in our case. They should also implement democracy in the international (relationship), and act to realize equality, integration, and freedom in relations between the states of the world."[4]

However, the collapse of the Soviet Union was not – as Asad perhaps had hoped – a passing event with merely symbolic or psychological significance. It caused more than a passing wave of graffiti, and sporadic demands for more political freedom and liberalization. No longer would Soviet political backing, economic aid or moral support help the Syrian regime to maintain the barricades it had erected against outside influences. Since the early 1990s Syria had found itself in the fast track toward exposure to the wider world. Economic and technological developments had started the process, and the collapse of international political barriers gave it momentum. Of course, the reverse might also have been true: increased exposure to the world at large could have led to the collapse of the old barriers, as satellite broadcasts, computerized communication, and the global economic market made them irrelevant.

The Syrian elite struggled against this process. It clearly feared the effects of exposure to the outside world, but at the same time became increasingly aware of its necessity. There could be no improvement in the country's regional and international status without progress in communications, technology and the economy. To achieve such progress, boost the economy and share in technological and scientific advances Syria had to open its doors to the world beyond its borders. The regime recognized that progress toward a market economy was essential to integration into the global economy. This recognition, coupled with its desire to foster economic ties with the West and receive economic aid, made it necessary to throw open the gates. Once the wonders of Western technology had begun to pass through those gates, the regime could not easily slam them shut.

Thus, readers of London's Arabic language *Al-Hayat* were surprised to read in October 1997 of Bashar al-Asad's proficiency in surfing the Internet. The President's son explained to the paper's correspondents that he recognized his country's pressing need to stay abreast of developments in computer technology. However, he also warned against unsupervised access to Internet sites because of the danger that they exposed the Syrian citizen to the values of a wider world.[5] Indeed only in late 1999 did ordinary Syrian citizens gain access to the Internet, apparently because the authorities had heeded Bashar's warning.[6]

The Internet was not, of course, the only problem keeping the Syrian leadership awake at night. As early as February 1994 the Information Minister, Muhammad Salman, granted an interview to the Saudi newspaper *Al-Majalla* in which he revealed that throughout Syria tens of thousands of unauthorized satellite dishes had been installed. He warned that the unsupervised watching of satellite television broadcasts from around the world presented a danger to the "morale, faith, and adherence to values" of the Syrian citizen.[7] To counter this problem the government hastened to establish a Syrian satellite television station (Channel 2) broadcasting Western movies and entertainment programs, even if only in rationed amounts to satisfy the Syrian information controllers (Channel 1 broadcasts mainly Arabic programmes).[8]

The concern provoked by technological advances among the Syrian political and security elite was not surprising. For many years the regime prevented the use of fax machines even for commercial and media purposes, but finally had to give way and allow their use after it became clear that thousands of machines had been smuggled into the country illegally from Lebanon. However the green light for the use of fax machines was given – so it was reported from Damascus – only after the security services acquired monitoring equipment that would enable them to keep track of the content of all faxes sent. A similar dilemma confronted the regime with the cellular telephone, the use of which it banned until late 1999.[9]

With voices at home calling for political and, in particular, socio-economic change, the regime adopted a series of steps designed to give the public a sense of increased political liberalization. Among these was the effort to give a democratic, popular flavor to the national referendums held to ratify the candidacy of President Asad for another term in December 1991 and February 1999, and to the elections for the People's Assembly (*Majlis al-Sh'ab*) in May 1990, August 1994 and November 1998. In addition, the regime broadened the Assembly's authority and areas of jurisdiction, and allowed candidates who were not members of the Ba'th or its satellite parties to run as independents. Another notable step was the release of thousands of political prisoners during the first half of the decade. Finally, the regime showed willingness to enlarge the dialogue with leaders of the Syrian Islamic movement, who in the past had been reckoned among its most bitter enemies.

The integration of independent, unaffiliated candidates to the People's Assembly and dialogue with parts of the Islamic movement reflected the regime's efforts to broaden its basis of support beyond its traditional strongholds (among the minority communities, the rural areas and the periphery, the military, and government and party apparatuses). Stability on the domestic front, or the establishment of "domestic harmony", was intended to enable the regime to turn its attention to regional and international problems, which it perceived as more pressing.

The steps taken by the regime were more than cosmetic and yet not enough to offer any substantial changes to the political reality and the structure of the governing system. The avoidance of any change in an effort to prevent domestic upheaval was clearly reflected in the regime's reluctance throughout the decade to convene a Ba'th Party Congress; according to the Party's constitution, one was required to meet every four years, but the last had been in January 1985. Past congresses had provided a forum for ideological and political deliberations, and a binding framework for the future policy path of the party. The congress also elected members of the party's senior institutions, namely the Central Committee and the Regional Command. Thus it seemed that the regime was seeking for the time being to prevent any discussion of its policies, having sensed that the path it had followed for so many years had led to a dead-end. Moreover, there was no ideologically appropriate replacement for its worldview, which had collapsed. It seemed also that the regime wished to avoid any discussion or decision on the manning of the party's senior institutions. Because these party institutions could influence the outcome of the struggle for the succession, it thus hoped to prevent political disquiet among its elite.[10] The Congress was finally convened in June 2000 following President Asad's death, and close Bashar as the Ba'th Party secretary-general.

*Release of political prisoners.* Between 1991 and 1995 over 5,000 political prisoners were released from Syrian prisons. In December 1991, on the occasion of Asad's election to his fourth term of office, 2,864 were freed; in March 1993 in honor of the start of this term, 600; and in November 1993 to mark the anniversary of the Corrective Revolution which had brought Asad to power, another 554. In November 1995, 5,300 prisoners were released, among them 1,200

cial and economic domain helped the latter to regulate
rol manifestations of dissatisfaction, anger and bitterness
e population generally. Lastly, the People's Assembly ena-
regime to outline and implement a policy of liberalization
er openness in economic life. The state's media exploited
ing deliberations in the Assembly, during which many
called for such a policy to be pushed forward, and for
ion concerning economic openness to be widely dissemi-
addition, the Assembly produced a great deal of legislation
implementing this policy, the high point of which was In-
Law no. 10 aimed at encouraging investment in the state,
May 1991 (see below).

olicy to accelerate economic liberalization drew criticism
ious sectors of the Syrian public – primarily from among
er strata, and the government and party bureaucracy. The
s of the People's Assembly resounded with such criticism,
presentatives of these sectors constituted the majority.
over these issues enabled the regime to steer the middle
etween these contradictory orientations toward economic
ation, however limited, and the desire to preserve the socio-
ic and political *status quo*.

## nd the economy – continuity and change

both the ability and the desire to introduce changes in the
's political life, the regime concentrated its efforts on the
nd economic spheres, which occupied a prominent place on
an agenda. This was after years in which they had been at
ttom of the national list of priorities, due mainly
lemands of the struggle with Israel. The regime focused on
allel goals: limited liberalization of the economy to encour-
nomic activity, and energetic efforts to raise the living standards
nasses, *inter alia* by broad investment in developing the eco-
nfrastructure.

*economic liberalization.* From the early 1990s, the Syrian gov-
nt adopted an economic policy characterized by more – if
tial – openness and readiness for a liberalization of the economy.
olicy was designed to encourage economic activity and create
urces of income and employment; also to ease Syria's inte-
into the world economy, an essential pre-condition in the
many for its future stability and economic prosperity. Such
nomic policy could also serve to win favor with various sectors
public, but in particular the Sunni urban elite whose political

political prisoners, this time to mark the twenty-fifth anniversary of
the Corrective Revolution.[11]

Among the prisoners released in the early 1990s were Asad's old
rivals from the time of the struggle for control in Syria (1966-70).
The former President, Nur al-Din al-Atasi, had spent over twenty
years in a Damascus jail since Asad ousted him in 1970, and having
been in poor health, died in December 1992 in Paris two weeks
after his release.[12] Also among those released were Muhammad
Rabbah al-Tawil, who had served as Minister of the Interior, and
Ahmad al-Suwaydani, Chief of Staff in1966-8.[13] Salah Jadid, Asad's
main rival from that period, remained behind bars until his death
on 19 August 1993.[14] The release – or demise – of these people had
only symbolic significance, but no practical implications since they
were too old and sick to pose any threat to the regime. It is unlikely
that they still enjoyed any support in Syria. More significant was
the release of thousands of members of the Muslim Brotherhood,
who had served time since the suppression of the Islamic Revolt in
the early 1980s. The regime's readiness to demonstrate "goodwill"
toward the Syrian Islamic circles was an important step in its efforts
to push forward its decade-long dialogue with their members – both
within Syria and beyond – with the goal of ensuring their support
(see below).

While the release of political prisoners was interpreted as a manifestation of the regime's self-confidence, it stemmed largely from
pressure both within Syria and from abroad. This gesture was an
attempt to demonstrate the new, more enlightened face of Syria
both toward the West and toward its own citizens. The regime's effort to revamp its image in the West also led to the decision in April
1992 to allow Syrian Jews to emigrate. Most of the community left,
leaving behind only a few hundred of its members.[15]

*More power to the People's Assembly.* For many years the conventional
view of the Syrian People's Assembly held it to be primarily a symbolic body devoid of decision-making power or ability to influence
the policy and measures of the regime. The past elections to it were
seen as lacking any political significance, and being at most cosmetic, to burnish the regime's supposedly democratic image. However,
since 1990 the importance and influence of the Assembly have
grown, if in a limited way, and it has begun playing a (relatively)
more prominent role in Syrian political life.

The People's Assembly thus began serving the regime as a tool
to advance its social and economic policy. The regime also began
to rely on the Assembly, more than it had done before, to release
existing pressures and tensions in Syrian society, in a controlled way,

or to soften the demand, restrained though it was, for greater democracy and the introduction of far-reaching social and economic reforms in the state.

In preparation for the elections to the Assembly that took place on 22 May 1990, the number of delegates was increased from 195 to 250. This was done in order to encourage additional forces that were not identified with the regime and were not part of it to take part in the Assembly. Eighty-four seats, or 40% overall, were set aside for candidates with no formal political affiliation. The remaining 166 were allotted to the National Progressive Front (*al-Jabha al-Wataniyya al-Taqaddumiyya*) – an umbrella organization comprising all the political parties active in Syria.[16] For the sake of comparison, in the 1986 Assembly elections only thirty-five seats were reserved for independent delegates (less than 20%).[17] These candidates ran as individuals rather than as members of political parties, and when citizens arrived at the polls they ticked off as many names on the ballot as were allotted to their voting district.

The Assembly that emerged from the August 1994 elections – and from the November 1998 elections as well – had almost the same proportion of independent delegates as the previous one (eighty-three delegates).[18] The regime prevented representatives of the National Progressive Front from running in the various electoral districts at the expense of seats set aside for independent candidates. Furthermore, it allowed independent candidates to form coalitions and alliances in preparation for the contest. In Aleppo, for example, in the August 1994 elections ten lists of independent candidates competed, while in Damascus manufacturers and merchants established a list called "*Dimashq al-Fayha*" (Damascus the great), and five of its thirteen candidates won seats. The press reported fierce competition among members on the list and between them and other lists.[19]

A significant proportion of the independent delegates elected to the People's Assembly represented a growing class of merchants and capitalists who had emerged in Syria following the policy of economic liberalization the regime had adopted since the early 1990s. This class set its sights on improving the economic situation, and was prepared to assist the regime to preserve political stability in the state, seeing it as a guarantee of the stability, growth and prosperity that characterized the Syrian economy in the first half of the 1990s. It was with the regime's encouragement that representatives of this class joined the Assembly and began playing a prominent role there, especially in economic deliberations. Dr Ihsan Sanqar, agent for the Mercedes Corporation in Syria, who chaired the Assembly from May 1990 onwards, was among the first

to propose establishing a stock exc
prominent representative was Riya
founded in partnership with the G
gust 1994 election Sayf won in his
more votes than any other Assembly
He was re-elected in the 1998 electio

The great diversity characteristic
egates contrasted starkly with the con
within in the framework of the Nati
perspective, the Front was somethin
the leftist parties were broadly repres
all. Before the 1990 elections the regi
establish a moderate Islamic party th
Front, to be headed by a cleric close to
Sa'id al-Buti.[21] But there were clerics w
dates and gained seats under the quo
These were moderates who, unlike th
ership in its time, were prepared to re
*fait accompli* and cooperate with it. One
from the Damascus district, explained
the Assembly was natural under the ci
he and his associates believed that reli
on the basis of justice", and that "Islam
terror, killing and violence."[22] 'Abd al-
the Assembly since 1987, praised the
sembly, noting that they fulfilled thei
reiterated the regime's position, where
do with state affairs – and where there i
in those affairs or religion is used to justi
to be a true faith."[23] (For the regime's att
in Syria, see below.)

The enhanced status of the People'
a profound change in the structure of
President Asad's regime continued to c
but nonetheless the process was not insign
Assembly granted representation and ex
have been – to various sectors of society
the margins of the state's political system
economic elite and moderate circles of
trend blended with the regime's efforts
mony by reconciling these sectors, which in th
among its critics and enemies, and integr
– into the day-to-day life of the state. Seco
to members of the Assembly to criticize th

in the so
and cont
among th
bled the
and grea
far-reach
delegate
informat
nated. In
aimed at
vestmen
passed in

The p
from va
the weal
corridor
since re
Debate
course
liberali
econom

*Society*

Lacking
country
social a
the Syr
the bo
to the
two pa
age ec
of the
nomic

*Limited*
ernme
still pa
This p
new s
gratio
view o
an ec
of the

support the regime wished to ensure.

The pride and glory of the regime's economic policy was Investment Law no. 10, passed in May 1991, with the intention of encouraging both foreign and local entrepreneurs to invest in the country. By the end of 1998, 1,494 projects, totaling some 366.7 billion Syrian pounds (approximately US $8.5 billion) and expected to create 100,000 jobs, were approved within the framework of this law.[24] However, official Syrian sources admitted that most of these projects – more than 75% – got no further than the planning stage, and most of the rest were carried out in or near Damascus and Aleppo, and not in the rural areas and the periphery, as the regime had hoped.[25]

Concurrently with the introduction of Investment Law no. 10, the Syrian government eased restrictions on commercial imports to Syria. This led to a real increase in the scope of imports because, among other things, the regime wanted to guarantee an abundance of goods in the markets and prevent the kinds of shortages that Syrians had had to endure in the past. In 1989 commercial imports were estimated at $2 billion; in 1991, $2.76 billion; and in 1993, $4.67 billion. Later years saw similar increases.[26] Increased imports led to a higher trade deficit and a rise in foreign debt to $16 billion (mostly to the former Soviet Union).[27]

Nonetheless, there was a limit to how much Law no. 10 could achieve, apparently because of the regime's reluctance to broaden and deepen the process of liberalization to the point where it would lose control of the state's economic life. The government refrained during the 1990s from establishing the necessary infrastructure to allow the trend of economic liberalization and openness to advance significantly. Nor did it set up a stock exchange, develop a computerization infrastructure in the state, or expand banking activity. Syria had no private banking services and most of the population were without bank accounts. The government also held back from privatizing various sectors of the economy, which mostly continued to be controlled by the government bureaucracy.[28]

*Change in the national order of priorities.* Along with limited liberalization of the economy, the regime put significant resources into raising the standard of living for the whole of society. In the first half of the 1990s, huge and unprecedented sums were invested in improving the infrastructure, especially electricity, water, communications, transport, education and health. Starting in 1993, the scope of the investment budget for improving the infrastructure was 60.75 billion Syrian pounds (US $6.4 billion) – approximately 51% of the total budget. This was a steep rise from the 1992 budget of 36.25

billion Syrian pounds ($3.23 billion).[29] In contrast, the published security budget (which does not necessarily include all security-related expenses, in particular those relating to the acquisition of arms) was frozen. The published security budget dropped from 29% of the overall budget in 1992 to 23% in 1993. These trends continued in the years that followed.[30]

The bulk of the growth in the investment budget was, as stated above, in the areas of transport, communications, water and electricity. Thus the investment budget for developing the water and electricity infrastructure in 1992-3 rose by 230% from the 4.12 billion Syrian pounds of 1992 ($475 million) to 13.69 billion pounds in 1993 ($1,217 million). This trend continued.[31] In these areas a real transformation took place. The number of telephone subscribers in the country grew, in the framework of a broad communications project carried out with Kuwaiti funding, from some 500,000 in 1992 to 3 million in 1999.[32] At the same time an effort was made to raise electricity production to supply increased demand, and a series of new power stations were established, worth a billion dollars, also with the aid of foreign grants and loans.[33] During the 1980s the regime had lengthy planned power stoppages every day in most cities, including Damascus, due to lack of supply.

In spite of impressive progress in these and other areas (e.g. the improvement of roads, railways and public transport), it seems that the regime's efforts were insufficient to overcome the growing backwardness resulting from years of neglect, the lack of a technological infrastructure, and the shortage of skilled and professional manpower. Moreover, the progress achieved fell short of meeting the rise in demand for these services because of the rapid population growth (see below). Infrastructural problems of water and electricity supply, transport and communications thus continued to preoccupy the regime in Damascus and draw sharp public criticism. From the second half of the 1990s it became clear that part of the achievements made in the infrastructure had been lost and Syrian citizens again had to cope with electricity and water shortages.

*Economic circumstances.* Favourable political and economic circumstances in the first half of the 1990s had eased the regime's efforts to improve the economy. First, there was a rise in oil revenues resulting from the discovery of new oil fields in the east of the country at the end of the 1980s. From the start of the 1990s, oil accounted for more than two-thirds of overall exports, bringing the state treasury some $3 billion annually.[34] Second, aid poured in from the Gulf countries: with the end of the Gulf War, Syria received, mostly from Saudi Arabia and Kuwait, a sizeable return (estimated at $2-3 bil-

lion) for its support during that conflict. These countries continued to aid Syria generously with the same level of grants and loans
in the years that followed.[35] Finally, the 1992-6 peace process made
Syria more attractive to foreign investment, and led countries and
economic bodies in the Far East and Western Europe to extend
financial aid. This was partly to encourage continued commitment
to the peace process and partly to acquire political and economic
status and influence.[36] The overall result was a short-term improvement in Syria's economic situation.

There is evidence of this improvement in the dry economic data,
which for the first half of the 1990s showed appreciable growth in
the gross domestic product and a broadening of economic activity.
According to official statistics, the GDP grew in 1992 by 10.6%, in
1993 by 6.7% and in 1994 by 7.6%.[37] The improvement in the economic situation also manifested itself in the impression of abundance
in the markets gained by foreign correspondents and visitors in
Syria: they were laden with foreign products after years of shortage
and austerity.[38] The inflation rate remained stable at approximately
10-20%, but official sources claimed a dramatic drop in inflation to
5-7% annually.[39] The balance of trade was stable thanks to a rise in
exports – primarily oil and its derivatives; in 1996 they reached a
peak of $4.3 billion dollars, compared to imports of $4.5 billion; the
trade deficit was then $200 million.[40] However, economic data from
the later 1990s show that this positive trend was a passing phenomenon. By the end of the decade, growth in the GDP was negative
and there was a sharp drop in foreign trade, reflecting the reces-
sion in the economy.[41] Further deterioration would have led to a
grave crisis.

Syria's problems, certainly for the long term, are demographic.
The country has the dubious distinction of holding the world's
record for natural population growth (3.3-3.5%). Official data for
1998 and 1999 show that this rate has dipped sharply, but their cre-
dibility is uncertain. Furthermore, the rate of natural increase in
the 1970s and '80s alone is enough to present a serious challenge to
the Syrian economy.[42] Whereas at the start of 1998 the country's population
was estimated at 17 million, by the year 2020 it is expected to pass
30 million.[43] In recent years the regime put the question of natural
increase on the public agenda, but unfortunately it also refrained
from presenting a clear plan of action to deal with the problem,
except for media campaigns, sex education in the schools, and more
active family planning centers in the rural regions and the periphery.[44]

Since the mid-1990s the first signs of crisis resulting from this
population explosion have appeared. They include a stalling in the

growth of the economy and, as a result, a retreat in the scope and depth of public services; pressure on an already ramshackle infrastructure; renewed shortages of water and electricity; a sharp rise in unemployment, especially among first-time job-seekers; a rise in illiteracy; and the by-products of poverty in the urban streets.[45] Then there is the fact that Syria is a Third World country characterized by a backward technological and economic infrastructure and still run by a regime committed – at least publicly – to a worldview taken from the long-defunct East European socialist regimes. These facts have unquestionably hindered Syrian society and the regime from coping with the emerging crisis.

*Unemployment.* The rise in unemployment was, as mentioned, a consequence of population growth. According to official data, the rate in the mid-1990s was a little under 10%, but unofficial estimates put it at 30% or more.[46] According to low estimates published in the Syrian press, the workforce in the year 2011 will number 7.21 million out of a total population of 25 million; in 1996 it numbered 4.225 million out of 16 million.[47] The significance of these figures is that the Syrian government, according to its own estimates, must create 3 million jobs within a decade – more than 300,000 annually – but the 1997 and 1998 budgets were designed to create only 85,000 jobs, i.e. no more than in earlier years. Law no. 10 to encourage investment, the jewel in the crown of economic reform efforts since the start of the 1990s, led in the course of the entire decade to the creation of only 100,000 jobs, and most of these were only on paper.[48] Political and economic developments in the Gulf states are likely to exacerbate the unemployment problem, since there are between a quarter and half a million Syrian 'guest' laborers in those countries. Between half a million and a million also work in Lebanon, where the political situation is also likely to influence employment in Syria.

Beginning in 1997, the GDP began to show signs of slowing significantly, and at the end of the decade, it was estimated at less than 1 per cent. Taking into account the population's rate of increase, the actual growth rate is negative.[49] A decline was also generated in the balance of payments because of the continued growth in imports as against the standstill, if not decrease, in exports that followed from the continued drop in oil revenues. Oil reserves in Syria are limited and, according to estimates, will be exhausted before 2010 if oil production in Syria maintains its present rate of some 600,000 barrels per day. Apart from this, the price of oil is subject to fluctuations and recent years has registered a continual drop. For instance, Syria's revenues from oil exports dropped in 1998 by some 30%. As political prisoners, this time to mark the twenty-fifth anniversary of the Corrective Revolution.[11]

Among the prisoners released in the early 1990s were Asad's old rivals from the time of the struggle for control in Syria (1966-70). The former President, Nur al-Din al-Atasi, had spent over twenty years in a Damascus jail since Asad ousted him in 1970, and having been in poor health, died in December 1992 in Paris two weeks after his release.[12] Also among those released were Muhammad Rabbah al-Tawil, who had served as Minister of the Interior, and Ahmad al-Suwaydani, Chief of Staff in1966-8.[13] Salah Jadid, Asad's main rival from that period, remained behind bars until his death on 19 August 1993.[14] The release – or demise – of these people had only symbolic significance, but no practical implications since they were too old and sick to pose any threat to the regime. It is unlikely that they still enjoyed any support in Syria. More significant was the release of thousands of members of the Muslim Brotherhood, who had served time since the suppression of the Islamic Revolt in the early 1980s. The regime's readiness to demonstrate "goodwill" toward the Syrian Islamic circles was an important step in its efforts to push forward its decade-long dialogue with their members – both within Syria and beyond – with the goal of ensuring their support (see below).

While the release of political prisoners was interpreted as a manifestation of the regime's self-confidence, it stemmed largely from pressure both within Syria and from abroad. This gesture was an attempt to demonstrate the new, more enlightened face of Syria both toward the West and toward its own citizens. The regime's effort to revamp its image in the West also led to the decision in April 1992 to allow Syrian Jews to emigrate. Most of the community left, leaving behind only a few hundred of its members.[15]

*More power to the People's Assembly.* For many years the conventional view of the Syrian People's Assembly held it to be primarily a symbolic body devoid of decision-making power or ability to influence the policy and measures of the regime. The past elections to it were seen as lacking any political significance, and being at most cosmetic, to burnish the regime's supposedly democratic image. However, since 1990 the importance and influence of the Assembly have grown, if in a limited way, and it has begun playing a (relatively) more prominent role in Syrian political life.

The People's Assembly thus began serving the regime as a tool to advance its social and economic policy. The regime also began to rely on the Assembly, more than it had done before, to release existing pressures and tensions in Syrian society, in a controlled way, or to soften the demand, restrained though it was, for greater democracy and the introduction of far-reaching social and economic reforms in the state.

In preparation for the elections to the Assembly that took place on 22 May 1990, the number of delegates was increased from 195 to 250. This was done in order to encourage additional forces that were not identified with the regime and were not part of it to take part in the Assembly. Eighty-four seats, or 40% overall, were set aside for candidates with no formal political affiliation. The remaining 166 were allotted to the National Progressive Front (*al-Jabha al-Wataniyya al-Taqaddumiyya*) – an umbrella organization comprising all the political parties active in Syria.[16] For the sake of comparison, in the 1986 Assembly elections only thirty-five seats were reserved for independent delegates (less than 20%).[17] These candidates ran as individuals rather than as members of political parties, and when citizens arrived at the polls they ticked off as many names on the ballot as were allotted to their voting district.

The Assembly that emerged from the August 1994 elections – and from the November 1998 elections as well – had almost the same proportion of independent delegates as the previous one (eighty-three delegates).[18] The regime prevented representatives of the National Progressive Front from running in the various electoral districts at the expense of seats set aside for independent candidates. Furthermore, it allowed independent candidates to form coalitions and alliances in preparation for the contest. In Aleppo, for example, in the August 1994 elections ten lists of independent candidates competed, while in Damascus manufacturers and merchants established a list called "*Dimashq al-Fayha*" (Damascus the great), and five of its thirteen candidates won seats. The press reported fierce competition among members on the list and between them and other lists.[19]

A significant proportion of the independent delegates elected to the People's Assembly represented a growing class of merchants and capitalists who had emerged in Syria following the policy of economic liberalization the regime had adopted since the early 1990s. This class set its sights on improving the economic situation, and was prepared to assist the regime to preserve political stability in the state, seeing it as a guarantee of the stability, growth and prosperity that characterized the Syrian economy in the first half of the 1990s. It was with the regime's encouragement that representatives of this class joined the Assembly and began playing a prominent role there, especially in economic deliberations. Dr Ihsan Sanqar, agent for the Mercedes Corporation in Syria, who chaired the Assembly from May 1990 onwards, was among the first to propose establishing a stock exchange in the country. Another prominent representative was Riyad Sayf, owner of a shoe factory founded in partnership with the German firm, Adidas. In the August 1994 election Sayf won in his voting district, Damascus, with more votes than any other Assembly delegate – 76,000 out of 250,000. He was re-elected in the 1998 elections.[20]

The great diversity characteristic of the list of independent delegates contrasted starkly with the composition of parties functioning within in the framework of the National Progressive Front. In this perspective, the Front was something of a historical anachronism: the leftist parties were broadly represented but Islamic forces not at all. Before the 1990 elections the regime had tried unsuccessfully to establish a moderate Islamic party that would function within the Front, to be headed by a cleric close to the government, Muhammad Sa'id al-Buti.[21] But there were clerics who ran as independent candidates and gained seats under the quota of independent candidates. These were moderates who, unlike the Muslim Brotherhood leadership in its time, were prepared to recognize the Ba'th regime as a *fait accompli* and cooperate with it. One of this group, Marwan Shihu from the Damascus district, explained that the election of clerics to the Assembly was natural under the circumstances, and added that he and his associates believed that religion "organizes life in society on the basis of justice", and that "Islam is a tolerant faith that rejects terror, killing and violence."[22] 'Abd al-Qadir Qaddura, Speaker of the Assembly since 1987, praised the clerical members of the Assembly, noting that they fulfilled their duties honorably. He also reiterated the regime's position, whereby "religion has nothing to do with state affairs – and where there is an involvement of religion in those affairs or religion is used to justify acts of terror, it has ceased to be a true faith."[23] (For the regime's attitude toward Islamic circles in Syria, see below.)

The enhanced status of the People's Assembly did not herald a profound change in the structure of the Syrian political system. President Asad's regime continued to control it with a firm hand, but nonetheless the process was not insignificant. First, the revamped Assembly granted representation and expression – limited as it may have been – to various sectors of society that till then had been on the margins of the state's political system, namely the Sunni urban economic elite and moderate circles of the religious camp. This trend blended with the regime's efforts to achieve domestic harmony by reconciling these sectors, which in the past had been numbered among its critics and enemies, and integrating them – if only partly – into the day-to-day life of the state. Second, the freedom granted to members of the Assembly to criticize the regime for its omissions in the social and economic domain helped the latter to regulate and control manifestations of dissatisfaction, anger and bitterness among the population generally. Lastly, the People's Assembly enabled the regime to outline and implement a policy of liberalization and greater openness in economic life. The state's media exploited far-reaching deliberations in the Assembly, during which many delegates called for such a policy to be pushed forward, and for information concerning economic openness to be widely disseminated. In addition, the Assembly produced a great deal of legislation aimed at implementing this policy, the high point of which was Investment Law no. 10 aimed at encouraging investment in the state, passed in May 1991 (see below).

The policy to accelerate economic liberalization drew criticism from various sectors of the Syrian public – primarily from among the weaker strata, and the government and party bureaucracy. The corridors of the People's Assembly resounded with such criticism, since representatives of these sectors constituted the majority. Debate over these issues enabled the regime to steer the middle course between these contradictory orientations toward economic liberalization, however limited, and the desire to preserve the socio-economic and political *status quo*.

## Society and the economy – continuity and change

Lacking both the ability and the desire to introduce changes in the country's political life, the regime concentrated its efforts on the social and economic spheres, which occupied a prominent place on the Syrian agenda. This was after years in which they had been at the bottom of the national list of priorities, due mainly to the demands of the struggle with Israel. The regime focused on two parallel goals: limited liberalization of the economy to encourage economic activity, and energetic efforts to raise the living standards of the masses, *inter alia* by broad investment in developing the economic infrastructure.

*Limited economic liberalization.* From the early 1990s, the Syrian government adopted an economic policy characterized by more – if still partial – openness and readiness for a liberalization of the economy. This policy was designed to encourage economic activity and create new sources of income and employment; also to ease Syria's integration into the world economy, an essential pre-condition in the view of many for its future stability and economic prosperity. Such an economic policy could also serve to win favor with various sectors of the public, but in particular the Sunni urban elite whose political support the regime wished to ensure.

The pride and glory of the regime's economic policy was Investment Law no. 10, passed in May 1991, with the intention of encouraging both foreign and local entrepreneurs to invest in the country. By the end of 1998, 1,494 projects, totaling some 366.7 billion Syrian pounds (approximately US $8.5 billion) and expected to create 100,000 jobs, were approved within the framework of this law.[24] However, official Syrian sources admitted that most of these projects – more than 75% – got no further than the planning stage, and most of the rest were carried out in or near Damascus and Aleppo, and not in the rural areas and the periphery, as the regime had hoped.[25]

Concurrently with the introduction of Investment Law no. 10, the Syrian government eased restrictions on commercial imports to Syria. This led to a real increase in the scope of imports because, among other things, the regime wanted to guarantee an abundance of goods in the markets and prevent the kinds of shortages that Syrians had had to endure in the past. In 1989 commercial imports were estimated at $2 billion; in 1991, $2.76 billion; and in 1993, $4.67 billion. Later years saw similar increases.[26] Increased imports led to a higher trade deficit and a rise in foreign debt to $16 billion (mostly to the former Soviet Union).[27]

Nonetheless, there was a limit to how much Law no. 10 could achieve, apparently because of the regime's reluctance to broaden and deepen the process of liberalization to the point where it would lose control of the state's economic life. The government refrained during the 1990s from establishing the necessary infrastructure to allow the trend of economic liberalization and openness to advance significantly. Nor did it set up a stock exchange, develop a computerization infrastructure in the state, or expand banking activity. Syria had no private banking services and most of the population were without bank accounts. The government also held back from privatizing various sectors of the economy, which mostly continued to be controlled by the government bureaucracy.[28]

*Change in the national order of priorities.* Along with limited liberalization of the economy, the regime put significant resources into raising the standard of living for the whole of society. In the first half of the 1990s, huge and unprecedented sums were invested in improving the infrastructure, especially electricity, water, communications, transport, education and health. Starting in 1993, the scope of the investment budget for improving the infrastructure was 60.75 billion Syrian pounds (US $6.4 billion) – approximately 51% of the total budget. This was a steep rise from the 1992 budget of 36.25

billion Syrian pounds ($3.23 billion).[29] In contrast, the published security budget (which does not necessarily include all security-related expenses, in particular those relating to the acquisition of arms) was frozen. The published security budget dropped from 29% of the overall budget in 1992 to 23% in 1993. These trends continued in the years that followed.[30]

The bulk of the growth in the investment budget was, as stated above, in the areas of transport, communications, water and electricity. Thus the investment budget for developing the water and electricity infrastructure in 1992-3 rose by 230% from the 4.12 billion Syrian pounds of 1992 ($475 million) to 13.69 billion pounds in 1993 ($1,217 million). This trend continued.[31] In these areas a real transformation took place. The number of telephone subscribers in the country grew, in the framework of a broad communications project carried out with Kuwaiti funding, from some 500,000 in 1992 to 3 million in 1999.[32] At the same time an effort was made to raise electricity production to supply increased demand, and a series of new power stations were established, worth a billion dollars, also with the aid of foreign grants and loans.[33] During the 1980s the regime had lengthy planned power stoppages every day in most cities, including Damascus, due to lack of supply.

In spite of impressive progress in these and other areas (e.g. the improvement of roads, railways and public transport), it seems that the regime's efforts were insufficient to overcome the growing backwardness resulting from years of neglect, the lack of a technological infrastructure, and the shortage of skilled and professional manpower. Moreover, the progress achieved fell short of meeting the rise in demand for these services because of the rapid population growth (see below). Infrastructural problems of water and electricity supply, transport and communications thus continued to preoccupy the regime in Damascus and draw sharp public criticism. From the second half of the 1990s it became clear that part of the achievements made in the infrastructure had been lost and Syrian citizens again had to cope with electricity and water shortages.

*Economic circumstances.* Favourable political and economic circumstances in the first half of the 1990s had eased the regime's efforts to improve the economy. First, there was a rise in oil revenues resulting from the discovery of new oil fields in the east of the country at the end of the 1980s. From the start of the 1990s, oil accounted for more than two-thirds of overall exports, bringing the state treasury some $3 billion annually.[34] Second, aid poured in from the Gulf countries: with the end of the Gulf War, Syria received, mostly from Saudi Arabia and Kuwait, a sizeable return (estimated at $2-3 bil-

lion) for its support during that conflict. These countries continued to aid Syria generously with the same level of grants and loans
in the years that followed.³⁵ Finally, the 1992-6 peace process made
Syria more attractive to foreign investment, and led countries and
economic bodies in the Far East and Western Europe to extend
financial aid. This was partly to encourage continued commitment
to the peace process and partly to acquire political and economic
status and influence.³⁶ The overall result was a short-term improvement in Syria's economic situation.

There is evidence of this improvement in the dry economic data,
which for the first half of the 1990s showed appreciable growth in
the gross domestic product and a broadening of economic activity.
According to official statistics, the GDP grew in 1992 by 10.6%, in
1993 by 6.7% and in 1994 by 7.6%.³⁷ The improvement in the economic situation also manifested itself in the impression of abundance
in the markets gained by foreign correspondents and visitors in
Syria: they were laden with foreign products after years of shortage
and austerity.³⁸ The inflation rate remained stable at approximately
10-20%, but official sources claimed a dramatic drop in inflation to
5-7% annually.³⁹ The balance of trade was stable thanks to a rise in
exports – primarily oil and its derivatives; in 1996 they reached a
peak of $4.3 billion dollars, compared to imports of $4.5 billion; the
trade deficit was then $200 million.⁴⁰ However, economic data from
the later 1990s show that this positive trend was a passing phenomenon. By the end of the decade, growth in the GDP was negative
and there was a sharp drop in foreign trade, reflecting the reces-
sion in the economy.⁴¹ Further deterioration would have led to a
grave crisis.

Syria's problems, certainly for the long term, are demographic.
The country has the dubious distinction of holding the world's
record for natural population growth (3.3-3.5%). Official data for
1998 and 1999 show that this rate has dipped sharply, but their cre-
dibility is uncertain. Furthermore, the rate of natural increase in
the 1970s and '80s alone is enough to present a serious challenge to
the Syrian economy.⁴² Whereas at the start of 1998 the country's population
was estimated at 17 million, by the year 2020 it is expected to pass
30 million.⁴³ In recent years the regime put the question of natural
increase on the public agenda, but unfortunately it also refrained
from presenting a clear plan of action to deal with the problem,
except for media campaigns, sex education in the schools, and more
active family planning centers in the rural regions and the periph-
ery.⁴⁴

Since the mid-1990s the first signs of crisis resulting from this
population explosion have appeared. They include a stalling in the

growth of the economy and, as a result, a retreat in the scope and depth of public services; pressure on an already ramshackle infrastructure; renewed shortages of water and electricity; a sharp rise in unemployment, especially among first-time jobseekers; a rise in illiteracy; and the by-products of poverty in the urban streets.[45] Then there is the fact that Syria is a Third World country characterized by a backward technological and economic infrastructure and still run by a regime committed – at least publicly – to a worldview taken from the long-defunct East European socialist regimes. These facts have unquestionably hindered Syrian society and the regime from coping with the emerging crisis.

*Unemployment.* The rise in unemployment was, as mentioned, a consequence of population growth. According to official data, the rate in the mid-1990s was a little under 10%, but unofficial estimates put it at 30% or more.[46] According to low estimates published in the Syrian press, the workforce in the year 2011 will number 7.21 million out of a total population of 25 million; in 1996 it numbered 4.225 million out of 16 million.[47] The significance of these figures is that the Syrian government, according to its own estimates, must create 3 million jobs within a decade – more than 300,000 annually – but the 1997 and 1998 budgets were designed to create only 85,000 jobs, i.e. no more than in earlier years. Law no. 10 to encourage investment, the jewel in the crown of economic reform efforts since the start of the 1990s, led in the course of the entire decade to the creation of only 100,000 jobs, and most of these were only on paper.[48] Political and economic developments in the Gulf states are likely to exacerbate the unemployment problem, since there are between a quarter and half a million Syrian 'guest' laborers in those countries. Between half a million and a million also work in Lebanon, where the political situation is also likely to influence employment in Syria.

Beginning in 1997, the GDP began to show signs of slowing significantly, and at the end of the decade, it was estimated at less than 1 per cent. Taking into account the population's rate of increase, the actual growth rate is negative.[49] A decline was also generated in the balance of payments because of the continued growth in imports as against the standstill, if not decrease, in exports that followed from the continued drop in oil revenues. Oil reserves in Syria are limited and, according to estimates, will be exhausted before 2010 if oil production in Syria maintains its present rate of some 600,000 barrels per day. Apart from this, the price of oil is subject to fluctuations and recent years has registered a continual drop. For instance, Syria's revenues from oil exports dropped in 1998 by some 30%. As mentioned above, the Syrian government has failed in its attempts to develop alternative sources of revenue.[30]

Against the backdrop of these figures, recognition grew among the business community, as well as among the economic and political elite, of the need to speed up changes in the economy. Even a transition to a market economy is feasible, considering the necessity of giving Syria economic strength to compete in and integrate into the world economy. This recognition found expression in public debate, unprecedented in Syrian terms, on the state's economic problems and ways to cope with them.

Sharp criticism began to appear in the Syrian press concerning the economic problems facing the country, as well as pointing to the imperative need for the government to adopt energetic economic steps that would enable it to cope with these difficulties. For example, in May 1997 *Al-Ba'th*, organ of the Ba'th Party, published a report written by the Syrian Association of Chambers of Commerce on the economic difficulties – which, it pointed out, were caused by the lack of competition, economic isolation, and an antiquated banking system.[51] Delegates to the People's Assembly also criticised the government's socio-economic policy, sometimes harshly. There were many complaints that the economy's rate of growth was not directly proportional to the rate of population increase, and warnings against a decline in the standard of living.[52] Other delegates pointed out the failure of Investment Law no. 10 and the bureaucratic obstacles facing would-be foreign investors. One even argued that Syria was the "world champion of bureaucracy".[53] Doubt was cast on the government's efforts to change the national priorities and put the economy and society at the forefront.

*Social gaps.* The economic changes in Syria from the start of the 1990s have led to the rise of a class of *nouveaux riches* – capitalists and businessmen who, protected by the economic reforms, began taking a growing part in the state's economic life. They came mostly from the Sunni urban elite who had previously controlled Syria but had been pushed to the sidelines after the March 1963 Ba'th revolution and as a result of the radical social and economic policy adopted by the neo-Ba'th regime in 1966-70. With Asad's rise to power in November 1970, his regime adopted a policy of economic openness – however limited – aimed at encouraging economic activity and reintegrating the economic elite and the Sunni urban middle class into Syria's economic life. However, the frequent reversals of economic policy during the 1970s and '80s as a result of the regime's economic and political difficulties prevented a truly open economy from developing and greatly limited the economic role these groups could play. Transformation thus began only in the early 1990s when the regime once again adopted a policy of economic openness, with the aid of the Sunni urban elite. This group and, alongside it, the urban middle class, became allies of Asad's regime, while remaining on the margins of the socio-political coalition he established. As will be recalled, apart from the growth – relative, of course – in the economic strength of this group, the regime had given it limited political power by integrating its representatives into the People's Assembly as independent delegates.

Still, the political power given to this group was clearly quite limited, and the claim was frequently heard that its leading figures were a band of close associates of the regime, such as the (Shi'ite) businessmen Sa'ib al-Nahhas, 'Uthman al-'A'idi (an 'Alawite) and 'Abd al-Rahman al-'Attar, whose economic links and cooperation with the elite of the regime enabled them to reap the fruits of the economic liberalization policy.[54] However, while this policy enriched the urban business elite, it had the side-effect of creating growing social and economic gaps which were new to Syrian society. These left behind precisely those sectors of the population which in the past had been the main bastions of support for the regime: the lower social classes, workers, peasants, residents of rural areas and the periphery, and finally the government and party bureaucracy. With the appearance and spread of social gulfs in Syria, a dilemma confronted the regime in everything connected with the continuation and acceleration of openness and liberalization of economic life.

In mid-1997 the government organ *Al-Thawra* published an article titled 'Blinded by the Light'. which gave prominence to this dilemma and the regime's search for a balance between those calling for continued liberalization and more profound economic reforms, and those liable to be hurt by these reforms. The article attacked the two existing economic schools in Syria – "that which seeks to ignore the existence of a world economy and the necessity of integrating into it, and also that which seeks to bring about Syria's integration into the world economy but ignores the danger that such a process will cause an economic and social shock, as well as dishonor and harm to economic and national sovereignty". It went on to claim that the path advocated by both schools led to ruin, and therefore Syria must adopt a middle way between them.[55]

Concern for the more vulnerable classes also arose in the People's Assembly. Many speakers – especially Ba'th Party delegates – representing workers, farmers and the government bureaucracy attacked the government and warned against further worsening the living conditions of these sectors. This was enough to balance pressure from the independent candidates, representing the commercial sector, in favor of accelerating economic reform.[56]

In June 1997 in an interview the then Prime Minister, Mahmud al-Zu'bi, addressed the public debate on this issue. He made it clear that the government's concept of privatization meant encouragement of the private sector to play a greater role in economic life by participating in the public sector, but not at its expense. Zu'bi stressed that Syria had learned a lesson from events in Eastern Europe, where rapid transition to a market economy and ill-considered privatization had led to economic depression, hyper-inflation, economic crime, and social and economic crisis. He said that Syria was taking balanced and gradual steps in the direction of reforms and changes, and would thus be able to prevent the phenomena of Islamic extremism, as well as hunger and shortages.[57]

In March 2000 a new government was formed under Mustafa Miru. This was portrayed as a clear sign of determination on the part of the Syrian regime, then under Hafiz al-Asad, to tread a new path of reform and modernization, mainly in the economy. It was also represented as Bashar al-Asad's personal choice, and thus expressing his desire to take over the management of Syria's day-to-day affairs.[58] The new government did indeed launch some reform initiatives, including limited changes in Law no. 10 to accommodate changing economic realities and thus make Syria more attractive to foreign investors. But these reforms were limited and were not followed by any real change in the economic system or economic realities in the country.[59]

We have already noted above (page 168) the character of the new prime minister, Mustafa Miru, and the composition of his cabinet, which did not seem to offer any prospect of a departure from the old ways. Following Asad's death there was a feeling of hope in Syria that his departure would remove an obstacle on the road to change, but at the time of writing it remains unclear whether Bashar can succeed, after stabilizing his rule, in leading the people towards a new openness, mainly in the economy. Because of his often stated intention to pursue a path of change combined with continuity, since too dramatic a change in a country ruled by an iron fist for so long would be liable to cause the Syrian structure to collapse,[60] Bashar must steer a course between the need for change on the one side and to maintain stability and the *status quo* on the other.

*The Islamic movement and the Ba'th regime – a pause in
the struggle?*

Late in February 1997 the Damascus press gave extensive coverage
to a letter sent to President Asad by the Abu Ghudda family of
Aleppo thanking him for his condolences following the death of
'Abd al-Fattah Abu Ghudda.[61] The President's condolences, like the
note from the bereaved family, were exceptional. 'Abd al-Fatah
Abu Ghudda had been a leader of the Muslim Brotherhood in Syria,
and between 1976 and 1982 had served as its "Inspector-General"
(*al-Muraqib al-'Amm*). After the Ba'th Revolution of 8 March 1963,
he left Syria for prolonged exile in Saudi Arabia, but continued to
fight the Syrian regime from abroad, and in his role as "Inspector-
General" led the Islamic Revolt against it. After the revolt failed, he
abandoned his political activity and immersed himself in teaching
and writing. He taught at Jiddah University and was known for
numerous theological works which he published.[62]

In December 1995 Abu Ghudda returned to Syria, apparently
under an arrangement with the Damascus authorities which permitted him to reside in Aleppo, the city of his birth, on condition
that he would concern himself solely with matters of education and
religion and avoid all political activity. But in mid-1996 he returned
to Saudi Arabia – perhaps because of a decline in his health, or out
of disappointment and frustration with political circumstances in
Syria that did not allow him and his associates to act freely to promote their worldview. He died on 16 February 1997[63] and the President
was quick to send his condolences to the bereaved family. An official delegation that included the Minister of the Awqaf, the governor
of Aleppo, and the city's chief of police visited the family and delivered the following message in Asad's name: "Abu Ghudda was a
man who inspired respect during his lifetime, and therefore it is
fitting that we preserve and honor his memory in death as well."
The President went so far as to offer the use of his personal aircraft
to fly Abu Ghudda's body to Syria for burial. He was ultimately buried in Madina, near the grave of the Prophet Muhammad, but Asad
earned the gratitude of the family.[64]

Abu Ghudda's willingness to return to Syria and the magnanimity
the Damascus authorities showed him attesting to the process of
reconciliation, or at least to a deepening of the more than decade-
long dialogue between the regime and the Syrian leaders of the
Muslim Brotherhood movement, who mostly lived in exile. This
process resulted from the willingness of the latter to accept the established Ba'th regime. The regime, for its part, also showed interest
in resolving the conflict with local Islamic circles with which it had

previously fought to the death. It seems that it wished in this way to broaden and deepen its support at home and to stabilize a "domestic front" against all the difficulties and challenges facing it in the domestic, regional and international arenas.

From 1976 to 1982, the Muslim Brotherhood had waged a violent campaign, known as the Islamic Revolt, against the Ba'th regime with the aim of establishing an Islamic state in Syria. The Brothers succeeded in mobilizing to their cause significant backing from among the Sunni community which formed a majority in the state, and when the revolt reached its climax in early 1980 took partial control of several cities in northern Syria. However, this was the extent of the Brothers' achievements, and from that point on, the heavy hand of the regime bore down upon them. The revolt began to dissipate, and ended in February 1982 after the suppression of the uprising in Hama during which Syrian military and security forces killed thousands of residents of the city. After the failure of the revolt, the Muslim Brotherhood ceased to exist as an organized and active movement. During its course hundreds of its activists had died, thousands were sent to prison, and most of its leaders escaped over the border.[65]

The violent campaign against the Ba'th regime was in many ways a deviation from the Muslim Brotherhood's traditional course. During the first years after its establishment in 1944, it had adopted for itself a middle path that sought to bridge the gap between religion and the state; the Brothers were willing to accept the existing political and socio-economic set-up in Syria and worked to blend into it. The movement took part in elections to the Parliament in the 1940s and 1950s, and its representatives served as ministers in several governments of that period. The Brothers thus concentrated their efforts on influencing the existing political system from within in favor of preserving and strengthening the Muslim character of the Syrian state.[66]

The path that the Muslim Brotherhood adopted for itself in Syria was the inevitable result of social, economic and political circumstances. These circumstances distinguished Syria from other Arab states – chiefly Egypt, of course. Support for the movement came only from members of the Sunni community, which made up some 60% of the overall population, while the minority communities in the state – Christians, 'Alawis and Druze – were, for obvious reasons, among its most obdurate opponents. However, even the Sunni were not monolithic in their support; many had reservations – particularly, but not only, the educated. These were attracted by the modernist-secular notions of "Arab nationalism" of the Ba'th Party school; by the "Syrian nationalism" of the school of Antun Sa'ada, a founder and leader of the Syrian Nationalist Party (PPS); and, finally, by communism. Even among the Sunni in the rural areas and the periphery – half of the total Syrian Sunni community – there was no recognizable enthusiasm for the messages of the Muslim Brotherhood. In those areas the Islamic presence – mosques and other religious institutions, and even clerics (*ulama*) – was very small if it existed at all. The main strongholds of support for the movement were among the Sunni middle class in the big cities, especially in the north of the country. However, as has been said, even this support was not complete.[67]

The challenge that the Ba'th regime presented to the Islamic movement and its supporters was ideological, political, and socioeconomic. This is what alienated the movement from the consensus in Syria and set it on the path of struggle. The Ba'th regime sought, as will be recalled, to designate to Islam a marginal if not negligible role in the society and the state, and as an alternative to Islam proposed "secular Arabism" of the school of Michel Aflaq, founder of the Ba'th, as a basis of identity for the individual, the political community and the entire Arab nation. This trend waxed stronger still between 1966 and 1970 under the rule of the neo-Ba'th regime, the radical faction of the Ba'th Party. Indeed, from 1963, when the Ba'th first took power, there were repeated confrontations between the authorities and activists of the movement, which had in the mean time been outlawed. These confrontations were mostly of a limited nature – strikes and demonstrations – and usually broke out as a local reaction to measures taken by the regime, yet they had a cumulative effect.

Asad's rise to power in November 1970 led to the regime's attempt under his leadership to start a fresh page in relations with Islamic circles in the country. In particular, Asad worked to mitigate the anti-Islamic line that had characterized his predecessors. He began to participate in prayers at Sunni mosques in Damascus, made a pilgrimage to Mecca, and actively tried to gain religious sanction for his community – the 'Alawi. In this he achieved some success in the form of a religious ruling (*fatwa*) delivered by the leader of the Lebanese Shi'i community, Musa Sadr: this stated that the 'Alawis were Shi'is, and as such were Muslims in every respect. However, the Muslim Brotherhood rejected Asad's efforts with the argument that his regime was one of coercion led by a non-Muslim ruler (because of his membership of the 'Alawi community).

A further factor contributing to the extremism that overcame the movement was generational – the emergence of a young and militant generation, distinct in its generally secular social background and education from the movement's founders. It was also under the influence of Sayyid Qutb. Several of these activists had met him while studying in Egypt, and now began preaching in the spirit of his ideas. They advocated open confrontation with the regime which they saw as heretical, i.e. secular and even non-Muslim (Ba'thist with shades of 'Alawism). They were willing to take the initiative and act independently once it became clear to them that the veteran leadership of the Brotherhood movement was in no hurry to adopt their notions and had reservations about a confrontational campaign against the Ba'thist regime. In the mid-1970s one of these activists, Marwan Hadid, established in the city of Hama the "Battalions of Muhammad" (*Kata'ib Muhammad*): this was an underground and fanatical organization which began violent activity against the regime. In retrospect, it can be seen as the vanguard of the Islamic camp preparing for a putsch – the Islamic Revolt. All that remained for the veteran leadership of the Muslim Brotherhood, which had lost its power and influence over rank and file activists, was to accept the inevitable and join the Revolt when it broke out.[68]

The Islamic Revolt against the regime failed utterly, leading to the liquidation of the Muslim Brotherhood as an organized political movement in Syria. After its downfall, those of the Brotherhood's leaders who remained alive began looking for ways to placate the regime. At the very least they hoped to establish a dialogue that would enable the Brotherhood to continue its activity in the state as an organized movement, or as individuals.

From the mid-1990s there was a recognizable improvement in the regime's attitude toward Islamic circles in Syria and beyond. First, the regime began to show more openness than before to manifestations of religious faith among its citizens, such as the wearing of traditional dress including the veil for women, maintaining a Muslim way of life, increased participation in festival and Friday prayer services in the mosques, and religious preaching. Foreign visitors to Syria reported that religious schools had begun to spring up, some with the government's encouragement, and some even named after the President (*Madaris al-Asad li-t'alim al-Qur'an*), and that textbooks and religious propaganda were offered for sale or distribution in the streets to all seekers; it was said that the works of Sayyid Qutb were available.[69] In these renewed manifestations of religious faith there was of course evidence that among various sectors of the population, especially residents of the big cities, deep Islamic sentiment existed which the regime had not succeeded in rooting out. It also seems that, faced with severe social and economic problems, chiefly the high natural rate of increase in the population, the rise in unemployment and increasing poverty among of society's weakest classes, this sentiment was likely to take deeper root, as happened in neighboring Arab states. Foreign visitors to

Syria in recent years left with the impression that Sunni concentrations in the big cities were slowly taking on a Muslim character, at least relative to the Syrian norm since the Ba'th Party took control, and in the period preceding it.[70]

Second, the regime released most of the Muslim Brotherhood members who had been in prison in Syria since the suppression of the Islamic Revolt at the start of the 1980s. Third, the regime permitted moderate clerics, including those outside the official religious establishment that was identified with it, to stand for election to the People's Assembly as independents in 1990, 1994 and 1998. With the help of these clerics, the Syrian regime worked to promote and preserve its notion of the place of religion in the life of the state – a milder version of the concept promoted by Michel Aflaq which sought, as will be recalled, to reduce its status.[71] The regime had thus come to recognize the power and status of Islam but, like neighboring Arab regimes such as Egypt and Jordan, sought to preserve a separation between religion and the state, and rejected the notion of "political Islam" – the basis of the Muslim Brotherhood revolt of 1976-82. An example of this trend was Muhammad Sa'id al-Buti, a cleric close to the regime, who published a book on the subject of *jihad*, in which he sharply attacked the Brotherhood as having acted in contravention to Islamic principles and for bringing about a civil war ( *fitna*) in Syria. He added that he opposed the establishment of a religious party: "There is always the fear that extreme elements will infiltrate such a party and turn it into a tool for sowing dissension and violence in society." The organ of the Brotherhood, *al-Nazir*, published in London and Vienna, was quick to claim in response that it was not the Muslim Brotherhood that had cut itself off from the nation; rather this had been done by the regime, to which Buti accorded religious legitimacy.[72]

Ahmad Kaftaru, the pro-regime mufti of Syria, granted an interview in June 1996 to the London Arabic newspaper, *Al-Wasat*, praising President Asad and his regime for their commitment to the faith and attacking the Muslim extremists whose actions had no basis in Islam. Kaftaru also expressed opposition to the involvement of clerics in politics. "In Islam", he said, "religion and state are bound together. Islam exists and there can be no denying it. It does not depend on the will of the ruler or of the state, and therefore the existence of Islam is not conditional on the existence of one or other party. In any case, there is no justification for such a party."[73] However, in the interview Kaftaru did not conceal that he and the Islamic extremists had no quarrel over their "vision of the last days" – or, in other words, the ultimate goal; they differed only as to the means to achieve this goal. Here Kaftaru exposed the limits of cooperation between establishment clerics like himself and the Arab regimes. Scrutiny of his remarks thus shows that it was in fact he, the authorities' designated religious leader, who deserved the title of "keeper of the path" of the Muslim Brotherhood movement. There was a clear link between him and the Brotherhood in its early days in the 1940s and '50s. They shared an adherence to goals combined with a willingness to show moderation, flexibility and patience on the way to realizing them. Kaftaru said, among other things:

Manifestations of extremism are neither wise nor logical, as anyone who tries to....hasten the coming of something risks losing it altogether.... Extremism is not for the good of the homeland or for the good of peace.... The Arab rulers and those who are not Arab accept Islam gradually – not all at once but in stages. The radical movements preach extremism, that is their way. I think their goal is [the victory of] Islam, but the question is not what they desire, but what can be achieved. I personally regard cooperation with the Muslim ruler as the only way to achieve our goal, and we should understand that these things will not be accomplished in an hour or even in a day."[74]

The change in the regime's handling of Islamic circles in the country led some Muslim Brotherhood leaders who had been in exile since the early 1980s or even longer to return to Syria. Among them were 'Adnan 'Uqla, a leader of the Islamic Revolt of 1976-82, and 'Abd al-Fattah Abu Ghudda. Those leaders of the movement who remained abroad began negotiations, as has been said, with representatives of the Syrian regime in the hope of being able to return home as well. However, it became clear that the regime's conditions for reconciliation were too hard for the Brotherhood to accept. For example, it demanded that the Brotherhood's leaders should repent, confess their guilt and express regret for the Islamic Revolt, and commit themselves not to renew their political activities as an organized movement in Syria. The Minister of Information, Muhammad Salman, declared in this context: "Anyone who renounces his past conduct is authorized to return and live a normal life in Syria and to conduct religious rites there. Abu Ghudda visited me in my office and I told him that we in Syria do not relate to the Muslim Brotherhood as to a political party but as to individuals."[75] The leaders of the Brotherhood rejected these demands, and the "Inspector-General" of the movement, 'Ali Sa'd al-Din al-Bayanuni, explained that the atmosphere was not yet appropriate for a deepening of the dialogue. The Brotherhood was ready to bear some of the responsibility for past events, but would not consent to return to Syria as private individuals. Later, in 1998, he began attacking the regime as sectarian and 'Alawi – another expression of his disappointment with the lack of progress in the dialogue his movement was conducting with it.[76] It was reported from Damascus, incidentally, that some figures in the regime, especially in the security apparatus, were still opposed to the Brotherhood leaders returning to Syria.[77]

Nonetheless, the Brotherhood began preparing ideologically for a possible decision to return to Syria and come to terms with the Ba'th regime. This was explained as follows:

First, Syria did not belong solely to the Muslim Brotherhood; it was ideo-logically, politically, religiously and ethnically heterogeneous. Second, cultural and economic developments in Syria in the last two decades created new circumstances that could not be ignored. Third, normalization of relations with Israel and the new world order had to be fought, not accepted as a natural development, and, furthermore this struggle should be at the top of the Arabs' list of priorities. Fourth, there was need for reconciliation among the various parts of the nation in the face of its current challenges. Therefore, it was time to turn over a new leaf, and there should be no return to the past.[78]

In this context it should be noted that the reconciliation between the Islamic movement in Syria and the Ba'th regime was in many ways the result of an increasing convergence of positions and views between the regime and other radical Islamic movements through-out the Arab world. Indeed, during recent years Damascus has become a pilgrimage site for the leaders of radical Islamic groups from all corners of the Arab world. Among visitors were Hasan Nasrallah, the secretary-general of Hizballah, and Husayn Fadlallah, the movement's spiritual leader; Hasan Turabi, leader of the Islamic movement in Sudan; Shaykh Ahmad Yasin, leader of the Palestin-ian Hamas movement, and Sunni Muslim leaders from Lebanon, Tunisia, Algeria and Jordan.[79] Ishaq al-Farahan, leader of the Jordan-ian Islamic Action Front, visited Damascus in January 1997, and signed a working paper determining a framework for cooperation between Islamic forces in Jordan and the Ba'th Party.[80] The Palestin-ian Islamic movement also made Damascus a center, with Islamic Jihad establishing its headquarters and Hamas its information office there.

To an observer the pilgrimage to Damascus seemed something of mirage. In the past the Syrian Ba'th regime had been seen as the stronghold of secularism in the Arab world, and to a great extent it continued to present itself as such, its secular outlook being one of the main reasons for its campaign against the Syrian Islamic move-ment. The transformation of Damascus into a beacon for the Islamic fundamentalist movements of the Arab world was thus inherent in an alliance of interests that grew out of Syria's position as the only Arab state still committed to the struggle with Israel. In the eyes of these movements, Asad and his regime remained the last bastion

## NOTES

[1] See Eyal Zisser, "Syria" in Bruce Maddy-Weitzman (ed.), MECS, vol. XXI (1997), pp. 647-65.
[2] See Patrick Seale's interview in the framework of the proceedings of the international conference on "Modern Syria" at Haifa University, 17-18 November 1997; see also Eberhard Kienle (ed.), *Contemporary Syria: Liberalization Between Cold War and Cold Peace.*
[3] See *Davar*, 8 March 1990; Eyal Zisser, "Syria" in Ami Ayalon (ed.), MECS, vol. XIV (1990), p. 653.
[4] *Tishrin*, 13 March 1992.
[5] *Al-Hayat*, 12 October 1997.
[6] *Ha'aretz*, 13 July 1998; and see the author's interview with a Syrian academic, Washington, DC, 11 June 1998.
[7] *Tishrin*, 19 April 1995; Eyal Zisser, "Syria" in Bruce Maddy-Weitzman (ed.), MECS, vol. XIX (1995), p. 596.
[8] *Tishrin*, 19 April 1995.
[9] *CF, Syria* –1995-6, pp. 38-40.
[10] *Al-Watan al-'Arabi*, 14 September 1998; Eyal Zisser, "Syria", Maddy-Weitzman (ed.), MECS, vol. XIX (1995), p. 594.
[11] See *Al-Ba'th*, 2 December 1991; 31 March 1992; *Al-Hayat*, 28 November 1995.
[12] *Ha'aretz*, 28, 29 November 1991.
[13] Radio Monte Carlo, 29 August – DR, 1 September 1992. Suwaydani was released in February 1994, see AFP, 22 February – DR, 23 February 1994.
[14] *Le Monde*, 24 August 1993.
[15] See *Ha'aretz*, 23 May 1992.
[16] See *Al-Ba'th*, 25 August 1994.
[17] Eyal Zisser, "Syria" in Ami Ayalon (ed.), MECS, vol. XIV (1990), pp. 654-5.
[18] See Eyal Zisser, "Syria – The Elections to the People's Assembly (August 1994) – Exercising Democracy?", paper presented at MESA Conference, San Francisco, 21–24 November 1997.
[19] *Al-Hayat*, 28 August 1994; *Tishrin*, 27 August 1994.
[20] *Al-'Alam*, October 1994; *Al-Hayat*, 28 August 1994; *Al-Hayat*, 12 December 1998.
[21] Eyal Zisser, "Syria" in Ami Ayalon (ed.), MECS, vol. XIV (1990), p. 665.
[22] *Al-Hayat*, 28 August 1994.
[23] *Ibid.*, 2 July 1994.
[24] *Ibid.*, 17 November 1997.
[25] *Al-Sharq al-'Awsat*, 15 August, 1997; *Al-Thawra*, 30 August 1997; see also *Al-Wasat*, 7 October 1997.
[26] Eyal Zisser, "Surya – Liqrat Seder Hadash miBayit" (Towards a Domestic "New Deal" in Syria), *HaMizrah haHadash*, 38, 1997, pp. 131-2.
[27] *CR, Syria – 1993*, no. 3, pp. 23-7.
[28] *Al-Hayat*, 17 February 1997; Eyal Zisser, "Syria" in Bruce Maddy-Weitzman (ed.), MECS, vol. XXI (1997), pp. 661-5.
[29] *Al-Thawra*, 16 May 1997; *Al-Jarida al-Rasmiyya* (Damascus), 28 May 1997
[30] *International Defense Review*, 1 May 1997; *CF*, Syria - 1993-4, pp. 40-2.
[31] See Eyal Zisser, "Toward a domestic new deal in Syria", pp. 129-31.
[32] *CR, Syria – 1998*, no. 3, pp. 19-20.
[33] *CF, Syria – 1995-6*, p. 26.
[34] *CR, Syria - 1997*, no. 4, p. 7.
[35] *Al-Hayat*, 6 July 1991; *CR, Syria – 1994*, no. 2, pp. 7, 24, 33.
[36] *Al-Hayat*, 6 July 1991; *CR, Syria – 1994*, no. 2, pp. 7, 24, 33.

against the peril of Western expansion, especially by Israel
and Muslim territory. In addition, the strategic pact be
mascus and Teheran helped to promote a favorable view of
regime among Islamic circles throughout the Arab world.

Examination of the relationship between the Islamic r
and the regime in Damascus leads to two basic conclusio
that for the foreseeable future the Islamic movement and
regime will be increasingly interested in continued dialog
out difficulties or, at least, to bring about an interruptio
prolonged ideological and political confrontation. Such
ruption would ensure calm and stability in the state, but u
state's protection the Muslim Brotherhood could recover i
Syria. It might not re-emerge as an organized power, but ir
clerics could begin acting in their own circles to foster the
sentiments already existing among the Syrian people, at lea
Sunni urban class.

The "Inspector-General" of the Muslim Brotherhood, 'Al
Din al-Bayanuni, alluded to this in a newspaper interview
1998:

"The goal of the Muslim Brotherhood is to act within Syria under
brella of the constitutional reality which will ensure freedom of
activity and the freedom to preach Islam… These conditions ar
case included in the demand of the movement for a guarantee
civil rights for all members of the Syrian people. These rights are de
in order to arrive at a national reconciliation based on respect for t
of the nation [Islam] and the granting of freedom of action to
sundry… and the abolition of any restriction on these freedom
among them the State of Emergency Laws and Law no. 49 of 1980
instituted the death penalty as punishment for membership of the l
Brotherhood]."[81]

Second, in the long term, the process of reviving the Islamic
ment's activity in Syria, however limited, is in itself enough to cha
the stability of the regime. Social and economic problems,
cially the high rate of natural population growth, are lik
strengthen religious sensibilities, at least in a section of the S
community. Islamic circles may become more demanding and
tant, as happened in Egypt and Algeria, but the regime has pref
to ignore this danger and to regard the glass as half-full rather
half-empty. Hence the Islamic movement's recognition of th
gime up to the end of President Asad's reign, and willingne
reach a compromise on its terms. However, the regime may ha
pay a heavy price for these short-term triumphs in the future.

[37] *CR, Syria - 1997*, no. 4, p. 3, 10.

[38] *Al-Hayat*, 21 February 1997; and see the author's interview with Syrian academics, Washington, DC, 23 June 1996; 11 June 1998.

[39] *Al-Ba'th*, 15 April 1997; and see *CR, Syria – 1997*, no. 3, p. 10.

[40] *CR, Syria – 1997*, no. 4, p. 8.

[41] *CR, Syria - 1999*, no. 4, p. 3, 4.

[42] *CR, Syria - 1997*, no. 2, pp. 2, 3; *Ha'aretz*, 28 February 1997; *Al-Sharq al-Awsat*, 5 April 1997. Also see Onn Winckler, *Demographic Developments and Population Policies in Ba'thist Syria* (Brighton: Sussex Academic Press, 1999).

[43] *Al-Sharq al-Awsat*, 5 April 1997; *Ha'aretz*, 28 February 1997; *Al-Thawra*, 11 June 1997.

[44] *Al-Thawra*, 11 June 1997; Eyal Zisser, "Syria", in Ami Ayalon (ed.), MECS, vol. XIX (1995), p. 599.

[45] See *Al-Thawra*, 7 June 1997; *Tishrin*, 9 September 1997; *Al-Ba'th*, 27 October 1997; *CR, Syria - 1997*, no. 3, p. 10.

[46] *Al-Quds al-'Arabi*, 20 February 1997, *Al-Sharq al-Awsat*, 5 April 1997; *Al-Wasat*, 7 October 1997.

[47] *Al-Sharq al-Aswat*, 5 April 1997.

[48] *Al-Thawra*, 14 May 1997; *Al-Sharq al-Awsat*, 14 April, 15 August 1997.

[49] *CR, Syria – 1998*, no. 3, pp. 5, 8.

[50] *Al-Hayat*, 9 April 1997; and see *CR, Syria – 1998*, no. 3, pp. 5, 8.

[51] *Al-Ba'th*, 12 May 1997; and see *Al-Ba'th*, 16 June 1997; *Tishrin*, 13 July 1997.

[52] *Al-Ba'th*, 30 March 1997; *Al-Thawra*, 5 April 1997; *Tishrin*, 6 April 1997.

[53] *Tishrin*, 6 April 1997.

[54] Eyal Zisser, "Syria" in Bruce Maddy Weitzman (ed.), MECS, vol. XX (1996), p. 636; Joseph Bahout, "The Syrian Business Community: Its Politics and Prospects", in Eberhard Kienle (ed.), *Contemporary Syria: Liberalization Between Cold War and Cold Peace*, pp. 72-80; Hans Hopfinger and Marc Boeckler, "Step by Step to an Economic System: Syria Sets Course for Liberalization", pp. 181-202.

[55] *Al-Thawra*, 13 August 1997.

[56] *Tishrin*, 13 July 1997.

[57] *Al-Quds al-'Arabi*, 17 June 1997.

[58] *Al-Watan al-'Arabi*, 22 February 1997; *Al-Hayat*, 25 February 1997.

[59] *Al-Hayat*, 8, 11, 13 March 2000.

[60] *Al-Hayat*, 15 May 2000.

[61] *Al-Wasat*, 29 August 1999.

[62] *Al-Hayat*, 17, 21 February 1997.

[63] *Ibid.*, 15 December 1995; 17, 21 February 1997.

[64] *Al-Watan al-'Arabi*, 22 February 1997.

[65] See Umar F. Abd-Allah, *The Islamic Struggle in Syria;* Thomas Mayer, "The Islamic Opposition in Syria, 1961-1982"; Eli Friedman, "HaAhim haMuslemim veMaavakam Neged Mishtaro shel Hafiz al-Asad" (The Muslim Brotherhood and Their Struggle against the Regime of Hafiz al-Asad, 1976-1982), M.A. thesis, Tel Aviv University, 1986.

[66] See Umar F. Abd-Allah, *The Islamic Struggle in Syria*; Eyal Zisser, "The Muslim Brotherhood Movement in Syria", pp. 96-114.

[67] *Ibid.*, and see Raymond A. Hinnebusch, *Authoritarian Power and State Formation in Ba'thist Syria*, p. 281.

[68] Umar F. Abd-Allah, *The Islamic Struggle in Syria*, pp. 103-7.

[69] *Al-Wasat*, 13 May 1996; author's interviews with Syrian academics, Washington, DC, 23 June 1996; and 11 June 1998.

[70] Author's interview with Patrick Seale, London, 24 September 1995.

[71] In this context see Moshe Maoz, *Surya haHadasha – Shinuyim Politiyim veTarbotiyim beTahalich Bniyat Kehila Politit* (The New Syria: Political and Cultural Changes in the

Process of Establishing a National Community) (Tel Aviv: Reshafim, 1974), pp. 85-6; and see Kamel Abu Jaber S., *The Arab Ba'th Socialist Party: History, Ideology, and Organization*; Majid Khadduri, *Political Trends in the Arab World* (Baltimore: Johns Hopkins University Press, 1972), pp. 176-211.

[72] *Ha'aretz*, 5 January 1997; *Risalat al-Ikhwan al-Muslimin*, 27 September 1996.

[73] *Al-Wasat*, 3 June 1997.

[74] *Ibid.*

[75] *Akhbar Wa-Ara'a*, 15 May 1997.

[76] *Al-Dustur*, 6 June 1998.

[77] *Al-Hayat*, 20 January 1997; *Al-Sharq al-Awsat*, 3 February, *MM*, 6 April 1997.

[78] See *Al-Shira'*, 16 March 1997; *MM*, 10 April 1997.

[79] See, for example, *Tishrin*, 6 January 1997; a*l-Diyyar*, 7 June 1997.

[80] *Tishrin*, 6 January 1997; *Al-Ba'th*, 8 January 1997.

[81] *Al-Quds al-'Arabi*, 9 May 1997.

CONCLUSION

# ASAD'S LEGACY: SYRIA IN TRANSITION

Over the course of the last three decades of the twentieth century, the Syrian President, Hafiz al-Asad, became one of the most prominent leaders in the Middle East. Under his leadership Syria was transformed from a weak and unstable state into a regional player with standing and influence. This was enough to turn Asad and his regime into an object of analysis that sought to understand the secret of how he had succeeded where so many others, in fact all his predecessors, failed. This analysis sought to define the man, the path he followed in administering Syria's affairs, his vision for the future, and his worldview.

However, despite the abundance of writings about him, Asad remained something of an enigma for many the West, in Israel, and even in the Arab world. The man himself, his worldview and, especially, the web of considerations by which he was guided in taking decisions were a puzzle. This of course, had implications for the effort to understand the regime he founded and the state over which he ruled for thirty years. It was the direct result of the deliberate obscurity into which he and his regime cast Syria and its people. Moreover, Asad was himself a reclusive leader who rarely left his palace to tour the country. He avoided encounters with his countrymen and only rarely gave media interviews or addresses to the nation. Asad ran Syria from his palace with a minimum of contact, which was mostly with those in his immediate circle – his family and close associates. On rare occasions he also met members of the second, wider circle: ministers, aides, and senior military commanders. In his biography *Asad of Syria* Patrick Seale attested that for many of his ministers the President was merely a voice on the telephone, seeking to clarify some detail or ordering them to carry out instructions. He did not even trouble to meet most of his cabinet ministers during their terms of office; only at their swearing-in did they see him face to face.[1]

Asad's few public statements regarding his vision and perspective

207

were in stark contrast to the cloud of obscurity surrounding him, and offered a rare opportunity to answer – if only partly and in a limited way – some of the fundamental questions underlying our study. Such an opportunity came about in February 1996 when Syria and the rest of the Muslim world were marking the month of Ramadan. During this holy month the President, in accordance with his annual custom, entertained clerics in his palace for an evening meal to break the day-long fast – an event that naturally drew the attention of the Syrian media. During the dinner the President boasted to his guests of the regime's strength on the domestic front in Syria and the significant progress that had been achieved in all areas of life since he came to power in November 1970. He declared: "Our domestic situation is strong and constantly improving.... Anyone comparing the circumstances in Syria before 1970 with today's reality knows that we are treading the right path, and that our situation has improved beyond recognition in all areas of our life." Still, Asad chose to present as his regime's most significant achievement the country's "strong stance" in relation to the challenges posed by its enemies in the regional and international arenas over the previous thirty years: this achievement could be summed up by saying that Syria had "preserved its independence, had not given in to pressures and campaigns of fear, and had refused to accept dictates contrary to its national interests".[2]

It was instructive that Asad chose to take stock of his regime's accomplishments and failures in this way at a relatively marginal event, a meeting with clerics during Ramadan. In April that year (1996) Syria had celebrated fifty years of independence (since 17 April 1946), and a year later the jubilee of the founding of the ruling Ba'th Party (7 April 1947). Asad refrained from addressing his countrymen on these occasions, and did not even attend the main commemorative ceremonies organized by the authorities, but in April 1977 he did nevertheless send a congratulatory letter to his fellow party members in honor of the occasion. In it he admitted: "The party's past is not free from failures and defeats. These were caused in part by objective factors, but in part they were the result of conspiracies by the forces of imperialism directed against the Arab nation. Furthermore, in some cases it was party members themselves who brought on defeat, since in every party internal disputes erupt over principles and perceptions." Asad nevertheless determined that "the party has always succeeded in overcoming the difficulties and courageously adhered to its path. This is becuase of the popular support it enjoyed and its ability to develop and change."[3]

It is, of course, debatable whether or not Asad believed Syria's situation to be as favourable as he painted it. In any case, the remarks he made to his guests or wrote to members of his party bear all the marks of a front, designed to give out a sense of "business as usual", especially in view of the grave difficulties which the Syrian state, society and economy face. But it seemed that Asad truly believed that the optimistic picture he painted for his listeners reflected the true condition of the Syrian state. At the start of the 1990s he did not hesitate to portray the dangers to Syria following the collapse of the Soviet Union in alarming terms,[4] but by the decade's end, he may have felt that the country's strategic position had improved and the dangers had dissipated.

Comments by the US Secretary of State, Warren Christopher, were instructive evidence of Asad's optimistic approach. He met the President often in the course of his shuttle diplomacy from 1992 to 1996 designed to push forward the Israeli-Syrian peace talks, and tried to explain in retrospect the reasons why the opportunity to achieve an Israeli-Syrian peace agreement in those years had gone sour. He complained that it was difficult, if not impossible, to persuade Asad – either by inducements or by pressures and threats – to advance on the path to peace: "It is hard to have a serious discussion with a leader of a state [Asad] who believes wholeheartedly that time is on his side."[5]

Asad was known as a leader with a deep historical awareness. His was always a far-seeing calculation; when necessary, he showed the patience and endurance to sustain a long-term policy with results measured in years and decades. He often said that eventually Syria would be able to put its problems behind it and overcome its rivals, the chief of which was of course Israel.

In his address to mark Revolution Day on 8 March 1988, Asad announced:

"We have no cause to worry, as the future belongs to us and not to Israel. Israel has sources of power and strength, but we too have sources from which we draw our strength. Even if Israel today enjoys superiority over us in certain areas, it is temporary. For the day will come, and it does not matter how long it is for this purpose, when the same power and ability that is today in Israel's hands will be at our disposal. Israel, on the other hand, can never achieve the same strength that is to be found in the hands of the Arabs. Such strength is far from its reach, and by this I mean faith in our rights and the existence of a great and vast Arab people."[6]

In the light of these remarks, Asad's speech in February 1996 to the clerics gathered in his palace to break the Ramadan fast with him is significant. It was not, like the above, a prophecy for the distant future concerning Syria's eternal battle with its enemies, in which ultimate victory – the triumph of the Arabs – was assured by historical inevitability. Rather, his praise of Syria's strength, and optimism about the future touched on the present and, at most, the immediate future. From these remarks it was clear that Asad felt Syria had survived the grave crisis of the late 1980s and emerged from it stronger than before.

The difference, sometimes profound, between the ways in which Asad perceived the circumstances surrounding his country and these circumstances are customarily described in the West (and, for example, in Israel in the pages of this work) arose primarily from his unique perspective – defensive, hesitant and above all inherently austere. In this perspective the story of Syria in the 1990s seems to have been one of great success. This, as even the regime's harshest critics admitted, was because the magnitude of the threats on Syria's doorstep was matched by the regime's success in extricating itself from them and surviving.

First, the standing of the regime at home seemed strong and stable; it faced no internal challenges – certainly not for as long as Hafiz al-Asad ruled in Damascus and there was no threat to its stability. The socio-political coalition on which it was based remained as strong as ever, and enjoyed more support at street level than was conventionally supposed – an important condition for securing political stability. Finally, it seemed that a satisfactory solution for the era following Asad existed in the person of his son Bashar, who indeed became Asad's successor.

Second, a significant portion of the regional and international threats which confronted Syria at the start of the 1990s either faded away or were dealt with. Iraq had its military strength critically impaired in the Gulf War, and ceased for the time being to constitute a threat to Syria. In addition, a possible threat from Israel and the United States – at least in the Syrian regime's perception – was neutralized. This threat grew in the wake of the Soviet collapse, but diminished thanks to Syria's siding with the United States in the Gulf War, and its readiness to open peace negotiations with Israel. In the summer of 1996, as a result of the impasse in the Israeli-Syrian peace process and the decline in its relations with Turkey, Syria again faced regional problems. Yet the improvement of its relations with Western Europe, the firming up of the alliance with Iran, and the development of ties with Russia all increased its maneuverability in the regional and international arena, and significantly improved its status. At the end of 1999 when the move toward peace resumed in the region following the Israeli elections, Asad adapted to the new circumstances and was ready to renew talks with Israel.

The regime's success in weathering the storms that battered it over the years can be attributed to several causes. First, it read correctly both the regional and international situations and was able to adapt to the changes in these arenas. In so doing it demonstrated political flexibility, but no more than was strictly necessary. Its success in coping with regional and international threats, at least in its own view, naturally affected its status inside the country as well. Second, the regime made certain to preserve economic stability in the state by exploiting the favourable circumstances of the first half of the 1990s. Third, it struck precisely the right chord to sway Arab public opinion, particularly within Syria, in everything connected to "the West" and Israel. In spite of the romance it carried on with the United States and its negotiations with Israel, the regime remained – in its own view and that of many in Syria and abroad – the Arab world's last bastion against the West and Zionism. (It served as a much more effective barrier than did Saddam Husayn, whose rash and reckless policy brought disaster on his country.) The regime's ability to mobilize the support of the radical Islamic forces in the Arab world was clear testimony to its success. Fourth, the regime continued to enjoy the backing of a broad coalition of social and political forces, and indeed of a majority of the Syrian population. For most of these forces questions of foreign policy, including that of peace with Israel as well as the demand for more political openness within Syria, remained secondary issues.

These forces thus continued to regard the continued rule of the Syrian regime as the preferred alternative or, more precisely, the lesser evil. The regime succeeded in mobilizing the support of additional social forces, chiefly the Sunni urban elite, a group which in the past had viewed it as an adversary but in recent years had begun to regard it as a guarantee of continued economic and political stability. Finally, as in previous years, luck favored the Syrian regime throughout most of the 1990s. Its good fortune included the discovery of oil fields in the east of the country, abundant rains that guaranteed good harvests, and finally the Gulf crisis, which it exploited to strengthen its position domestically and abroad. These "gifts from heaven" were not to last – it is estimated that the oil will run out before 2010, and the late 1990s were marred by drought. Still, the favorable conditions of the early '90s helped Syria overcome, if temporarily, a significant proportion of the challenges facing it, which actually turned out to be less severe than they had seemed at first. However, it was vital that the stability that Asad gave Syria after seizing power in the early 1970s should continue, and at the time of writing a question-mark inevitably hovers over the future course of the Ba'th regime without Asad.

Itamar Rabinovich, Israel's Ambassador to the United States and head of the delegation to the peace talks with the Syrians in 1992-6, was asked on a number of occasions if he felt that the Syrian President had had the upper hand in the Israeli-Syrian peace talks. After all, Asad apparently succeeded in forcing Israel to accept, if only in principle, his demand for a full Israeli withdrawal from the Golan Heights without any accompanying obligation on his part. Rabinovich responded: "One can indeed debate whether and to what extent Asad's path in the negotiations with Israel succeeded, but the real question that needs to be asked is where Asad's so-called successes have led Syria. Was there a clear and intelligible strategy hidden behind the tactics he adopted in the course of the peace talks with Israel between 1992 and 1996? To this", he concluded, "the answer is clearly negative."[7]

It is possible to extrapolate from the Israeli-Syrian negotiations of 1992-6 to explain Syria's general situation. Asad's gains in the 1990s, of which he frequently boasted, were mainly tactical, and it is doubtful that they led the Syrian state anywhere. Moreover, he seemed to have no answer to the fundamental long-term problems of the state he headed since, apart from the "end of days" vision of a united Arab nation triumphing over all its foes, he had nothing to offer for the future. With this in mind, the dilemma facing Syria today appears all the more acute. Will it choose to follow the new path in a direction that has begun to be clear since the start of the 1990s? Or will it continue to mark time, adhering meticulously to the *status quo* that has lasted for three decades? It appears that the steps the regime has taken have brought Syria to the start of a new path, but they were designed in principle to preserve the *status quo* in the state, which the regime sees as the best guarantee of its stability and of its very existence.

It seemed to many that with Asad's coming to power in November 1970 the "struggle for Syria", as Patrick Seale later termed it, had ended. However, Asad himself told his biographer: "The struggle continues."[8] He meant, of course, the struggle with imperialism, Zionism and other enemies of the Arab nation, but the remark is especially true of the domestic struggle for the soul and future course of the Syrian state. But this struggle is not yet decided in spite of the passage of time. Past experience in the region and at home suggests that Syria may emulate the Egyptian model, as it did in many areas in the past, although there was a delay of two decades in the political sphere where every aspect of the conflict with Israel was concerned. The Egyptian model is that of an autocratic regime that maintains a policy of economic and even, to a limited extent, political openness, and for that reason enjoys relative political and economic stability. However, Egypt has achieved only partial success, and its society has to cope with social and economic problems that pose an escalating challenge to political stability. It is doubtful that Syria, with its much more diverse and complex society, can withstand similar problems.

In Syria much was said and written in the 1990s in praise of the Chinese model – the model of a state that succeeded in turning to a market economy without paying any political price. In other words, China's ruling regime did not have to abandon the ideological worldview to which it was committed, and never lost its grip on the state.[9]

President Asad, for his part, boasted more than once of the uniqueness of the Syrian model that he himself fashioned and the many advantages inherent in it.[10] He was unquestionably referring to the democracy and pluralism which, in his eyes at least, exist in Syria. Yet his era is unlikely to be remembered for its civil society, which does not yet exist in Syria, or for the state institutions he established, which have mostly remained precarious and unstable.[11] The model of Syria under Asad was that of a centralized regime of vast might – with, at its apex, a group of military officers of clear ethnic identity, and at its foundation "a broad coalition" of political and social forces representing broad sectors of the Syrian people who back the regime. A similar model, incidentally, existed in medieval Islamic cities where local dynasties of military officers, most of Turkish extraction, seized power after the decline of the centralized government. They were backed mostly by the urban economic elite, who in return enjoyed political stability and physical and economic security.

Whether Syria follows the Egyptian or the Chinese path, or the unique Syrian one as charted by Asad since November 1970, naturally depends in the short term on Bashar al-Asad's ability to hold the reins of power firmly. In the intermediate term the path will be influenced by what kind of agreement emerges to resolve the conflict with Israel – should one even be signed. Finally, the path will be determined by, *inter alia*, the way in which the regime copes with the problems of society and the economy – and by domestic policy, in which the demographic problem will loom large. There are also the questions of economic and political openness to the West and of the status of Islam in Syria.

Thus Syria stands at a crossroads. Will it choose a new path, a path of change, or will it turn back and adhere to the *status quo* of the decades since President Asad seized control in November 1970? What, then, does the future hold for Syria? Even in Damascus, where many have adopted Bashar's slogan "change within stability and continuity",[12] there is no easy answer.

## NOTES

[1] Patrick Seale, *Asad of Syria*, p. 341.

[2] *Al-Thawra*, 17 February 1996.

[3] *Al-Ba'th*, 7 April 1997.

[4] See, for example, Asad's speech of 8 March 1990, *Tishrin*, 9 March 1990.

[5] Interview with Warren Christopher, *Ha'aretz*, 24 October 1997.

[6] *Tishrin*, 9 March 1989.

[7] Interview with Itamar Rabinovich, Voice of Israel, 23 June 1998.

[8] Seale, *Asad of Syria*, p. 495.

[9] See, for example, the series of articles published in *Al-Ba'th* in late 1992. The writer, Turki Saqr, the editor of the newspaper, included in these articles many of his notes from his tour of China. *Al-Ba'th*, 22, 23 November 1992.

[10] *Tishrin*, 13 March 1992.

[11] See Seale, *Asad of Syria*, pp. 492-5; Moshe Maoz, *Asad*, pp. 203-8.

[12] *Al-Wasat*, 29 August 1999.

# INDEX